LIMKOKWING

The man who designed the future

Ambi Mathe

PRIME MINISTER
MALAYSIA

FOREWORD

LIMKOKWING The man who designed the future is an appropriate description of him. He is a man who has influenced many in the course of his life and over the last three decades the influence has extended across the globe to touch millions of lives.

I have known Tan Sri Dato' Sri Dr Limkokwing for many years. A creative thinker he always responds with sincerity to assist the Government overcome many socio-economic issues. A strong supporter of 1Malaysia drive he has always championed causes that promote national unity. I remember the cartoons he created called Guli Guli that took humorous jibes at the common foibles of Malaysians. He did it without offending people, something that is not easy to achieve.

The title recently bestowed upon him as Father of Innovation in Creative Education by the Ministry of Science, Technology and Innovation, speaks volumes of his endeavours in shaping the delivery of education to produce the calibre required to move industry to new levels of excellence.

This is a unique publication in that the life journey of Tan Sri Limkokwing illustrates the changes one person can create in the lives of millions by simply doing what is best and pursuing the outcome, even if it may seem impossible to others.

(DATO' SRI MOHD NAJIB)

PRIME MINISTER
MALAYSIA

MESSAGE

I am one of the few people who still remember living in Malaysia when it was a British colony. I cannot forget how inferior I felt to the British officials including my teachers. I never really thought that we could be otherwise than inferior. Of course, I never dreamt I would ever be in a position to do anything to bring honour back to the Malays, in particular, and Malaysians, in general.

But Allah be praised for, by a quirk of fate, I was put in a position to help retrieve the honour of the people of this country. But between having the opportunity and achieving the objective, there is a wide gap. Probably many Malaysians have the same desire but found they were not able to do anything.

Tan Sri Dato' Sri Dr Lim Kok Wing is among the people who shared my views. He believed, as I do, in the abilities of the Malaysians. This enabled us to get along very well and to work together on the process of convincing the Malaysians and in particular the Malays that they can do what others can do and probably do it better. He espoused the belief in 'Malaysia Boleh' and helped to make it a credible slogan.

He was particularly interested in the Rakan Muda project and immediately recognised how it could turn the aimless 'lepak' youths into responsible dedicated citizens. He came up with numerous ideas on how to promote the Rakan Muda programme. I know that he was disappointed because he could not be put in charge but he never stinted when asked to help.

Kok Wing believed in what I believe in terms of developing the country and bringing about racial harmony long before others overcame their suspicions of me as a Malay ultra. He helped me to overcome my bad image. His faith in my ideas never diminished even when the whole world's media condemned my tirade against the currency traders. He was up front fighting my battles. One of the results was the book 'The Hidden Agenda' which defended my belief that the attack on Malaysia's finances was deliberate and meant to force this country to submit to a form of Western imperialism. Apart from his interest in creative art, which resulted in his setting up the Limkokwing Institute of Creative Technology he has always been involved in charity work.

Kok Wing is a good friend and he can be relied upon to help with ideas and solid work in order to materialise some of my ideas. I hope this biography will inspire others, particularly the young, to dedicate their lives to the betterment of the society in which they live.

Dr Mahathir bin Mohamad
Putrajaya, June 6, 2000

The essential Malaysian

"I practically discovered him. I listened to him. I was quite impressed with his ideas. I thought he would be able to translate my ideas into something more tangible, something more easily understood by people. That is his strong point, his forte. He makes the language more simple. And I think his ability to read you, and read you correctly is his strength. The other part of him, of course, is having read you he is able to translate whatever you had in mind into ways that will enable other people to appreciate the way he appreciates. So I think it is good to listen to him because he comes up with ideas and he sees things from a different angle.

He has a lot of ideas and the way he puts his ideas forward makes them very interesting. I was quite impressed with his ability to communicate and because of that I thought he would be very useful for the Government. I think he and his ideas have given me ideas myself.

His innovative ideas can come out if he studies anything. If say the Government has got a plan, and the way the plan is to be implemented is spelt out but if he were to study the plan, he might be able to come out

Above: Tun Dr Mahathir bin Mohamad has been the inspiration behind many of Tan Sri Lim's endeavours. Their relationship goes back some three decades to the time when Tun took office as Malaysia's fourth Prime Minister in 1981.

with other ways of carrying forward the plan. This, I think, is something not many people have. The ability to see, understand the plan and see its implementation in ways other than what has been spelt out.

Tan Sri Lim is not the image of the Chinese that we have. He has this correct balance. While he wants to help himself, he also feels an obligation to help the country and he understands the racial composition, he understands the disparities and he wants to help correct the disparities. I think, because of that, he has given a lot of opportunities to Malays in his University. So he is truly a Malaysian because he understands the needs of Malaysia. He is the essential Malaysian who is concerned that everybody should move forward together.

He does not take sides. He has contacts with both sides. In mediation you must have the ability to approach both sides. He is not committed to any particular person or ideas. He has the idea that he should be able to explain to both sides why there needs to be reconciliation, for example. Why there shouldn't be this confrontation. So in that sense, because he was able to meet both sides I could communicate with both sides through him.

The ordinary person will see only the front but he is able to see not only the sides, sometimes from the back also. So this gives him an advantage in terms of understanding things.

He is someone I could trust to convey my views to the different parties."

YABhg Tun Dr Mahathir bin Mohamad
Fourth Prime Minister of Malaysia
Extracted from an interview conducted on 29 January 2010

Actions and outcomes

Essentially this book is about actions and consequences. They are illustrated through the life of a man called Lim Kok Wing. He has filled his life with actions that have had great consequences. Each success that he achieved along a remarkable journey opened up new opportunities and carried him further and higher up. Today, he stands at the precise point where he had planned to be, where he can influence the thinking of millions of people. Through them, he is reaching out to change mindsets and to design the future.

The reader will learn that the more actions we are able to implement the more we are able to shape the outcomes. If every action is well thought through and implemented with the right timing and determination, then the outcome will be exactly what we want to achieve and maybe more.

Past = Present = Future

The Past is a series of actions that we have no means of reversing but it contains lessons that can guide us in deciding the form of actions we take in the Present. Those who are aware of this will find that they can determine their own Future to a certain extent.

The life of Lim Kok Wing is presented here within the context of Past, Present and Future. The Past describes his journey where his creativity, discipline, perseverance and vision were the driving factors that brought him singular success in a career in advertising and communications. The same traits led him into the corridors of political power as he contributed his expertise to the government in helping to promote unity, change mindset, increase awareness, and strengthen the faith of Malaysians in their ability to compete with the best in the world.

The lessons that he learnt from his journey were applied to design a university that pioneered a new kind of education. This forms the basis for Part Two covered in The Present. He refused to be bound by the traditional rules in providing education. He broke the norms and innovated the ways knowledge was delivered and acquired. The model that he created excited young people and they came from all over the world to study at his university. Part Two journeys with him as he launched the global expansion of the university to set up campuses across the world. Many developing countries have rushed to embrace his "New Vision of Education" model that focuses on empowering young people with the knowledge and skills needed to build capacity to effectively drive the transformation of their countries.

Part Three is about The Future. In The Present he has designed a creative learning environment at his campuses that is moulding a new generation of youths who are motivated to be the best persons they can be; an environment that inspires new ideas; one where the students are encouraged to challenge the norm, to explore new ways that will result in new things that will work better, look better and last longer. Part Three also explores what the future can be if Lim Kok Wing has his way and realises his vision to create a global network that will bring his innovative education to deprived people so as to give them a better shot at building a higher quality of life.

Ambi Mathe

Contents

Designing the future

The future exists.

It evolves in the same fascinating way as the Google machine that tracks every nanosecond of interactions in cyberspace. The brightest and most vibrant portions on the globe that Google has installed in its headquarters in the United States indicate where people are actively engaged in some form of action. The darkest areas are where the infrastructure is the weakest, revealing the areas where people are not part of this global activity, and they stagnate, perhaps regress, as the world leaps into another exciting new era.

Today we are living the future that was imagined and created in the past. The world as it exists today is the product of past actions. The conflicts, the violence and the destruction occurring around the world co-exist with the marvels of technology, innovation and invention. We are living today the future of people long dead and gone.

The future is about people.

People's lives are interconnected. The things we do are interrelated. It is a difficult resource to work with because people are such complex beings. But while we may be complicated as individuals, as a society we can be manipulated because we play by a different set of rules.

The future is created in the present.

This makes the now, this moment, today, a very precious and priceless commodity possessed by us all. Very few of us are conscious of this power that we possess. Very few of us are conscious of the fact that we are the architects of the future. In every action we lay the seeds of something that will become tangible in the future.

The future is determined by action.

The future is the consequence of what we do in the present time. Everything that we do, consciously or unconsciously, creates the future. The future is not some distant time ahead of us. It is tomorrow, next week, next month, next year. The future starts with the next thing that we do. It solidifies and becomes more real with each continuous action.

That brings us to the question of action. What is action? How does it create the future? Action is our response to life's questions that appear to us in the form of problems or issues. They prompt us to think deeply and those who respond well are like chess players who plot every move knowing the consequences and desiring the outcome. But life is not as simple as a game of chess. It can spring some surprises because life is about people who can be unpredictable. Life is also about nature which is equally capricious.

Architects of the Future

The chaos theory explains that the flutter of a butterfly's wings in Brazil can cause a tornado in America. Therefore, actions that we put into motion have power not merely creating the future but actually engaged in designin it. These are the ones who understand the value of time and use every minute of their waking hour thinking of the future, planning the strategies and persevering to ensure the outcome they want. They are the true architects of the future.

Such a person is Tan Sri Dato' Sri Dr Lim Kok Wing, a Malaysian, whose personal style and thinking have influenced all who have come in contact with him. He works to change people, directly or indirectly.

But he has little more power than other ordinary citizens. Yet he has attempted to make a difference to the future of his country and in doing so found a way to influence the future of the world through the thousands of young people who travel thousands of kilometres to study at the university that bears his name. He built an institution for a new kind of education. He created a university unlike any other, one that is charting its own pathway despite the many obstacles. This book presents his journey, telling it differently so it may have value to others wanting to emulate his style and adopt his methods.

Lim Kok Wing

The Man

Few people are able to understand the energy and the drive of this man. What they see of him today seems incredible as he continues to move forward by leaps and bounds. He never takes a break and strives on propelled by the vision that he sees in front of him. It is a puzzle that he is putting together creating vistas that he had envisioned in the distance and which now make sense to those following behind.

His is a pioneering spirit. His early years shaped his opinions and moulded his conclusions about how far he could go. But those who have followed his life closely can see the pattern of what he wants to achieve emerging. It is a jigsaw puzzle of a landscape that keeps growing and growing. But before we can understand the vision we must first understand Lim Kok Wing.

Antiques and the colour black

His love for antiques and quaint artefacts is obvious, as is his love for the colour black. He has managed a unique fusion of the past and the contemporary. He enjoys the intricate craftsmanship and creative genius of these works of art that he surrounds himself with. In his mind's eye he can imagine the process when a piece of stone or wood is magically transformed into a masterpiece.

Black is the corporate colour of his company. All his staff, right down to the tea ladies, are dressed in black. The way to his office is through the covered Wings Plaza that is dominated at the driveway entrance by a giant metal bird with wings outstretched for flight. The theme of flight is emphasised by the massive panels held up by beams that make up the layered roof, creating the impression of wings spread and poised to lift up the entire building. Tiny sparrows play 'catch-me-if-you-can' games and dart from the roof to the circular aluminium tables arranged around the interior of the arena-shaped plaza for students and university staff to take their meals, alfresco. Young people swarm the place throughout the day engaged in all kinds of activities – perusing an exhibition, watching a performance on a stage, surfing the Net on their notebooks, having their hair styled in a salon, jogging on a treadmill in the gym or even shooting a video. This is the "most happening" place in the campus, the most important place for the students to meet each other and learn to make friends. A campus, you say? Looks more like a mini United Nations. You catch glimpses of blonde and brown amongst the dominant black-haired students from Asia and Africa that throng the plaza. The visible creativity is simply stunning. It is clear in the way the students dress and the way they style their hair. It is in the décor of the place with huge banners that hang down from the third and topmost floor. It is in the music that floats through the air from the campus radio station. It is in the cloth posters printed with colourful motifs

Above: This graphic served as the logo to represent the philosophy of his Wings Creative Consultancy which he set up in 1975. It was inspired by a book called Jonathan Livingston Seagull about a seagull that broke free from tradition and conformity to discover new meaning to life.

depicting creative industries that adorn the walls. It is in the explosion of ideas exhibited in the galleries. The most eye-catching design feature – remarkable for both its size and breathtaking in its conception – is a spectacular multi-hued cloth wrap, bearing giant images reflecting the creative and multinational environment of the campus, that covers the length and breadth of one side of the 4-storey black building that houses the academic wing next to the plaza. Totalling 150 metres long, the digitally composed "skin" is among the biggest in the world and visible kilometres away from the campus which sits on the side of a hillock commanding a panoramic view of the tree-clad rolling terrain.

An active past, present and future

Enter his spacious office and you see him as he talks into his mobile phone. As he talks he writes instructions to his staff. A tray is full of letters that demand response. There are appeals for funds from charitable organisations, both foreign and local, and invitations to ministerial functions, business symposiums and conferences. Another tray is full of documents in clear holders that are from the various key people he works with to run his many businesses and campuses. There are memos regarding work in progress, new designs for publications, new concepts for advertising, PowerPoint document presentations in hard copy, and new video scripts to market his university that await his comments. A pile of diplomas await his signature. Graduation of another batch of students is around the corner. His favourite design publications are within easy reach.

What is he reading right now? A few books apparently. One is about Quiet Leadership. Another is about the Quran and another is Bridging the Innovation Gap.

"The Quran?" I ask him. He replies, "Three-quarters of my staff are Muslims. I need to understand them better," he quips.

The tops of his low cupboards hold trophies and photographs of his son Tim and daughter Tiffanee and cherished moments with famous dignitaries. The trophies are very impressive. They come from all over the world – Geneva, London, Frankfurt, New York, Paris, Madrid, Doha, Kuala Lumpur – for all kinds of reasons, from visionary leadership and innovative education to entrepreneurship. There is a crown of gold and jade from the chairman of a Korean university, an admirer of the creative pioneering spirit he has brought to education.

He used to adorn his walls with some of the 100 national and international advertising awards he won over 35 years in the business. He has put them away to replace them with more recent work done by his group of companies. He also finds space for excellent work created by students of Limkokwing University of Creative Technology. A huge Chinese drum takes centre stage on the floor while a large painting of Buddha looks peacefully down on his conference table. Here and there you see gifts from all over the world – an exquisite painting from Iran, a jade antique from China, an intricate carving from Africa, a work of art turned into a table from Bali.

Of politics and men

As he writes his memos, his personal assistant walks in with a message that says he has to leave in ten minutes for an appointment outside the campus. He has to rush off to lunch with a Minister. At the moment of writing the particular Minister was in the midst of a party crisis. Over the past years a number of Ministers and others in similar situations have sought Tan Sri Lim's mediating ability to settle disputes. He is, however, tight-lipped about these meetings. He just smiles and changes the subject. He walks the middle line, not taking sides. He is a friend to all.

When Tun Dr Mahathir Mohamad was Prime Minister of Malaysia he was often asked to look into intricate political situations and come up with creative solutions. There were times when Dr Mahathir could not make the same request to someone within the party or his office. These were occasions when a neutral party was needed to smooth ruffled feathers and deliver the former Prime Minister's messages.

Tan Sri Lim is highly respected as an ideas man and a very creative person. What separates him from others is his ability to produce solutions that are practical and workable.

But it was not always smooth sailing for him. Often his ideas were taken up and carried out by ministries but only sometimes did he receive the credit. There was a case of a ministry so hobbled by internal politics that its operations were adversely affected.

> *Nature had concealed at the bottom of his mind, talent and ability of which he was not aware. But his passions have aroused them and brought them to light, giving us, sometimes, views more certain, more perfect than art could possibly produce.*
>
> *City Mode Magazine*
> *November 1990*

When Tun Dr Mahathir asked him to see what he could do, Tan Sri Lim provided ideas to build and develop a vital section of the ministry that dealt with the public. The ministry's officials listened to his ideas very politely and simply told him that they were already doing what was suggested. Five months later the ministry announced its projects for the year and, unsurprisingly, the projects were exactly what Tan Sri Lim had earlier proposed.

He shrugged off the incident as part of the politics that he had to deal with. However hurt he might have been, he never spoke to Tun Dr Mahathir about these transgressions as he felt they were too petty. In any case, he said, he felt he had achieved what Tun Dr Mahathir had wanted, even if he was not given the credit.

There were also ministries that were very receptive to his ideas but lacked the implementation power to see them through. These had irritated Tan Sri Lim a lot because he felt very strongly about the viability of the ideas and was confident they could help people but when the ministries dragged their feet, the timing was lost and the whole exercise became a waste of time and effort.

These days he faces a different breed of politicians. The young, raring-to-go type, intent on establishing their grassroots support that will ensure their political survival and ascent. These are the types who possess little understanding of the communications process and seem more interested in the hype rather than the substance.

So a lot of time is spent in creating the fireworks to dazzle that they want. Tan Sri Lim reckons he is getting too old to deal with these new types because there is the need to educate and he simply has no time for it. Because they do not understand the communications process he often finds himself working backwards – the cart before the horse kind of situation. He says they want to see the gimmicks and the glitter first, and once they are satisfied they then begin to look at the content. It is frustrating for his people, many of them young professionals who spend long hours in rendering the animation and composing the music.

What happens at the tail end has now to be placed upfront. Then when the content is revised time and time again, the rendering has to start from scratch.

Working from dawn to midnight

He works hard, up by 4 a.m. every day and goes to bed only after midnight. And because he works himself hard he expects the same of his staff. He takes little time off. Even Sundays he can be seen holding marketing meetings during crucial recruitment periods.

There are those who even go so far as to say he is impossible to work with. The long hours of work and the dedication to quality are something many of his staff find difficult to sustain. But it is upon these very principles he has built his life and staked his reputation. These are also the very principles that hold him prisoner. These days you will find him fatigued and less energetic than he used to be. A case of the spirit is willing but the flesh is weak. His empire has grown and the projects are many. There is still vision and mission to continue but he admits he needs to loosen the reins of control to let others take up the torch.

If he could, he would clone himself for there is much to be done and no one that shares the same degree of passion to do what he does. He is excited by technology and what it can do. He sees in his students a promise of the future. He enjoys their attempts at creating and lectures his staff to go beyond the ordinary to provide the impetus these young minds need to give their best. Therein lies the secret of the university's success. Students revel in the freedom. After the initial shock when they are asked to think – really think – they enjoy the challenge and often outdo themselves. He takes pride in all their achievements. Through them he is, in fact, cloning himself.

Blood, sweat and tears

He pushes and prods. He insists on outstanding work, frontier thinking and quality finish – all the time. High flying executives from other companies who join him often find themselves lacking in innovative thinking as they find their proposals returned with remarks that ask them to tell him something new and not something he already knows.

Working with Tan Sri Lim is to discover oneself. He demands full commitment and pushes so hard that it is either you sink or you swim. There is no in-between. The ego is the first to bruise but as the person begins to grasp the intricacies of working at Limkokwing he or she discovers capabilities undreamed of. There is growth, both internal and external. A writer finds out he or she is able to whip up a video script within hours, a media manager is able to convince a newspaper to give a good position for an ad even though it is past the booking deadline, a supplier finds that he can print a leaflet overnight, a film editor is able to complete a commercial just minutes before airing date! Indeed, most of those who work with and for him learn patience, acquire calm and find they work well under stress and sometimes achieve what they thought was impossible!

Challenging the norm

He is an enigma to many who also find him eccentric. A Chinese, he respects the culture of his ancestors but at the same time he brazenly breaks traditions. He used to drive a black Mercedes Benz that had 40 as the plate number – a number most Chinese shudder to use because it shares the same sound as the word for death in some Chinese dialects. He uses black openly and some would even say defiantly. The traditional Chinese shun numbers and colours that allude to death and gloom. He feels this adherence to such symbols shackles the mind and dampens creativity. His life, he says, should stand as an inspiration to the young who should not be afraid to explore and go beyond the past. Learn, unlearn, re-learn, he insists.

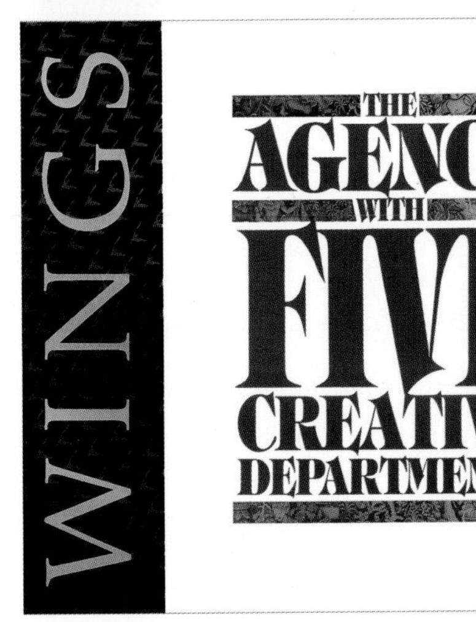

Wings Creative Consultants was the business he set up in 1975, then a young man of 29. He had his own ideas about the advertising industry and developed his company in a unique way that resulted in his astounding success. He built his business to be among the top ten in the country outshining multinationals and stamping his mark on the industry. Featured here are extracted portions from the brochures he created to communicate his philosophy.

Guli-Guli (marbles in Malay) by Tan Sri Lim was the first locally produced cartoon series commissioned by a local newspaper, the New Straits Times. It had an admirer in Tun Dr Mahathir who liked the subtle jibes taken against fellow Malaysians to deliver larger messages. The Prime Minister used Guli-Guli on billboards nationwide as part of a national courtesy campaign.

Top: *In the international arena Tan Sri Lim has spared no effort to promote Malaysia as a haven for investment. In these books – Malaysia Incorporated and Malaysia Branding For The World he has set out to build a quality image for the country.*

Bottom: *At the same time when the country was besieged he also contributed in the best way he could to correct misinformation and misconception about Malaysia. He worked to produce these books – Hidden Agenda and Currency Turmoil to help the world understand that Malaysia's controversial policy of pegging the Ringgit to the Dollar was aimed at preventing the total collapse of its economy as had happened to other Asian economies.*

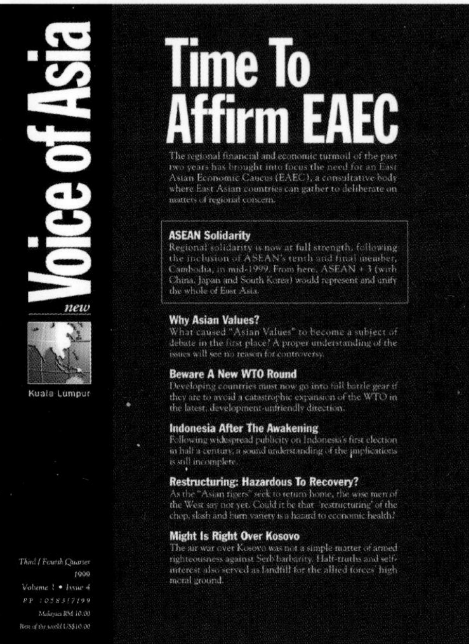

***Top:** Tan Sri Lim was often sought out by the Government when faced with thorny issues. The Green Horizon book was a strategic move to counter foreign allegations that Malaysia had destroyed its rainforest. The book was a pictorial journey that proved otherwise.*

The Mission 2020 publication was produced to help Malaysians understand Tun Abdullah Badawi's strategy on achieving Vision 2020, a landmark blueprint that was designed by his predecessor Tun Mahathir in the early 1990s to take Malaysia into fully-developed nation status.

***Bottom:** At the height of the Asian Financial Crisis Tan Sri Lim found the biased reporting by western media hurting Malaysia's image. With no other avenue to set the records straight and tell the story from an Asian point of view, he set out to create the New Voice of Asia as an alternative channel for an Asian take on international current affairs.*

Tan Sri Lim mooted the Leadership magazine to provide a vital link between Corporate Malaysia and the Malaysian Government to bring up issues where solutions could be presented and thus help to move the country forward.

Top: *Tan Sri Lim loves crafts in whatever form or format. In the early 1990s he took over a pre-war historical building called Loke Mansion in the heart of Kuala Lumpur and refurbished at a whopping RM1 million to create a haven for antiques and crafts from around the world. He called it Artiquarium.*

The journey of batik was for the first time documented on the research of its obscure origins to its latest application. Tan Sri Lim produced an exhibition as well as a publication tracing its journey across the continents and through the centuries.

Bottom: *Positioning Malaysia as a producer of quality products and services has been an on-going crusade for Tan Sri Lim. He worked with the Malaysia Trade Development Corporation (Matrade) to promote top Malaysian brands to the world.*

When Tun Mahathir created the Putrajaya township Tan Sri Lim could not resist capturing its beauty through large format photographs which he set into a coffee-table book that explained the concept and philosophy of the city.

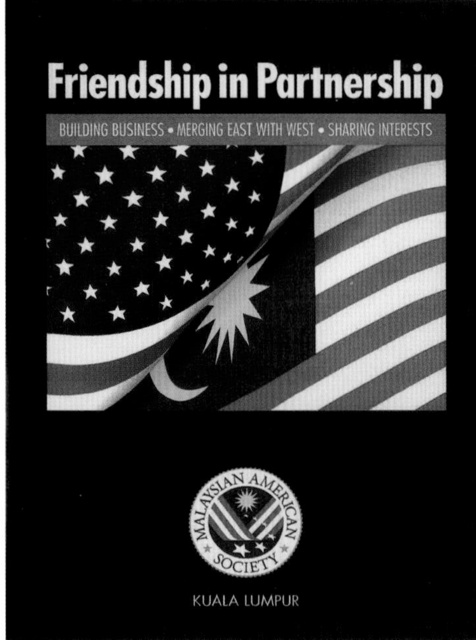

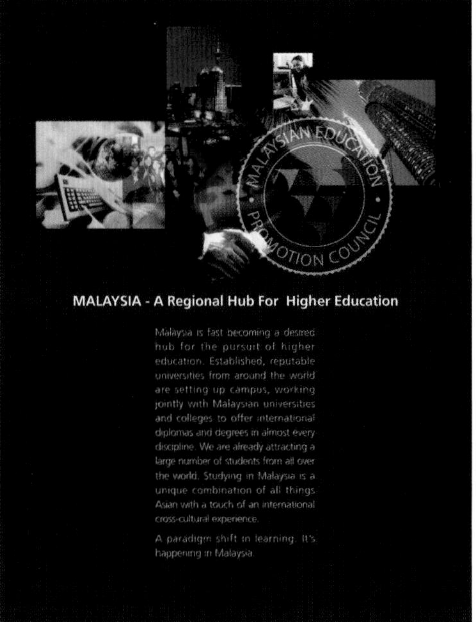

Tan Sri Lim's artistry has always been consistent. The words are always clearly communicated no matter what the event or the occasion is. His signature style can be seen in these brochures produced in 1974 till now with every event organized and every project begun. His design style has always been sharp and clean.

Part 1

Lessons From The Past

Our upbringing, family background, circumstances, the decisions we make and our responses to situations - whether they are opportunities or crises - will decide the turns we take in our lives. Every experience changes us, for the better or worse. In the case of Tan Sri Dato' Sri Dr Lim Kok Wing he leads a life enriched by experiences because he is the kind of person who is always restless, always planning something, always selecting his options and implementing them. He has come a long way and learnt many lessons. In this section, travel with him and marvel at the manner in which he climbed up the ladder to success.

- ***The journey***
- ***The creative maestro***
- ***The philanthropist***
- ***Designing a nation***
- ***Designing a people***
- ***Winning hearts at home***
- ***Winning battles abroad***

The journey

He was born in Kuala Lumpur on October 22, 1946, to a Chinese carpenter and his wife. Just nine months earlier the Japanese had surrendered after occupying British-ruled Malaya, as Peninsular Malaysia was then known, since 1941.

Being the only son among four daughters Tan Sri Lim enjoyed an elevated place in the family hierarchy. Even the poorest Chinese families would spare no effort to ensure the son enjoyed the best of everything because the son would carry on the family name. Little did they know that the family name would be carried on in a manner that would surpass even the expectations of the wealthiest Chinese!

At that time the best for him meant being sent to an English-medium school which his parents had to pay for, while his sisters attended the local Chinese school which was free. Malaya was still under British control and English was the favoured language to succeed in life. Even after Malaya's independence in 1957 and all through his school years English would remain as the medium of instruction.

Tan Sri Lim attended Cochrane Road School in Kuala Lumpur, the capital city of Malaya and now Malaysia, the name for the new country formed through the merger of Malaya, Sabah and Sarawak in 1963 (Singapore was a part of the Federation of Malaysia until its expulsion in 1965). The choice of the type of school he was sent to was instrumental in laying the foundation to build his future; if he had gone to a Chinese-medium school, his life would have gone in a different direction.

Nurturing a passion

The most significant detail about his early life was his extraordinary passion for art and how he nurtured it against the wishes of his parents who saw no future in the discipline. He kept it a secret from his parents.

His parents were not amused and tried to stop him from "wasting" his time on art. There was no motivation from his parents. "When I won awards, invariably it was always for painting or designing or drawing. I never brought these awards home because my mother never liked to see them. She thought that kind of pursuit was a complete waste of time. She kept saying that every good artist died a pauper. It was only years later that people would discover that these people actually had talent. That was stuck in her mind and she wouldn't change it."

But at school Tan Sri Lim's artistic activities were gaining attention. When there was no art teacher available, he was called upon to teach the class. As his "reputation" grew, he was asked to teach other classes too. Soon, he had a small entrepreneurial business going on the side as he tutored his classmates who paid him RM10 for an art lesson.

Tan Sri Lim found encouragement from a most unexpected source.

"We had a strict headmaster whom we nicknamed Bulldog because he was very fierce," he remembers.

"I went to see him the day I left school. He said something that I remember to this day, and it gave me the conviction to follow my heart. He said: *'If you were to do what you most like to do, you are most likely to succeed. You have always been good at art. If I were you, that's where I would go."*

This was a lesson that he carried with him throughout his life and he never fails to pass on the lesson to inspire others to follow their own dreams.

He has always said that if you have a passion for something then this is the gift given to you to make something of your life.

He left school in 1964 – choosing not to continue with two more years of pre-university education – because he felt it did not have anything more to teach him about what he was really interested in. He also knew his parents did not have the money to put him through university. It was his love for art that would open the door for him to achieve amazing success.

Malaysia's first serial cartoonist

His first jobs included selling encyclopaedias and cars, using the income he earned to produce cartoons and posters to build a portfolio. Within six months, he had enough materials to show to a publishing firm. On the strength of this work, he landed a job as an illustrator, earning RM150 a month designing book covers. It was hard work, and the hours were long, but he did not mind because it was the start he needed.

But the repetitive work soon bored him. He took the cartoon strips he had been working on and approached the Eastern Sun newspaper about serialising it.

They agreed, and Tan Sri Lim attained his first major milestone when his strip – ABU – became Malaysia's first local daily cartoon strip. This spurred him to try his hand at reporting and he became a stringer for the Eastern Sun for two years until the paper folded. It was a sign for him to move on.

Trailblazing in advertising

It was 1970, and Tan Sri Lim felt confident that he had accumulated a sufficient portfolio to go for the big time. He decided he would join an advertising agency, and a friend got him an appointment with the art director at a multinational agency, McCann-Erickson. At the interview, the art director bluntly told him his portfolio wasn't strong enough and it was unlikely he would get a job in an advertising agency with what he had. "I was really disturbed by what he said," said Lim. "I was never one who didn't do enough. I was never one not to do my homework. But on hindsight, I felt he actually had done me a favour." Tan Sri Lim swore he would never again be told he hadn't done enough, and developed so much work for his next interview "that I think I just overwhelmed them!"

He got the job, and within a year had risen up the ranks to become art director. It was a historic breakthrough. Until his appointment, in the early 1970s, no Malaysian had ever held such a key post in an international advertising agency.

Four years later, he notched another first when he was named the agency's regional creative director. All that in a span of five years from the time he was told he didn't have what it took to work in an agency! Tan Sri Lim honed his skills and learned everything he could about agency operations while with McCann-Erickson. By the end of the fifth year, he felt he was ready to make real a dream he harboured – to start the first professional Malaysian advertising agency.

It was 1975. He was just 29 years old.

First Malaysian ad agency

The founding of Wings Creative Consultants was a bold move because he was muscling into an industry controlled by expatriates and multinationals. At that time, there was no such thing as a local advertising agency. There were sign painters and sign makers, but no one was producing campaigns and television commercials. He knew the business. He knew the market. And he had fire in his belly.

He was supremely confident that his agency provided a crucial niche to the Malaysian advertiser. "There was never the fear or the concern that we would not be able to compete with the big boys. I wasn't uneasy or afraid in the least when I started the business because I knew the business was there. I was determined to prove that local people could communicate better through advertising. My goal was to become the most creative agency in the country," he said.

Again there were barriers to overcome. He could not find financing from banks to start the company, because banks considered the advertising business 'high-risk'. But his credibility and creativity in advertising circles proved to be a valuable asset. Former clients followed him and in the first year alone, he handled RM150,000 worth of advertising. He only had four employees then. "I was the managing director, copywriter – everything!" he remembered with a laugh. But he persevered, working late into the night. One former employee remembered: "He was always the first in the office, and the last to leave. He was a workaholic even then!"

He broke new ground, and added to his accolades by consistently winning awards. Within three years of its inception, Wings was one of the top 10 leading agencies in the country and the most prolific award winner. In just four years, business had grown so big that Tan Sri Lim ran a large agency with 30 employees. Turnover had reached RM4 million a year and increased to RM19 million in less than a decade.

There was one frustration though. Clients wanted better work from him but expected to pay him far less for the effort than they would to the international agencies. "I used to reprimand potential clients," he said. "I told them, you expect us to run faster and shoot farther. You expect us to be better and yet cheaper (than international agencies). You're just not being fair to us."

Even then he was battling the widespread misconception among Malaysians that foreigners were better than locals. He still is. He would constantly return to this theme over the years, stressing that Malaysians must have faith and confidence in the ability of their own people to succeed and achieve greatness.

Others in the industry were watching Tan Sri Lim's rapid progress closely. One was BBDO, one of the world's largest multinational advertising agencies based in the United States. Like many other international agencies at that time, it sought to gain quick access into the Malaysian market by buying into local agencies. In 1988, it came knocking at his door with a dream deal that would catapult Tan Sri Lim and his agency into the big league.

Malaysia's first global advertising agency

The Wings/BBDO alliance was formed with Tan Sri Lim as Executive Chairman as well as Creative Director. It was now among the top agencies in the country. Tan Sri Lim's decision to go into a partnership with a foreign agency was a realistic one. A more sophisticated Malaysian clientele required a full-service agency, and his staff needed training and new opportunities to grow. Tan Sri Lim himself was tired of being bogged down with the day-to-day financial and operational management of Wings.

In an interview in 1989, Tan Sri Lim said: "What is important is that this is a locally-driven agency," he said. "It is not just any other agency but one that contributes and works for the growth of the local industry."

In his role as Executive Chairman and Creative Director, Tan Sri Lim relished the opportunity to do what he really loved – creative work. He swiftly brought international acclaim through *Ceasefire '89*, a one-minute filmlet produced in 1989 as part of a worldwide drive against the nuclear buildup, which was honoured by the International Physicians for the Prevention of Nuclear War. Another campaign, called *Unity is Everyone*, included a 30-second video clip that won an award at the 34th International Advertising Festival of New York in 1991. It featured a group of Malay, Indian and Chinese children working together to build a playhouse. The public service message was that all Malaysians were needed to build the nation, and that unity was the foundation of the nation's continued growth. It was his sixth campaign. The others included *Good Neighbourliness, Caring for Children, Malaysian Red Crescent and AIDS.*

Billings of Wings/BBDO reached RM26 million in 1989; by 1992, billings rose to nearly RM40 million. New accounts such as Tourism Malaysia and Malayan Railway were added.

He ended his partnership with BBDO in 1992 to set up Limkokwing Integrated. He needed to be a fully Malaysian company for his next phase of expansion.

With this new company, he diversified and expanded to cover the full range of communications services. It became an international strategic communications group providing services in design, advertising, international relations, corporate communications, multimedia, audio-visual production, publications and public relations, and film and photography resources. Many of his most memorable and outstanding achievements on branding of Malaysia were created in Limkokwing Integrated. It was also at this time that he set up what later became Malaysia's first global university.

The creative maestro

Just consider for a moment the possibilities that will arise for people in the future and you will glimpse a little of what goes on in the mind of Lim Kok Wing. He is concerned now with moving creativity to new levels. The University that he set up is a centre for creativity, innovation and content creation. He sees it as a gathering of mind power to build a new world that combines the best of both East and West to forge new directions in all areas of life.

It is a habitat where creativity lives, and where innovation results. It moves now by what it needs to do to make it a success. But the intent is far-reaching. It is there in the distant future. A place where those with ideas will find the funds and the facilities to incubate and give birth to new content that will make this world a better place.

It is a place of innovation providing the thinking and thrust that will build national competitiveness.

The University has within its midst a professional centre known as the Malaysian Design Innovation Centre (MDI). MDI has a foundation that goes back to 1975 when Tan Sri Lim set up Wings Creative Consultants. Its core business was to produce creative content in the form of brand promotion for industry and government. This became sharply focused when it evolved into Wings BBDO in 1988, a collaboration with an international advertising conglomerate. By 1992 creative content development expanded with the founding of Limkokwing Integrated where he was able to offer the whole gamut of creative content from printed, electronic to outdoor communication. His work with industry and government had taken on new proportions, a number of which were ground-breaking and global.

The setting up of the University moved content creation downstream to the areas of education and training. This brought Tan Sri Lim to the source of creativity, making him understand its inner workings and how to stimulate creative thinking. It was also a world of the young and the uninitiated. He was astounded by the energy and the explosion of new ideas from students exposed to the cross-cultural experience of a multi-national and multi-cultural campus. He saw the need to harness this energy and connect it to industry and promote enterprise.

Flexing Asian creative muscles

"I have always put my faith in the creativity of people," said Tan Sri Lim as he sat back to reflect. He was convinced that creativity will provide the strength for new regional cohesion in Southeast Asia and believed that Malaysia could provide the lead. But first, he saw a need to educate the local businessman.

"Malaysian businesses as well as others must change their attitude towards design and the use of design services. Design is an important business activity like any other, such as marketing, engineering and finance. It is unfortunate that many fail to make that vital connection," he said.

When he first began designing the complex that now flourishes in Cyberjaya, the satellite city to Putrajaya (seat of the Malaysian Federal Government) he wanted it to exude creativity. "This is a complex devoted to design and creativity. So it cannot be just like any other complex. The creative input has to be higher, more exciting, more visible."

He wanted every inch of the complex to be supported by the creativity of industry. He pitched his idea to industry. "This is a showcase complex," he explained, again and again to a number of Malaysian businesses. "We will have visitors from all over the world coming to the place. This is an opportunity for new ideas and capabilities to be put on show."

His timing, however, was not perfect as the country was plunged into an economic crisis as a result of the Asian Financial Crisis and industry was slow in seeing the vision in the mind of Tan Sri Lim.

"I felt that simply dedicating a space to exhibit new products just won't do. The experience has to be total and therefore I have tried to make the industry understand the vision that is in my mind. In the end it is they who will benefit," he said with a sigh.

His sigh was very telling and when asked why he had to push so hard he suddenly found new energy to talk about the real aim of the complex.

"It's about building competitiveness and innovation is at the heart of this thrust," he said. "If you look at the United States, if you study the trend from way back in 1900 to 1999 you can see that there is a new class of people called the Creative Class.

"In 1900 they comprised only 10% of the US workforce. The majority then was the 37% working in agriculture. By the turn of the new millennium the creative class comprised 30% of the workforce and agriculture was reduced to only 0.4%."

Fully energised now Tan Sri Lim explained the correlation between the US, intellectual property and the world economy. "Intellectual property is a good indication of innovative trends. In 1999 world spending on R&D was USD545 billion. Of that figure the US share was USD243 billion which was 44.6 %.

"In terms of total creative output the US was responsible for producing USD960 billion or 42.8% in areas that include science, research, entertainment, fashion, software and many others," he said.

So what does it all mean?

The point is, he said, these figures show the world economy is actually dependent on the economic strength of the US and the US depends on innovation to surge forward. "We must learn from all this and move forward."

"We can," he insists.

"We don't lack in any way in terms of knowledge and expertise. We just need to provide the climate that will encourage people to invest in innovation, which in simpler terms means investing in research and development,"

He had planned for the entire complex to reverberate with creative energy. In one section there was the University bringing together creative minds from all over the world. Adjacent to this sphere MDI was to have a dedicated museum showcasing prototypes of great design ideas from all over the world. And amidst this he had planned for retailers to create their concept stores.

Pushing all things Asian

Lim wanted MDI to be successful. He saw this as an opportunity to create content that highlighted the best of Asian culture, history and values.

"The cultures of Asia are old, reaching back aeons. Asians were then the visionaries, the builders and the leaders. The Asian civilizations provided the framework for the world to emerge from barbaric society structures and build their empires. From astronomy, art, science, engineering and design, Asia has provided the foundation for the world to evolve and improve," he pointed out.

There are many inventions credited to the West that had actually originated in Asia. "The Chinese had actually made a lot of discoveries for which it is only now that they are being given the recognition. They were very advanced, thousands of years more advanced than the West. It was the Chinese who introduced new irrigation systems, invented the decimal place system, the first law of motion, the invention of paper, agricultural innovations, even simple things like pest control and hundreds of other solutions.

"The intelligence of these ancient people was very high and the innovations were a natural progression. They were solutions that eased the way of life," he said.

It is a different scenario today. Today it is the Western world that dominates. They have the technology, the media control, financial clout and most of all military might.

"For too long we have looked to the West as the market to penetrate," says Lim. "For too long we have allowed the West to dictate the terms by which we set our standards in many areas of business, education, entertainment, in fact life, in general. This has become so pervasive that we are in danger of losing our cultural identities, our unique values and our individual styles.

"Consider this. Of late we have been witnessing a surge of interest in Asian legends, folklore, history and traditions. Millions are being poured by Western nations to convert this information into movies, cartoons and documentaries. It is great to see Mulan come to life in a full-length animation by no less than the world-famous and highly reputable movie producer - Disney Studios. It is a pleasure to see documentaries about local festivals, the limestone caves of Sarawak or our wonderful scuba diving resorts shown over National Geographic.

"What pains me, however, is that these are presentations made palatable for a Western audience. These are presented with Western viewpoints and perceptions. Who can blame them for what they do because the funding often comes from their own shores. And these are raw materials that have no copyright. Anyone can take them and do with them what they wish. Sure some people will protest here and there. So we have Mulan packaged in American expression even though the audience is worldwide. We have Keanu Reeves playing Buddha. And what does it matter if Entrapment distorts Kuala Lumpur as a haven for thugs living in squatter settlements directly below what was then the tallest buildings in the world.

"But, excuse me, we do care about how we are presented to the world. And yes, we do care because our children and our youths are absorbing this misinformation. These movies care little about Asian values. They care little about Asian traditions and expressions. Asian legends are just stories to the West but they are part of our culture and in some instances communicate Asian values such as respect for elders, filial piety etc."

Developing design consciousness

Tan Sri Lim wants very badly to give Asian creativity greater expression through the University. "It is a long road. I am in a long tunnel and I am seeing glimpses of the light in the end," he smiles.

Another area of concern that he has put into the mission for the University is in moving ahead in improving the design consciousness of the business community in Malaysia as well as its neighbouring countries. He laments the fact that Asians are still far behind in strategic use of design.

"Design is the process by which actions are taken to improve products and services by taking into account new market trends, customers' demands and new available technology and materials. Successful corporations around the world invest in design knowing the competitive advantage it gives their services and their products. They take the time to develop their brands, building consumer loyalty by ensuring the quality.

"It is a well-known fact that often the products are manufactured elsewhere, like Asia, for example and are sold at a premium because of the branding. Perhaps now is the time to consider brand-building and look at Asia as the market to conquer."

He pointed out that ASEAN has eleven member countries. Between them the population is more than half a billion. Asia has 48 countries with a population of almost 4 billion. "This is the market base we must look at. This is a market we, as Asians, understand because these are countries rich in cultures and tradition that are not alien to us.

We must tap this richness."

Lim said the University can provide the base to host ASEAN discussions. "Often we compete with each other when we can collaborate and make strategic use of our skills, our knowledge, our resources. The University has the right environment and philosophy to play an active role in enabling technology transfer, research for innovation, design management, new product development, training of required skills and in the production of content."

He said he was very keen to develop content for the world market.

He said the Western media has for long decades presented Asia with a Western viewpoint. "In so doing many things right about Asia to Asians appear wrong to the West. Their viewpoint has a global audience. To date Asia has been getting a raw deal where coverage of its news, views and issues are concerned. Asian content and quality of design are largely being reported within a framework of Western news values and agendas, which limit the issues covered. Often, these are rooted in colonial and snobbish perceptions of Asia."

He said it was important for Asia to control information outflow through content creation. "By controlling outflow Asia can influence inflow of information. Content creation comes in various forms – movies, television serials and documentaries, music albums, websites, virtual games, books, newspapers, magazines, CD Roms and printed promotional materials.

"Controlling information outflow will influence perception of the quality of products designed in Asian countries. However Asia needs to engage in designing products for an Asian market and in the process invest in developing brands and building brand awareness," he said.

Through content creation, said Tan Sri Lim, Asia can achieve the following:

• Sharpen Asian economic competitiveness
Develop brands for the Asian market because we have the natural advantage. In developing Asian brands the region is able to sharpen market competitiveness. Through government to government negotiations Asian countries can create smart partnerships that have mutual benefit.

• Raise design quality
Within Asia there are advanced economies with the infrastructure and the capability to upgrade skills and thereby raise product quality. Both are vital in a brand building initiative. This is a vital area of product development that can be explored in greater detail. A number of collaborations can be effected beginning with training, research and development that will lead to new product development.

• Preserve Asian culture and traditions

Increasingly many of Asia's ancient practices are fading away as youths show marked preference for Western ideals and lifestyle.

• Provide accurate presentations and viewpoints

Much of the research that has been documented over decades were initiated and created by Westerners. Asians are beginning to do more of these but documentation does not enjoy high visibility because of poor presentation. There is opportunity to expose Asian research which will not be coloured by Western perceptions and values.

• Prevent misconception

Incidents get distorted owing to hidden agendas of the media moguls of the West. An alternative avenue must be available and propagated to cut the sensationalism that the Western media seeks. But the avenue must be created and sustained perhaps by joint action of the countries that make up Asia.

• Educate on Asian values

Simple presentations giving insights to Asian ideals and way of life is needed to balance the distortions being aired over Western media.

• Bridge digital divide

Immersing into content and brand creation using new technology will help to upgrade capability. By creating a demand for content and developing our own brands it will naturally boost creative skills and the harnessing of techno-capability.

• Change Western and Eastern mindsets

Asia must have representation in terms of content and brands. It must start with changing mindsets at home to better appreciate our own cultures. In the process of information gathering and content creation for home audiences the content can be re-positioned to educate Western audiences.

• Expedite intellectual growth

The process of content and brand creation will help to stem outflow of talent and capability. Injecting new energy into industry that is involved in content creation will increase output and thereby expedite intellectual growth.

Championing the solution

Tan Sri Lim believes very strongly that Malaysia can champion the cause. "We understand the Asian psyche. We appreciate its diversity of culture and tradition. We respect the unique differences. Malaysia can provide the leadership for Asia by applying methodology, harnessing new technology to produce our own brands and content for worldwide markets."

He said many Asian countries have their own documentation of events and stories that we can gather to provide acceptable versions or format for worldwide audience. The same goes for creation of Asian brands which in fact will be easier because many countries are already producing export quality products.

It is a bold thought and workable considering that Malaysia has already moved in the right direction with the set up of the Multimedia Super Corridor and the global expansion of the Limkokwing University.

"Of course it is workable," insists Tan Sri Lim. "We have the infrastructure and we can obtain the technology but far more crucial is to create the content and the products to power ahead.

Building competitiveness

The bigger agenda for the University is in building competitiveness. Tan Sri Lim said if the University succeeded in fulfilling its objectives, the bigger picture that will emerge will be competitiveness.

"The overall competitiveness of Malaysia has been declining for some time now. Competitiveness is needed to create wealth. But to build competitiveness we need to harness knowledge and innovation," says Lim.

He explained it simply by saying, "the greater the innovation the higher the competitiveness. In a K-economy innovation is very important."

He said he was very concerned because many of the companies were holding the wrong end of the stick. "By this I mean that we are investing in technologies that are not considered sunrise. We are getting into areas that will soon be obsolete which is why we are falling behind."

The University's thrust in this area is aimed at building up SMI strength. "SMIs are important because they constitute over 90% of the Malaysian manufacturing sector. They form the backbone of our economy. If they are strong then the Malaysian economy will be strong.

"But SMIs face a lot of problems. They are what we say flying without a radar. This is what we want to address through the University. SMIs need market intelligence, they need technology innovation foresight, they need to keep up with global trends.

"In addition they have financial constraints. The average SMI will only look to the bottomline and will hesitate to venture forward.

"They have limited technology capability and do not know how to source the funds to conduct R&D. SMIs face several challenges, chief among them is increasing production costs and bigger than that is the market liberalisation as well as globalisation trends that are bringing new and bigger players that cut their market share," says Lim.

"SMIs will not survive if they do not innovate," he warned.

The Innovation thrust

Lim explained that there are many types of innovation. "Innovation is in all aspects of business – there is innovation that is technology-based, there are new business models, new distribution and marketing, post-sales support."

Technology-based innovation especially involving inventions, he said, would be difficult for SMIs. "This is an area that is expensive and time consuming and mostly left to universities and multinational companies to explore."

"What we should be looking at is in Applied Creative R&D. This is about using existing inventions in unique ways to create new or differentiated products. This is an area that can be explored."

He said he was very keen to work with local manufacturers to bridge the creativity and technology gap needed to incubate innovative new products. "There are many building blocks to innovation. It starts with creativity or an idea, it needs knowledge of how you are going to make the idea work and of course this idea has to make money."

Innovation is something least understood by most people. "It is true that not many people are well-versed in this area. It needs commitment and dedication. It needs passion."

He is a highly sought speaker on branding and his views are helping the SMI community understand the value of innovation.

Speaking at a function jointly organised by the Branding Association of Malaysia and the SMI Development Corporation in May 2009 he said:

"It is the quality of the product that makes a brand famous. It is never the other way round. It was the music of the Beatles that made them famous. It was cars that made Toyota a global brand. It was shoes that made Nike famous.

"The branding of Malaysia started a long time ago. Brand Malaysia is nothing more than being who we are as a people and how progressive we are as a nation. To succeed in the long term, Malaysia must be branded for innovation. Here and now, corporate and enterprise Malaysia must work shoulder to shoulder with the Government of Malaysia to build for the nation a big passion for innovation."

In December 2009 Prime Minister Dato' Sri Najib Tun Abdul Razak declared that 2010 would be a year of Creativity and Innovation.

After years of pushing for creativity and innovation to be brought to the fore, it was a moment of exhilaration for Tan Sri Lim.

He celebrated by launching the third edition of his Innovation Enabling Transformation book which gathered together all his speeches and writings regarding innovation. The book has been adopted by the Ministry of Science, Technology and Innovation and widely distributed.

"The rise of innovation to the top of the agenda of many countries today has resulted in a profound shift in the nature of global competition," he said when speaking in July, 2009 at a conference of District Education Officers national management conference in Seremban.

He warned that economic advantage no longer depended on natural resources, raw materials, trade of goods and services, giant factories, or even growing consumer markets. "Instead creativity is now driving the new economy and regenerating the old economy. At the cutting edge of this shift is the creative sector of the economy – science and technology, software engineering, web publishing, digital media and design innovation, culture and entertainment, and the knowledge-based professions.

"Because these industries rely primarily on talent, countries around the world have stepped up their efforts to attract the brightest scientists and most innovative thinkers. Countries with the right conditions stand a better chance of moving ahead through innovation than those countries that still hold on to traditional and obsolete methods of governance."

Innovation can only happen in places where there is encouragement for new ideas. Without the right conditions the most talented and most creative brains will migrate to places where they are able to do their best work.

Limkokwing
1998

Despite his many attempts to explain the nature of innovation and the kind of eco-system needed to nurture it he was disappointed to glimpse the lack of understanding among key government bureaucrats when he was asked to assist in launching the Malaysia Inovatif drive in January 2010.

The drive to push creativity and innovation had been reduced to holding carnivals to celebrate creativity.

He felt it was a very serious undertaking which required careful thought and planning to educate people on the kind of mindset needed to become innovative. In his blog he hinted at the need to have vision and a mission with a set of objectives to ensure that a road map was in place.

"Simply put, without Vision we will be blind. We will be blind to the opportunities in front of us and at the same time we will be blind to the dangers that surround us. Vision is a destination in the future. But to get there we need Mission."

He said Malaysia desperately needed to put in the ecosystem for innovation to take place. "Such a system would be interdependent and interactive, no different from an ecological system except that it is not natural. The processes have to be put in place to allow for specific outcomes.

The mapping has to be extensive and expansive, touching the lives of every Malaysian from cradle to career."

He further explained that research and development must be tied to specific outcomes and that innovation cannot simply be for the sake of innovating something. "There has to be values attached to the whole exercise," he said.

He said an invention cannot be termed as an innovation if it was of no use to people. Using the automobile as an example he said that while it was a great invention value was not in the invention itself but in the way it revolutionized people's lives.

"The value was in the changes that came about half a century later – in the urbanization that was triggered, the refrigerated trucks, the distribution network, the hotel industry. The value migrated from the invention itself to the way the invention was used to create other things of value to people."

The philanthropist

Tan Sri Dato Sri Lim Kok Wing is a generous man. You can touch his heart very easily. But many find him perplexing because he is both a hard-nosed businessman while at the same time he gives unstintingly to those in need. The two sides of his character are actually very natural given the circumstances in which he grew up and the success he has achieved.

He describes the poverty days in his youth as a *banquet.* "If you haven't been there you would not know anything about it. You wouldn't know the value of success in the first place. Certainly you wouldn't know the value of money. You therefore wouldn't know the value of charity."

Many experiences in his charitable work touched his life and made deep impressions that have strengthened his determination to pursue philanthropy. "I remember going to rubber estates with the Rotary Club to give Indian students shoes. While I was giving them shoes, I discovered many of them couldn't read.

"I asked why after three years they couldn't read. Actually they were short-sighted. They couldn't read because they couldn't see properly. They needed spectacles but couldn't afford them. Many of them were from broken homes."

In 2009 he was singled out by Forbes magazine as one of four Malaysians among 48 Asian Heroes of Philanthropy. But the magazine's editors saw only one aspect of his generosity. They noted the financial contributions that he made and that too of a recent nature. But Tan Sri Lim sees philanthropy as part and parcel of a company's corporate philosophy as well as in the projects that it initiates. He thinks it is hypocritical for organisations to keep their corporate responsibilities separate from its business development by calling it Corporate Social Responsibility or CSR.

He wants philanthropy to embrace a wider perspective. "Even if you are a bank, every aspect of the organisation's business or its relationship with customers can be designed to include something that will benefit the public. That would be CSR instead of setting aside time for staff to visit an old folk's home or organise a New Year's party for orphans or just give money to the WWF and then claim that you are helping to protect endangered animals," he says.

"Don't get me wrong," he explains. "You can contribute to the orphanages and NGOs but companies should re-look the way they view CSR and give it more meaning within the sphere of what they do."

The late Dato' Ruby Lee, who was Secretary-General of the Malaysian Red Crescent Society in 1965, spoke of Tan Sri Lim as a young man eager to help in the movement which he joined in his 20s.

"He was the quiet type…very humble but committed," she said. "I could sense that he was interested in helping out and I invited him to join us. He started off handling our publicity, fundraising, and then all these brochures throughout the years. Whilst he was doing various other things, he still had time for MRCS because he believed in our fundamental principles and the work we were doing."

The work with the Malaysian Red Crescent was the start of a lifelong involvement in charity and humanitarian efforts that continue to this day. He started as a member of the organising committee for the World Red Cross Day in the 1960s, and rose through the ranks to eventually become Vice-Chairman of the society.

Dato' Ruby Lee pointed out that Tan Sri Lim's greatest strength in charity work was no different from his professional strength. "He had this ability to get the message across - either to the doers within the committees or the donors," she related. "So, on one hand, he was getting the doers to work on implementation, and on the other hand he was raising money. Through all of this, he had a knack of not pushing himself out front. He is a very good example of someone not needing a leadership position to get things done."

Beyond assisting in service organisations Tan Sri Lim contributed monetarily where he could. In 1990, he footed the RM15,000 bill to provide plastic surgery to a 10-year-old burn victim from a poor Malay family. The victim's face and body had been horribly scarred in a fire when he was three years old.

In 1987, the proceeds from the sale of the second edition of his book containing his cartoon strips called Guli-Guli (Marbles) at RM1,000 a copy were donated to the Society for the Rehabilitation of the Handicapped, the Ex-Policemen's Association, the Ex-Servicemen's Association and the Women's Aid Organisation. Only 300 copies of the hardcover edition were printed.

Cancerlink Foundation

In 1988, following the death of his mother-in-law from cancer, he helped to found Cancerlink, a non-profit foundation offering counselling services and day-care centre for those suffering from cancer as well as their families. It also provided free lodging for low-income patients from out of town who had to come to the capital city for treatment.

He was driven to start Cancerlink after seeing how his mother-in-law suffered from misdiagnosis and lack of proper care and attention from the hospital. It was, he said, to ensure that those suffering from cancer were treated with dignity and their families helped through the process with care and sensitivity.

"My mother-in-law had been a teacher all her adult life, so she felt she had earned the privilege of going to a government hospital to be taken care of," he said. "She was at a local hospital and I was really taken aback by the scenes I saw whilst visiting her.

"I saw a lot of cancer patients waiting there, many of them from out of town, waiting hours for a doctor to attend to them. They were in pain and they had no choice but to wait. It really troubled me."

After being treated, Tan Sri Lim's mother-in-law was told she had no more traces of the cancer and was released.

She later complained of bleeding and was taken to a private hospital. The family was told her condition was terminal. The cancer had spread to her lungs and she was given not more than three months to live.

When Tan Sri Lim – in an effort to find out how his mother-in-law was given a clean bill of health earlier – sought an explanation from the public hospital, he ran into a bureaucratic maze.

"When I said I wanted to see her records, I was told I had to write in formally. I did, but was then told I could not have the records. The only way he could get them, he was told, was if the hospital was 'compelled' to give them to him.

"In other words, sue us," said Tan Sri Lim. "When we asked a lawyer about suing the hospital, we were advised against it. He told us we would be taking on the whole government and that would be risky."

Frustrated, he channelled his energy into starting Cancerlink so that other cancer sufferers and their families would have a place to turn to that would help them through the ordeal.

"I have always wanted to leave something behind, because life isn't just about making money," he said. "I always see what I do for others as part of what I do. For instance, when I was building the advertising business, I did not see it as a business per se. To me, it was a craft. And I just wanted to do it very well. What you do for others – whether it's Cancerlink, whether it's the neighbours, whether it's somebody who needed money to have a transplant – you just need to do what you have to do."

Society for the Severely Mentally Handicapped

Tan Sri Lim founded the Society for the Severely Mentally Handicapped in 1984. It was a spin-off from his work with the Rotary Club after he was approached by some parents to help set up a home for severely mentally handicapped children.

When the Rotary Club could not commit itself to a project that required RM200,000-300,000 a year to run, Tan Sri Lim offered to help register and set it up and then help from behind the scenes.

Right from the beginning, he faced obstacles. He was discouraged from setting it up by the then Ministry of Welfare.

"I think they meant to be considerate to me," he said. "They said I should channel my time and energy into an organisation where the people could be helped because the children with severe mental handicap are not people you can do much for. So it took me a while to convince them that money would not be wasted. I assured them that I would not come to them for money, and that I would raise it myself."

Tan Sri Lim's heart goes out to these children because he said such children and their families have a stigma to contend with.

"Chinese parents believe a child born with mental handicap is the result of some kind of jinx or a curse," he said. "Therefore, they keep the children behind closed doors. In the past, you even read in the newspapers about them being chained."

While publicity is often seen as a tool to create reform of such behaviour, Tan Sri Lim pleaded with newspapers not to print such photographs. "The Society needed time to overcome this and it took us some time to convince the newspapers – especially Chinese ones - to stop publishing such photographs."

The idea behind SSMH is to have centres around the country, supported by the community. This is to remove the misconception and stigma associated with mental retardation and to create greater understanding. The SSMH is more than a care centre. It offers training to parents and family members on how to care for such children.

Scholarships for the creatively inclined

When Tan Sri Lim set up the Limkokwing Institute of Creative Technology he wanted humanitarian activities to form part of its culture. The Foundation for Creative Excellence was mobilized to provide scholarships for talented but underprivileged school-leavers. This was a unique scholarship scheme that has given to students from all backgrounds -

regardless of race - the opportunity to gain a tertiary education.

In 2003 the school was given special recognition by the Ministry of Education for the most number of scholarships given.

Among the recipients of the Foundation's scholarship was athlete Anastasia Karen, 25. Winner of numerous individual gold awards in national and international race walking events, her tenacity and commitment to her goals was an example to young people everywhere. Despite also having represented Malaysia in the Atlanta Olympics in 1996, she discovered that no one was willing to help her get the tertiary education she needed when she retired from professional race walking.

Anastasia remembered that she was at an emotional low point after numerous rejections by public and private colleges that she had approached. After having dedicated years to represent the country internationally, and with numerous commendations and recommendations from national sporting associations, she kept getting the cold shoulder from tertiary institutions.

Anastasia's plea for assistance in a local newspaper caught Tan Sri Lim's attention, and he immediately offered her a full scholarship to study at the College. He was frustrated and irate with the way she had been treated, calling it "ridiculous" and a "sorry state of affairs" that someone like Anastasia found no support from the very country she represented with such commitment for so many years.

The Limkokwing Foundation for Creative Excellence is a one-of-its-kind scholarship facility in the country. It offers an opportunity for those who excel in various areas - not just academic - to pursue a tertiary education. It provides scholarships for those with talent, but facing financial constraints.

What makes the Foundation unique is that besides offering scholarships to academic high achievers, those with promising achievements in other areas such as sports, art and design, writing, and other creative areas are also eligible. Additionally, those who are physically challenged but able to produce a portfolio that shows talent, can also apply for a scholarship. Almost every year you will see hearing-impaired young people graduating with Diplomas and Degrees.

"Every Malaysian has a role to play and no one should be excluded, as long as they are capable and committed," says Tan Sri Lim of his Foundation's mission.

Limkokwing Institute for Tomorrow

Tan Sri Lim has spoken many times about the harsh inequalities in the world in speeches he made around the world. He points to the huge divide between rich and poor, literate and illiterate, developed and developing countries. "Clearly this is a divide we don't need and don't want," he says.

Poverty, he warns, undermines social and political stability. In many regions, poverty is the cause as well as the consequence of conflict.

He is convinced that the eradication of poverty is the first step to a more peaceful world; and that education is the most effective key to poverty eradication.

"Knowledge is an indispensable economic resource. It empowers people and expands their range of choice. Educated people are more likely to be employed, and to remain employed. The better qualified they are, the higher their income is likely to be. Thus, by dismantling the barriers to education and increasing access to knowledge and skills, we will be helping to create more economic winners," he reasons.

To help drive his vision, he established the Limkokwing Institute for Tomorrow (LIFT) in 2007.

LIFT will work initially with local communities and political leaders in Africa to operate free ICT Training Centres.

The programme has two primary thrusts. Firstly, it is to use ICT as an enabler to provide disadvantaged communities new knowledge and technological skills. The purpose is to help bridge the digital divide, promote the use of technology in improving lives, and to teach marketable skills to people who are deprived of a good education because they are too poor to go to school or the districts where they live are too poor to build good schools. Secondly, by creating ICT-trained human capital, LIFT will play the role of a catalyst to attract investments in industries that expand employment and business opportunities.

Through its programme, LIFT aims to contribute to strengthening capacity-building efforts so as to enable the transformation of countries in Africa.

Pesta Pembangunan (Development Carnival) was a landmark exhibition presenting the country's plans for the future. It was the biggest organized in the country, occupying the length and breadth of the national stadium. It provided the main thrust of the election manifesto developed by Tun Abdul Razak as he faced a country recovering from the racial riots of May 13, 1969. Tan Sri Lim, at that time a young man in his 20s, was given only a few days to visualize the concept of the exhibition and develop a story in a way that would be palatable to a divided nation.

Top: *Malaysia's second Prime Minister Tun Abdul Razak during his official visit of Pesta Pembangunan, the vehicle that helped Malaysian Chinese and Indians grasp the full import of the New Economic Policy which was the Prime Minister's strategy to address Malay concerns that they were losing out on economic opportunities.*

Bottom: *Malaysia's King – DYMM Seri Paduka Baginda Yang di-Pertuan Agung Sultan Abdul Halim Muazzam Shah Ibni Almarhum Sultan Badlishah with his consort DYMM Permaisuri Agung Almarhum Sultanah Bahiyah Binti Tuanku Abdul Rahman during their official visit to the exhibition.*

Designing A Nation

Designing a nation is to get involved in its politics and its people

What do I mean when I refer to a nation? Essentially I refer to its people and its environment. By people I am referring to the mindset, the prevailing traditions and culture that influence the tendencies of the people who live in a country. By environment I am alluding to the infrastructure as well as the political leadership and policies that influence the lives of the people. To design a nation is to become absorbed in its politics and its culture. To design a nation is to aspire to change the way politics is played, policies are made and how people think and act.

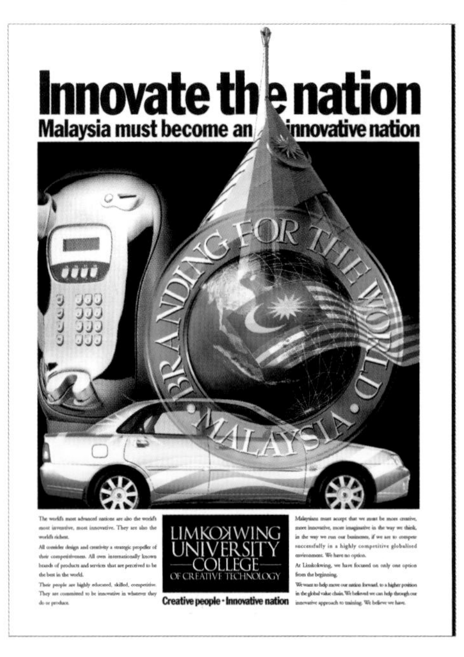

Designing a nation begins with the desire to change people

Before an individual engages in designing a nation, he or she must have the desire to change people and their environment and thereby alter their circumstances. That desire is present in almost everyone.

We must now focus on creating transformational systems that will prepare the country for a quantum leap from where we are to where we must be - an innovation economy - capable of competing with the best in the world.

Limkokwing
2007

It is weak in some and stronger in others. In an individual with a driving passion and commitment, the desire can energise him or her to perform feats of greatness. It can galvanise the person to reach out to new areas, to chart new frontiers, to set new benchmarks. To make possible the impossible. All the world's great leaders in the past were driven by such a burning desire; what they did changed the course of history.

Using perseverance and determination to build success and transform lives

Tan Sri Dato' Sri Dr Lim Kok Wing transformed his life using the golden principles of perseverance and determination. He understands the power of these qualities and he applies them throughout his life to reap success in everything that he does.

Having lifted his life out of the cycle of poverty that he was born into, he wanted to change the lives of others. As a young man his hard work and talent created milestones within the advertising industry that he worked in. He has the distinction of being the first Malaysian to become an art director in a multinational agency and later he became the first Malaysian and first Asian regional creative director. But he was one man and he saw that he was not making much of a dent in the way the world perceived Malaysia and Malaysians. Not many people around the world knew the country existed. The work he produced won accolades for the agency he worked for. The credit was seldom, if ever, attributed to Malaysian talent.

Using energy and drive to build talent and to blaze ahead

He left the multinational agency to set up on his own. Here he gathered together young Malaysian talent and groomed them. He started small but aimed big. He pitched against foreign agencies for blue-chip accounts. He was very confident of his ability and he persevered; even when he was continuously turned down, he never gave up. Within months of starting his business he succeeded in proving that Malaysian talent was as good as any out there. One by one, international brands such as Standard & Chartered Bank, Proctor & Gamble, Castrol, Mercedes Benz and many others, began to see the value of his strategy and embraced his ideas. As his business grew he looked for other avenues where he could make a difference in bringing change to Malaysians. He knew there was more he could do. He plunged into humanitarian work but was swept up by the political leadership which turned to him to help build the nation.

Tan Sri Lim has the ability to understand Government intentions and translate them into communications that are easily understood by people. Tun Dr Mahathir recognized this ability very early in his tenure as Prime Minister. He drew Tan Sri Lim into his circle of professionals who could assist in building bridges between Government and people. Here you see outdoor media that were used on various occasions to deliver messages on unity.

Rakan Muda was a solution provided by Tan Sri Lim to overcome a youth-related issue. The philosophy of Rakan Muda (Young Friend in Malay) was to provide a wide range of sports and recreational activities that would appeal to youths. Rakan Muda became a controversial issue when thousands of youths responded to the campaign, catching the Ministry of Youth and Sports unprepared for the deluge. The Ministry re-organised itself to channel responses to existing sports clubs and recreational societies.

The Yakin Boleh signature line of the Rakan Muda campaign became the aspiration for the Malaysia Boleh battle cry that was heard the loudest during the 16th Commonwealth Games hosted by Kuala Lumpur in 1998, the first to be held in an Asian city.

Top: *Tun Dr Mahathir dotting the eye of the bird that was drawn by a child studying at the Wings of Creativity children's centre. The Prime Minister in January 2002 launched the publication Wings of Creativity which encapsulated the 3-decade journey of Tan Sri Lim.*

Bottom: *A brochure promoting the children's centre called Wings of Creativity. The centre was an innovative venture that changed the way people viewed the education of young children. The centre broke away from the norm building children's skills in using the computer to flesh out their ideas about the world around them. Being a pioneering venture the authorities had no category to place it in providing the centre a permit to practice. It was not a kindergarten neither was it a tuition centre.*

Top: *When Tan Sri Lim was asked to design the uniform for the National Service programme he was strategic in using the tiger stripes as the inspiration. He wanted to anchor an identity that would belong to Malaysia. Here you see Dato' Seri Najib, Deputy Prime Minister in 2005 with new recruits wearing the blue tiger stripes.*

Middle: *Invited to design the official attire for the Malaysian national sports team he again used the tiger stripes as the inspiration. By doing so he was consciously developing a Malaysian identity, one that was filled with competitive spirit, power and stamina to symbolize the aspirations of the Malaysian sportsmen and sportswomen.*

Bottom: *Tak Nak (Don't Want in Malay) became a brand that stood for anti-smoking. For a year a dedicated campaign to build awareness about the dangers of smoking began to pick up momentum. However politics nipped it in the bud, losing the Government a valuable opportunity to address a serious issue.*

***Top:** The University's branding gallery has now become a showcase gallery for small and medium sized entrepreneurs keen to upgrade their product branding. In 2010 the government agency - SMECORP Malaysia - signed a collaboration with the University to provide training for SMEs.*

***Middle:** A key feature of the University's branding gallery was the now and new section which has been translated into a mobile gallery designed to bring new ideas in packaging right to the doorstep of entrepreneurs living in remote parts of the country.*

***Bottom:** The Prime Minister Dato' Sri Mohd Najib Tun Abdul Razak and Dato Seri Dr Ahmad Zahid Hamidi, Minister of Defence check out the packaging designs in the mobile gallery. Dato' Dania, Vice-President of Limkokwing University was there to facilitate the visit.*

Top: *In July 1995 Tun Mahathir launched the Malaysia Incorporated publication, a road map to investment in Malaysia. Mooted and managed by Tan Sri Lim it pooled the knowledge and expertise of leading players in both public and private sectors in presenting the country's prospects for the future.*

Middle: *Tan Sri Lim with veteran politician and former Cabinet Minister the late Tan Sri Dr Muhammad Ghazali Shafie and Dato' Sri Najib Tun Abdul Razak, Minister of Defence, who launched the Hidden Agenda publication. Also in the picture is Datin Seri Rosmah Abu Mansor, wife of Dato' Sri Najib.*

Bottom: *In January 2010 the Deputy Minister of Science, Technology and Innovation, Tuan Haji Fadillah bin Yusof (fifth from left) launched Tan Sri Lim's Innovation Enabling Transformation book which was a compilation of his speeches and articles on creativity and innovation.*

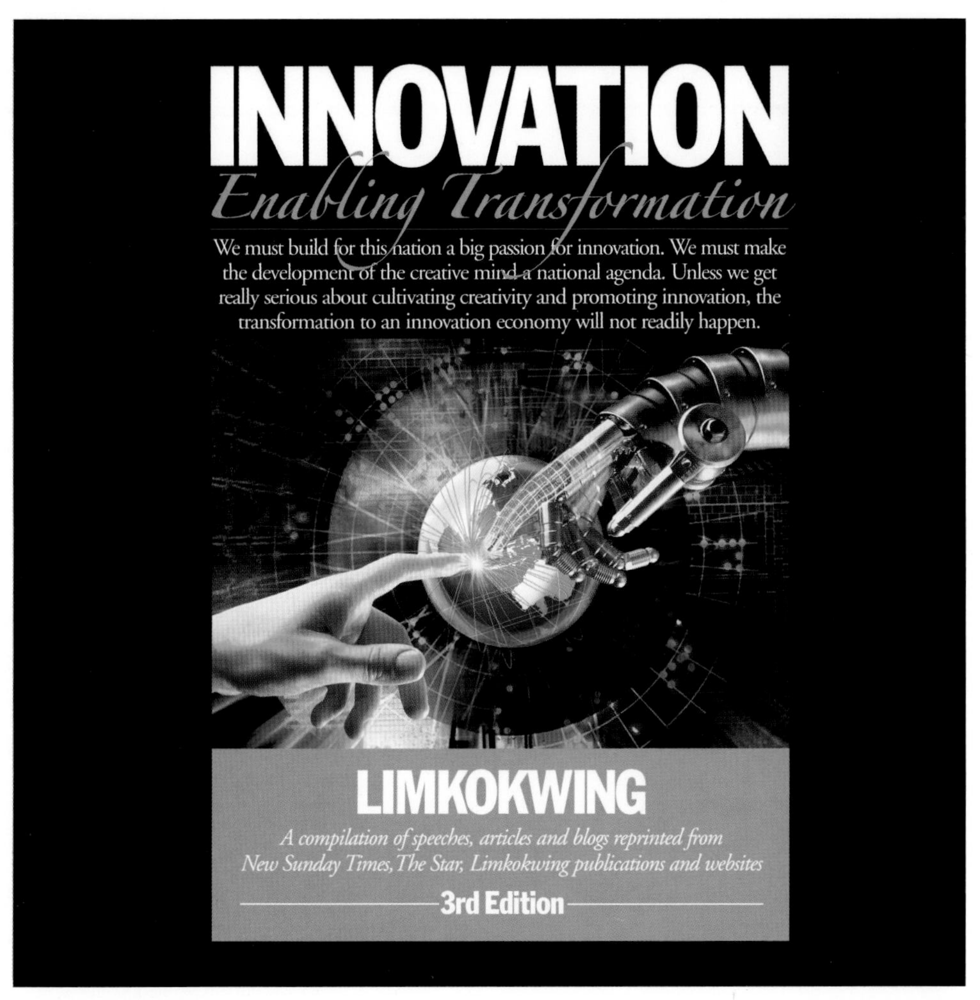

A highly sought-after speaker Tan Sri Lim is also a prolific writer especially on the topic of innovation. This publication also included many of his views from his blog, his newspaper and magazine articles as well as his speeches dating back 15 years.

Political Baptism

Malaysia is a nation young in age but built upon a unique historical foundation that reaches back thousands of years to the great civilisations of Asia and Europe. This is a kaleidoscopic nation nourished and enriched by a diversity of cultures, religions, languages and ethnicity that is a mirror of the world. Its diversity is the country's greatest strength. It pulls together the talents and knowledge of almost all the races in the world which have made Malaysia their home. "In other countries, you will find many different races but they don't live and integrate like those in Malaysia," says Tan Sri Lim.

Peninsular Malaya, then known as the Federation of Malaya, gained its independence from the British in 1957. It later joined with the British-administered territories of North Borneo (now Sabah), Sarawak and Singapore to form the Federation of Malaysia in 1963. Singapore was expelled from the federation in 1965.

The British had left behind a fairly sound infrastructure but that was built mainly to facilitate the exploitation of the nation's rich natural resources of tin and rubber. Basic amenities did not reach much of the population living in the rural heartland. With Malaysians at the helm, the nation began to forge forward.

The first three Prime Ministers – Tunku Abdul Rahman Al Haj, Tun Abdul Razak Hussein and Tun Hussein Onn - diversified and expanded the economic base from concentration on tin and rubber to include oil palm, timber products, oil and gas, and industrial manufacturing. There was progress. There was prosperity.

Then came the fourth Prime Minister – Tun Dr Mahathir Mohamad – who took office in 1981. He charted the way forward for Malaysia as far ahead as 2020. His Vision 2020, enunciated in 1991, was cast as the catalyst to lift the nation to fully developed status. Soon after he took the helm, he began to expand steel production capacity to facilitate the manufacture of a national car, Proton. It was a move unheard of in the developing world and much derided by critics in the West but he persisted. The national car project was the first of many controversial decisions to accelerate Malaysia's transformation from agriculture-led to industry-driven, from export of raw commodities to export of manufactured products that originated in this country.

But first the Prime Minister needed to bring Malaysians on board his vision. He needed to change Malaysians' conservative mindset. He needed to build faith and confidence in Malaysians. He needed to move a whole population to see themselves through his eyes – as people who are as capable as anyone, anywhere, in the world, if not better. And he wanted the world to see his nation as skilful, innovative, knowledgeable and quality-conscious.

The Mahathir Years

A meeting of like minds

Tan Sri Lim did not know Mahathir personally when the latter took office as Prime Minister in 1981. He was already six years into managing his own advertising and communications business called Wings Creative Consultants. He was 35 years old and winning his own battle to prove that Malaysians were as talented as the best in the world in the advertising business.

Tan Sri Lim's advertising genius put him in the spotlight. His award-winning prowess, his vocal opinions on a host of Malaysian advertising, social and humanitarian issues, and his determination to prove that Malaysian creativity was just as good, if not better, than Western ideas caught Tun Dr Mahathir's attention.

What got the two together was a weekly cartoon series begun in 1981 by Tan Sri Lim called *Guli-Guli* - Malay for Marbles - which featured the heartwarming traits of the Malaysian character through the conversation of three friends - Bakar, a Malay, Ah Boo, a Chinese and Muthu, an Indian. He skilfully used humour to point out Malaysian eccentricities while advocating in his narrative a goodwill message to build cohesion among the races and promote acceptance of our multicultural diversity. The crafty satirical strips had a follower in the new Prime Minister.

"He was never a man of many words, so the idea of delivering messages with simple caricatures appealed to him because he felt they were more effective than a thousand words," recalled Tan Sri Lim. "He was very good at conceptualising. He was very innovative and very willing to challenge the norm, push the boundaries. He was also very strategic and very creative."

It was a meeting of creative minds and the beginning of a long relationship.

In 1982 *Guli-Guli* strips were featured on billboards all over the country. It was a public relations message to foster courtesy and good behaviour among people of different races. These were messages in tandem with the prevailing socio-political thrust.

It was the start he was looking for. With the accomplishment of each task that Tun Dr Mahathir brought to Tan Sri Lim, confidence grew in the Prime Minister that he had harnessed a brilliant mind that could assist him in many ways.

Tan Sri Lim relished the challenges. In Tun Dr Mahathir he found an exceptional leader and gladly contributed his expertise to create campaigns that were among the most memorable in Malaysia. His great admiration for Tun Dr Mahathir was very clear when he spoke during a ceremony at which his university awarded the former premier an Honorary Doctorate of Humanity in June 2008. Said Tan Sri Lim, "He created a revolution that he accomplished in stages and by phases over 22 years. He built the tallest buildings and the longest bridges. He built them with every Malaysian in mind. With every steel frame of their construction he lifted the spirit of every Malaysian. He re-engineered their hearts and minds to leap from impossible to possible. He moved mountains that stood in the way as he moved the nation forward. He embedded the maxim "Yes We Can!" 10 years before it became a slogan of the winning campaign for presidency in a far-away country."

While Tun Dr Mahathir designed ground-breaking policies and implemented mammoth projects, Tan Sri Lim designed campaigns to warm hearts, change mindsets and win battles.

Branding Malaysia

The branding of Malaysia – this discovery of self and identity – was driven by Tun Dr Mahathir Mohamad. He set in motion the birth of a new, modern Malaysia. Not just of the landscape and infrastructure, but of a generation that believed anything was possible. It was a generation that believed it was inferior to none.

He saw in Tan Sri Lim a man who understood what he was trying to achieve. Their working together was surely predetermined. Tan Sri Lim was by all accounts a trusted confidante to Tun Dr Mahathir. In addition to working on voter education campaigns during general elections for the ruling party, Tan Sri Lim's portfolio of projects - spanning the two decades when Tun Dr Mahathir was Prime Minister - had been intimately linked to the rebranding of major national entities and the branding of new corporate entities. His expertise was also called upon to create public information campaigns such as the Anti-Piracy, Anti-Inflation and Anti-Smoking campaigns.

Tan Sri Lim pioneered new fields in the branding and promotion of sports and events marketing in the Kuala Lumpur Commonwealth Games, the Asian Games bid by Malaysia and a national youth development programme called Rakan Muda.

His expertise was at the forefront of many national campaigns to 'sell' Malaysia's capability to the world – such as the work he did for Tourism Promotion Board of Malaysia and the Made-in-Malaysia for the World campaign for the Ministry of International Trade and Industry.

Why was his work so popular with government agencies? Tan Sri Lim had an uncanny ability to grasp the 'big picture' of where the country was headed and what it needed to do to get there.

He had helped to hone the country's competitive edge by giving visual identity, personality and shape to its national policies and initiatives. These were campaigns that made the nation sit up and take notice; campaigns that made the people think; campaigns that motivated and inspired.

It was this that became the essence of Tan Sri Lim's work – to brand the nation. It became his most important mission. It has become his lifelong passion.

Straddling power bases

Despite his many years of working within the political circles, Tan Sri Lim had no illusions about how he was viewed and where he stood. He was an outsider and that meant what he could do was limited.

Without official standing, he relied on his own credibility and acceptability to move with the government, media, NGOs and the public. Working to communicate the government's policies and actions in that environment was akin to negotiating an obstacle course. He had to tread cautiously so as not to trip up; yet he had to show results.

Tan Sri Lim created this logo for Matrade in 1995 to communicate Malaysia's pride, in the global quality of its products and services.

But the outsider tag didn't get him off the merry-go-round of suspicions and paranoia surrounding the political establishment.

"This is a very protocol-conscious society," he said. "To move forward on things that required the support of many people often turned out to be monumental tasks and I did get tired of it sometimes."

He long ago decided that to do what he wanted, he had to remain 'unseen' in the background. Thus, little of what he did in various election campaigns or other government campaigns found their way into media reports.

"I prefer it that way so that whatever campaign I worked on would not be linked to a person," he said.

"Because of the obstacles, I failed in some of the things I had set out to do. When things get too difficult, you simply have to move on to something else. It's a very fluid environment but, on the bright side, I had a chance to work with practically everyone in the Mahathir Cabinet, and very closely with most of them."

The prevalent perception of Tan Sri Lim – both within political circles as well as outside – was that he was staunchly loyal to Tun Dr Mahathir. It was to affect his relationship with the political leadership when Tun Abdullah Ahmad Badawi took over as Prime Minister from Tun Dr Mahathir. Tan Sri Lim was kept at arms length for some time by Tun Abdullah's advisers during the transition of power.

Tan Sri Lim acknowledged with a wry grin that he was said to be a Mahathir 'crony' but dismissed accusations of blind loyalty to him.

"If you know me, you will know I do not trade my principles in order to become popular or to gain anything," he said. "It's not about blind loyalty to Tun Dr Mahathir; I was loyal to the chair. I performed the same role when Tun Abdullah became Prime Minister and again now when Dato' Sri Najib is the Prime Minister because I contribute my services to the country and not solely to an individual."

He never referred to Tun Dr Mahathir as his friend. "I don't go horse riding with him. I am seldom seen in public with him, and that's by design. I do not take his friendship for granted. But we do have a close rapport – an intellectual, purpose-driven rapport. It's not what Malaysians would call a 'friend-friend' thing.

"For instance, I have only invited him to my own functions three times. Once was when we opened the Artiquarium Gallery because he had expressed a desire to visit Loke Mansion, a beautiful heritage building in KL. The second was when I invited him to visit the university at its (former) Mayang campus and he did come." The third occasion was when the university conferred an Honorary Doctorate of Humanity on Tun Dr Mahathir in June 2009.

The Artiquarium, which showcased Asian arts and culture crafts, was the largest and most reputable private art and antique gallery in the country.

Tan Sri Lim described his relationship with Tun Dr Mahathir as a "long-running working one".

"We work consciously to build harmony, cohesion and encouraging Malaysians to move forward, to have more confidence in their own abilities. It's been many years now."

Tan Sri Lim believes Malaysia is unlikely to see another leader in the mould of Tun Dr Mahathir for a long time to come.

Mahathir and the Western media

The incessant attacks by the foreign media on Tun Dr Mahathir in the last years of his tenure – especially since 1997 – was evidence of the global standing he enjoyed despite being the leader of a tiny Third World nation. Mahathir's Malaysia was punching way above its weight in the world. Tun Dr Mahathir was given many cover stories in leading international publications. The Western media – while often uncomplimentary to him – still found him a fascinating Asian icon.

Hong Kong-based The Far Eastern Economic Review, in a cover story in January 2001 headlined *Mahathir: Declining Powers*, wrote: "His approach to leading Malaysia has been to browbeat, cajole and, if necessary, persecute those who don't share his vision of progress and development."

Yet, it gave Mahathir credit, albeit grudgingly.

"In the end, Mahathir will be judged as a great Asian leader. But his legacy will be coloured by his uncompromising political views and the way that he recast Malaysia's democratic institutions in a more authoritarian mould."

Asiaweek, another news magazine published in Hong Kong, was more balanced in its judgment, describing him as the Great Survivor in a June 2001 cover story entitled *Rebranding Mahathir* that painted him as a leader that kept coming back to fight battle after battle.

"At perhaps his weakest ebb in two decades," pronounced Asiaweek in reference to the erosion of electoral support in the 1999 general election following the ruthless sacking of his deputy prime minister and heir apparent, Dato' Seri Anwar Ibrahim, from the government and his party Umno, the year before, "the Malaysian Prime Minister came surging home like a spring tide."

The writer of the cover story, that analysed Tun Dr Mahathir's no-nonsense presidential speech at the annual Umno General Assembly, added: "At his most vulnerable, he was at his best."

"So when he stands up to debate or criticise them (foreign media) – something hardly any Third World leader will do – they take it as an affront. I think that has been at the crux of this orchestrated campaign to vilify him in the international media."

Tan Sri Lim, although frustrated by the jaundiced reporting, never gave up hope of getting the international media to see the story of Tun Dr Mahathir from the reality on the ground. As someone who was looking in, up close and personal, he knew the reports in the local media were distorted when picked up by the international press.

"I remember at one stage he just didn't want to talk to them, even though they kept seeking interviews. I think he was just tired because every time he spoke to them, he was misquoted," he said.

Tan Sri Lim said he convinced Tun Dr Mahathir that he needed to keep talking to the foreign media even though the latter disliked giving interviews and talking about himself. "He asked me, 'You still want me to talk to them?' and I said, 'Yes.' And he said: 'I will still call a spade a spade'."

And so Tun Dr Mahathir continued to talk to the foreign media, but

Tan Sri Lim admitted that "things didn't get any better".

Still, despite his great resentment at the negative treatment by the international media, Tun Dr Mahathir never wielded the powers he had to clamp down on their operations in the country.

The International Herald Tribune was printed in Malaysia, yet they carried articles that attacked Tun Dr Mahathir viciously. One which appeared in the last quarter of 2000 was headlined to the effect of "*A Doctor Divides a Nation*".

"The writer began the story by narrating about a hawker holding up a coconut and smashing it into two as if it was someone's head. And writing that the hawker was thinking of Mahathir when he did it.

"How can they do that!" exclaimed Tan Sri Lim. "The paper was printed here and it would be so easy for Tun Dr Mahathir to withdraw the approval to print it here. After all, this is our country and why should we allow someone else to come here and rail against our leader like that?"

But Tun Dr Mahathir never gave any such order. He allowed the IHT to continue. This was just one of many contradictions in the Western media that many in the outside world did not see, Tan Sri Lim said regretfully.

Above: Tan Sri Lim designed this tribute to Tun Dr Mahathir Mohamad which was produced by the Ministry of Foreign Affairs.

Tan Sri Lim reckoned that a big part of the dislike the Western media had against Tun Dr Mahathir was his outspokenness. Ironically, he added, that was the very thing that drew them like moths to the flame in wanting to do interviews and features on him.

However, Tun Dr Mahathir's steadfastness in his views earned him some good reports, such as the good reviews by regional media of the book, *The Malaysian Currency Crisis: How and Why it Happened* (not published by Tan Sri Lim), which chronicled Malaysia's handling of the 1997-98 Asian financial crisis during which the Malaysian Ringgit and other regional currencies came under sustained attacks by currency speculators. The Ringgit lost half of its value, falling from above 2.50 to under 4.10 to the US dollar. Inflation jumped and the Kuala Lumpur stock exchange slumped. The crisis spread rapidly across East Asian economies. While Indonesia, Thailand and South Korea turned to the International Monetary Fund to bail out their drastically devalued currencies, Tun Dr Mahathir refused IMF aid which risked mass shutdown of Malaysian companies, escalating job losses and destabilising the country politically. Instead, he chose a radical solution by imposing strict capital controls and pegging the Ringgit to the US dollar. The measures worked, returning Malaysia more quickly to economic stability and growth than those countries that took the IMF route.

Asiaweek in its July 23, 1999 review said the book was "...a chastening read...Dr Mahathir says much that needs to be said. He says publicly what many leaders think, but don't have the guts to enunciate. Indeed, the evidence for his argument grows as time passes. He is worth listening to and he does provoke. The Prime Minister's capacity for provocation is perhaps his greatest attribute."

The Far Eastern Economic Review in its June 17, 1999 review said: "For those who consider his anti-Western convictions vindicated by the Asian economic crisis, the book offers a timely and readable affirmation. What comes through loud and clear is Mahathir's utter dismay at the power of global economic sentiment, and his unflinching belief that Malaysia and the rest of Asia are victims of a new form of imperialism."

Mahathir and the local media

Tan Sri Lim believed that the misreporting by the Western media could have been due to the sometimes simplistic interpretations of Tun Dr Mahathir's remarks by the local media.

"Very often – where the local media is concerned – he talked to an audience made up of people who were not very sophisticated. Because of that, he had a tendency to reduce things to the simplest form and use very simple words to explain things. This was also very often done in Malay."

He quoted the example of Tun Dr Mahathir's comments that if Malaysians didn't take care of the economy, the country could be taken over by others.

"It was a simple way of talking about maintaining independence. What he meant was if you could not stand on your own feet, your companies and banks would be taken over, and you would come under the influence of others," said Tan Sri Lim.

"But because it was reported in a simplistic way in the local papers, the Western media picked it up and scoffed at Tun Dr Mahathir's references to economic colonisation.

Mahathir: Voice of the Third World

Few would dispute that Tun Dr Mahathir was greatly respected by leaders of Third World nations. Tan Sri Lim was very much aware of this admiration as he travelled extensively, both as part of Tun Dr Mahathir's delegation on official visits or to attend business and trade promotion events, as well as during his private business trips. He had also worked in South Africa on the African National Congress' (ANC) voter education exercise for the country's first democratic elections won by Nelson Mandela. The admiration for Tun Dr Mahathir was obvious.

"In countries like South Africa, Botswana and Lesotho, he is a world hero," said Tan Sri Lim. "People were amazed by his ability to develop Malaysia, build unity, and get on stage to hold a debate with leaders of the most powerful countries in the world – and had the audacity to disagree with them publicly."

He was bold and he was outspoken. He set the tone that rallied the developing world. He became the voice of conscience in a conflict-driven, painfully divided world.

Tan Sri Lim recalled the words of former South African President Nelson Mandela, a good friend of Tun Dr Mahathir, who said to him, 'Your Prime Minister is a very tall man'.

"I corrected him by saying, 'Not really. He is no taller than me'. He then said more assertively, 'I mean your Prime Minister is a very tall leader'. This time I corrected myself by saying, 'Sure, in that sense, he is at least a hundred times taller than me'!"

A new leader and new priorities

Tan Sri Lim has known Tun Abdullah Ahmad Badawi, or Pak Lah (Uncle Lah) as he is known to most Malaysians because of his friendly and kindly nature, much longer than Tun Dr Mahathir. "About 30 years," he recalled. "We worked together in the Malaysian Vocational Guidance Association. We used to spend a lot of time chatting. When I was President of the Bandaraya Association in Bangsar, he would come to our gatherings. We once ate durians by the roadside."

Tan Sri Lim said his first royal award came through Tun Abdullah's recommendation.

Tun Abdullah, then a Vice President of Umno, was appointed Deputy Prime Minister by Tun Dr Mahathir on January 8, 1999 to replace Dato' Seri Anwar Ibrahim after the latter was sacked as deputy premier and deputy president of Umno. The appointment came as a surprise to many but those who knew Tun Abdullah well considered him a "timely stabilising factor" in Umno which was, and still is, the leading party in the ruling Barisan Nasional (National Front) coalition. Tun Abdullah became deputy president of Umno the following year.

In an interview just before Tun Abdullah succeeded Tun Dr Mahathir as Prime Minister on October 31, 2003, Tan Sri Lim described him as

It is for people like Tan Sri Lim, who understands the art of communication, to package our ideas so that they are better understood and thus, become more acceptable. Tan Sri Lim's creative mind enables him to see things from many perspectives. He is able to get to the heart of the matter and, thereby, help rally public support.

Tun Abdullah Haji Ahmad Badawi
Prime Minister, Malaysia, 2004

"a soft spoken, no-frills type who does what is right, is loyal to a fault, a gentleman by nature, diplomatic by character."

As deputy premier Tun Abdullah helped to bring stability to the storm-tossed politics that roiled Umno and the Barisan Nasional in the wake of the Anwar controversy. At the helm was the ultra-modern, technology-loving Tun Dr Mahathir and by his side was Tun Abdullah, a pious Muslim nicknamed by the media as 'Mr Nice' whose more easy-going personality appealed to the people of the rural Malay heartland who were the decision makers in every general election.

Tun Abdullah was seen as more approachable than the stern-faced Tun Dr Mahathir; a soft-spoken, sincere and smiling leader with a strong record of public service and administrative experience dating back to the 1960s. He resigned from government service in 1978 to enter politics and was elected Member of Parliament for Kepala Batas in the northern state of Penang. He has held the seat since then and was re-elected in the 2008 general election.

His rise to the top had not been spectacular but it was steady. While factions within Umno fought each other, he had remained cool and level-headed and stayed true to his party's ideals.

But after so many years of working with a personality such as Tun Dr Mahathir how did Tan Sri Lim fare with the new Prime Minister?

It started out as a difficult time for him as he was seen to be a Mahathir loyalist but his friendship with Tun Abdullah helped him cross the barrier. Even then it wasn't overnight because those close to Tun Abdullah made it tough for Tan Sri Lim to play the role that he had been used to for so many years.

For Tan Sri Lim, so used to a Mahathir-led government, it was hard to adjust. But he persevered and managed to find his balance although the new role was a far cry from the heady Mahathir days of major nation-building projects.

The Endon factor

Working with Tun Abdullah meant there was always his wife, the late Datin Seri Endon (now Tun, an award conferred to her posthumously by the King), to consider. "She was a very strong woman. Her passion was in pushing for the resurgence of batik and songket, both traditional fabrics, and she was very successful at it. Her resilience was phenomenal because she worked very hard alongside Tun Abdullah to help him in his political career while strategising to position batik in the global fashion market. And all that time she was fighting breast cancer. She was a pillar of strength to him and when she passed away it almost broke him," he said.

Tun Endon passed away on 20 October 2005. One month later Tan Sri Lim held a special banquet as President of the Malaysian Institute of Directors to show support to Tun Abdullah's leadership. His son, Kamaluddin, thanked Tan Sri Lim and described the event as a turning point for Tun Abdullah as he struggled to make up his mind about continuing his work as Prime Minister. Kamaluddin told Tan Sri Lim that the event had renewed his father's faith and confidence.

The Vision to transform a nation

There was speculation regarding Vision 2020, a broad set of ideals aimed at ultimately achieving fully developed nation status for Malaysia by the year 2020 introduced by Tun Dr Mahathir in 1991, and what the new administration was going to do with it. In March 2006 Tun Abdullah tabled the 9th Malaysia Plan - the first 5-year development plan prepared by the Tun Abdullah administration. He put forward a new set of ideas designed to realise the aspirations of Vision 2020. He called it the National Mission – a framework for the country's development agenda which outlined the key steps that must be taken in the remaining 15 years to achieve the goals of Vision 2020.

He said the National Mission was similar to ascending a mountain. "The first half of the climb to the base camp is challenging, but the real test lies in scaling the peak. As we enter the next phase – the final assault – we face greater challenges and more intense competition."

A year later, in August 2007 Tan Sri Lim organised a banquet attended by industry leaders where the book *Mission 2020: The Final Stretch,* published by Tan Sri Lim, was launched. The book, provided an overview of the National Mission's five thrusts. It was translated into three languages

Tan Sri Lim understands that to move forward we need the drive. His main contribution is about moving society, inviting people into innovation. He is recognized as a paradigm pioneer, a leader who brings about shifts in thinking about realities.

Prof. Dato' Ibrahim Ahmad Bajunid, President, Malaysian Association of Leadership Management, 2010

and widely distributed to enable more Malaysians, as well as foreigners, to understand Tun Abdullah's plans for his administration.

A priority within the National Mission was to build the 'software' of the country after the successful development of the 'hardware' – the physical and economic infrastructure under the Mahathir administration. By 'software', Tun Abdullah had plans directed to raise the country's capacity for knowledge, creativity and innovation and nurture a 'first class mentality' to match the 'first class infrastructure'. He believed Malaysia's future success depended on the quality of its human capital, not only in terms of intellect but also character. Sought comprehensive improvement of the country's education system, from pre-school to tertiary and vocational institutions. At the same time, heavier emphasis would be placed on the shaping of values to create more well-rounded individuals.

Tan Sri Lim began to strategise on how he could assist in achieving the new Prime Minister's goals.

He looked at the vista that Tun Abdullah was focusing on, which was rural Malaysia and came up with a few plans to bridge the digital divide.

He presented document after document covering a wide range of topics – from bringing ICT to the villages, enhancing education and training for bumiputeras (Malays and the native ethnic groups in Sabah and Sarawak), taking rural entrepreneurship to a new level plus recommendations on how to set up an integrated halal hub. (Halal is an Arabic term used to describe anything permissible under Islamic law, commonly used to refer to food and its preparation that Muslims consume).

All the plans were part of a vision to transform the whole nation. It was well-planned with recommendations on how to implement these ideas. And they were given freely.

Tan Sri Lim was still on the "Mahathir mode" where the private sector was encouraged to make recommendations for the improvement of the economy and the government would work in partnership to carry them out.

But this was a new administration that he was facing and the process was not so straightforward – getting the Prime Minister to give the green light and then it proceeding with all systems go.

There were layers of decision-making to go through. Tan Sri Lim had to peel his way through, layer by layer. There were projects that he proposed that never saw the light of day because the delays grew into months and then years.

The huge losses suffered by the Barisan Nasional in the 2008 general election could have been prevented if the powers-that-be had taken a closer look at the proposals from Tan Sri Lim and implemented them strategically to create early results.

Given the responsibility, he would have been able to create the desired change in the rural heartland. "The strategy to transform the rural heart of the country was already voiced by Tun Lah early in his term of office. He was right on target. He was the right man at that moment. The people, especially those in the villages were looking to him to lead them. But five years later the promises still remained promises and people lost confidence in his administration," said Tan Sri Lim.

Tan Sri Lim did try to help. To show exactly what he could do for the country, he spent RM1 million to set up a branding and packaging gallery at his university campus in Cyberjaya. It became a project for his students and their task was to create 1,000 designs using 100 newly created brand names.

It was turned into an unusual exhibition, planned the way only he can. Giant packs carrying key branding messages provide immediate lessons for visitors. Taking centre-stage is a Now and New section, much like a show-and-tell of how the packaging that is being used now for products from small towns and rural places can easily be turned around by using smart packaging to enable the products to reach supermarket shelves in city centres and thus command a premium pricing.

It is a unique exhibition that until today is still used by government agencies to help educate small and medium sized enterprises on how to build their branding. It has triggered collaborations with private entities such as British-owned hypermarket chain Tesco where work-shops have been held to enlighten their suppliers on how they can improve their product packaging and branding. The idea is also being

This country is full of talented people. Our cultural diversity is our magic wand. The industry must make the best use of it in all that you do, and protect it well with all the means that you have. Not only is it important for the growth of our industry it is essential for our society.

Limkokwing
2007

taken up in his other campuses in Africa and elsewhere in Asia to mobilise the creativity of students from the local population to migrate the country's small industries to a higher level.

Tan Sri Lim is disappointed that the country failed to use its strengths to position itself strongly in the global marketplace. He often refers to the multi-racial composition of Malaysia's population - the presence of Muslim Malays, Chinese, Indians and the large number of indigenous ethnic groups in Sabah and Sarawak. He sees this diversity as the country's greatest strength and an opportunity for it to connect with the world's new economic powers – China, India and the Middle-East. The main ethnic groups in Malaysia are the inheritors of ancient innovative civilisations from the three regions. Today, China and India are again driving ahead as the engines of growth of the global economy, while the capital-rich Muslim nations of the Middle-East are being courted by countries around the world.

With their cultural and linguistic advantages, Malaysian Malay, Chinese and Indian business people have built solid connections with their counterparts in China, India and the Middle-East. They could go further and do more with the government fully behind them.

From Razak to Razak: coming full circle

A year after the huge losses suffered by Barisan Nasional Tun Abdullah Badawi stepped down making way for the ascension of his Deputy, Dato' Sri Mohd Najib Tun Abdul Razak who became the country's sixth Prime Minister on 3 April 2009.

Just by ascending to the Premiership he achieved a few firsts. Dato' Sri Najib is the first son of a former Prime Minister to be elected into the same office. His father Tun Abdul Razak was Malaysia's second Prime Minister.

Dato' Sri Najib is also the first baby boomer to hold this high office and one who has fonder memories of the British than his predecessors. Of all the previous Prime Ministers he has fully embraced new media technology using the various tools available online to connect with people. He tweets. He blogs and has a Facebook following of fans and friends. He has more than 118,000 fans in his Facebook account and 6,000 followers in Twitter.

Facebook is a social networking website launched in February 2004 and over 400 million people worldwide (as of February 2010, according to Wikipedia) use the service to keep their friends updated on their activities and opinions.

Twitter is a social networking and microblogging service sometimes referred to as the SMS (short messaging service) of the Internet. It was launched in July 2006 and by the first quarter of 2010 four billion tweets have been posted.

In using new media technology extensively he became, within the space of a few months in 2009, the most popular politician among netizens in the country. He had grasped the fact that the web had created an alternative reality where space, time and distance became totally irrelevant. Borders had dissolved and priorities changed. "Dato' Sri Najib has charted a new way forward for a new breed of politicians who must be savvy with the connecting power of the worldwide web. He provides more details of his daily movements and shares opinions through Facebook and Twitter than any newspaper or online website can match. This personal touch makes him more approachable and builds loyalty among the people," said Tan Sri Lim.

To Tan Sri Lim Dato' Sri Najib as Prime Minister was a significant sign. It meant his life had come full circle. Back in 1974 a major milestone in his life was when he produced the country's largest exhibition as part of voter education for the general election for the then Prime Minister Tun Abdul Razak. Now, close to four decades later, he finds himself working with another Razak.

Walking the future with Najib

Tan Sri Lim has known Dato' Sri Najib, who has been in the political limelight since Tun Abdul Razak's demise in 1976, for a long time. He became his father's torch-bearer at a very young age of 23, just seven years younger than Tan Sri Lim. Over the last four decades Dato' Sri Najib held almost every portfolio in government, understanding its ebb and flow in a way very few can claim to know.

Both their paths crossed many times as Tan Sri Lim worked with the government to address many of the country's socio-economic and political challenges.

And as was his style Tan Sri Lim continued presenting his views and solutions on these issues just as he had done with Tun Dr Mahathir bin Mohamad and Tun Abdullah Badawi.

When Dato' Sri Najib came into power, the new Prime Minister arrived with a bag full of solutions for many of the woes faced by the

> *Tan Sri Lim has long been an advocate for change through creativity and innovation. He has spoken extensively on the subject. There is no doubt that this is a Malaysian who is passionate about the nation moving forward.*
>
> *YAB Dato' Sri Mohd Najib Tun Abdul Razak*
> *Prime Minister Malaysia 2010*

country. However the major setback suffered by the Barisan Nasional influenced his views and tempered his actions. He had to get his priorities in order.

He formulated the 1Malaysia drive as the roadmap upon which all other activities must base their success. He followed this through with the Government Transformation Plan to improve public sector delivery and by June 2010 he was ready to unveil the 10th Malaysia Plan which spelt out the areas for government focus over the next five years.

"The concept of national unity has always been on the agenda of every Prime Minister. His, now famous, walkabouts define his 1 Malaysia concept better than anything else. He has brought a new sense of openness that is refreshing in a leader. His digital walkabout, on the other hand, brings him in touch with Malaysian netizens who may be otherwise not so easily reachable," commented Tan Sri Lim on the change that Dato' Sri Najib was bringing into Malaysian politics.

Dato' Sri Najib speaks about the same things that concern Tan Sri Lim who is convinced that he is setting the right tone for the country to move forward. His first year as Prime Minister was peppered with economic reforms aimed at transforming the country.

Tan Sri Lim attempts to assist wherever he can because he knows Dato' Sri Najib faces a difficult task of uniting a divided nation.

The political disaster of 2008 still rankles and he has the unenviable task of building credibility for the Barisan Nasional.

Tan Sri Lim knows that a lot of the change that Dato' Sri Najib is planning must begin within the government as well as within the Barisan Nasional.

"Many within Government do not see the dangers that are already taking shape outside of our borders. The global economic landscape has already changed. We are not performing as well as we should. Countries that were considered as poor and backward are now moving forward very rapidly. They are competing with Malaysia for foreign direct investment and that is very worrying," said Tan Sri Lim.

However, he applauded Dato' Sri Najib's move in liberalizing the capital market allowing foreign investors to use Malaysia as a base for their regional and international operations. The Prime Minister has said that growth for Malaysia would be driven by investments in technology, talent, infrastructure, R&D and marketing to maximize long-term revenue growth and enhance market vibrancy.

Tan Sri Lim said there were many good ideas raised in the 10th Malaysia Plan. "The only concern is the implementation. The transformation of Malaysia is inevitable because global trends in technology and politics will demand change. The question that arises is whether the process will be a comfortable shift or a painful one. The Prime Minister is doing the right thing. He is setting the right directions. But it is for those down the line in both public and private sectors who must embrace it and translate his vision into action."

He added that the only way they can achieve the best results was by walking together and not sit at opposite sides of the table. "By walking together both sides will see the same vision, the same picture. By walking together they will speak with one voice and work as one team."

Tan Sri Lim feels very strongly that both public and private sectors have to succeed in working together. "For the private sector to succeed in growing the economy to become higher-value-added and higher-income-generating, the public sector must act less as a facilitator and more as a partner."

He warned that global conditions had reached such a state where Malaysia has to speed up just to remain competitive. "We have no choice because neighbouring countries are already making the push. If we want to lead then we have to move at breakneck speed to do so."

Vindicated: creativity and innovation become national priorities

In December 2009, when Dato' Sri Najib announced that 2010 would be declared as the year of creativity and innovation, Tan Sri Lim felt truly vindicated. Rightly so because he has been the country's foremost champion for these twin propellers of growth.

For over two decades he has been advocating for change based on these two factors. He set up a university to do his part to produce the creative intelligence he knew the country would need to match the pace of growth within the country to that which was taking place abroad.

"Malaysia has to move the economy up the innovation value chain because we face a highly competitive and aggressive global marketplace. We have to move quickly because we have been in decline for too long. Innovation is about competition and competition is about innovation. We have no choice but to go this way because the future of the nation depends on our ability to manage the competition that comes from across our borders.

"Innovative human capital is what every economy is looking for and fighting to keep because of the enormous value that is now attached to new ideas," said Tan Sri Lim.

In January 2010 he worked with the Ministry of Science, Technology and Innovation to officially launch the Malaysia Inovatif 2010 campaign. This interaction with the Ministry gave him valuable lessons on the prevalent mindset of those within public service.

"Innovation is not clearly grasped and therefore the responses of those down the line are still very much old school," said Tan Sri Lim, very concerned that while the public sector was performance-driven through its system of Key Performance Indicators (KPI) to track progress, they were not outcome-come focused.

"Simply fulfilling their responsibilities in carrying out the actions in no way guarantees that they will achieve the objectives. The change in mindset must therefore start with the rank and file of government before the country can see any kind of progress in transformation," he said.

He stressed that innovation, essentially, was about making things better. "Change inevitably means challenging the norm and often in this country it is a battle that cannot be won. But it is a battle that the country simply cannot afford to lose.

"The traditional or old school way of doing things rely on compliance. Therefore challenging the status quo means you can never win. Until this attitude or mindset changes the country simply will remain where it stands today," he said.

Designing a people

> *I am very glad Tan Sri Lim Kok Wing is a citizen of Malaysia. I have been in contact with Tan Sri Lim Kok Wing and he has been extremely helpful in solving some of our communications problems.*
>
> *Tun Dr Mahathir bin Mohamad*
> *January 2002*

Every country has a strong image characterised by its geography, the nature of its politics, the culture of its people and the quality of its products. No one will dispute the precision of German-made cars, the beauty and style of Italian fashion, or the exquisite intricacy of Persian carpets. These have all endured through the ages and created impressions that have influenced the world's view of the people from the countries that made these wonderful products.

It is true that the quality of these products reflects the brand image of these countries. It is something that has concerned Tan Sri Lim for the major part of his life. The years that he spent within the advertising industry opened his eyes to how others viewed Malaysia and Malaysians. He felt a burning desire to mould this perception.

When his path crossed that of Tun Dr Mahathir, he found a like-minded man with the political will and leadership to bring about changes to Malaysia and Malaysians. Tun Dr Mahathir provided the leadership and the national platform for Tan Sri Lim to work alongside to direct Malaysian capability into new directions by building confidence in themselves.

Winning hearts at home

In the country today, Tan Sri Lim is the most experienced and skilful strategist who is able to advise both the public and private sectors on a wide range of issues and challenges. Winning hearts at home has a lot of meaning for him because he would translate it to mean many things – from economic, political and sports to education and social issues. Each challenge has been complex because this is a multi-racial country and to work within the political and social culture of this country requires agility and sensitivity.

It has been a long journey and the challenges have been many. Yet he strives on, responding with ideas and solutions to the many individuals, organisations and governments who seek his assistance. In the midst of it all he has juggled his businesses and working for the government, succeeding in a way no one else has in this country or this region.

Working on 6 election campaigns

Tan Sri Lim is, perhaps, the only Malaysian to have worked on six election campaigns for the ruling party, Barisan Nasional. He got his feet wet in the political communications arena by producing an exhibition and a booklet explaining the New Economic Policy, in simple terms, with illustrations and caricatures. This was in 1974 when the government, headed by the second Prime Minister Tun Abdul Razak Hussein, was facing a general election after the disastrous 1969 elections which had resulted in racial clashes in the notorious May 13 Incident. The election results, which saw the ruling Alliance Party – subsequently enlarged with more member parties to become the present Barisan Nasional – losing heavily in the federal Parliament and several state assemblies. A state of emergency was imposed to restore law and order, Parliament was suspended and a National Operations Council (NOC) took over the running of the country. The NOC, headed by the Deputy Prime Minister Tun Abdul Razak, governed from 1969 until 1971 when parliamentary democracy was restored. The first Prime Minister Tunku Abdul Rahman Al Haj was forced to resign to make way for Tun Razak just before the NOC was dissolved.

Tun Abdul Razak introduced the New Economic Policy, an affirmative action programme favouring the majority Malays, whose frustration and anger at being left out of commercial and economic development contributed to the racial riots. Tan Sri Lim recalled helping to organise an exhibition to explain the salient points of the NEP. Called *Pesta Pembangunan* (Development Fest), it was then the biggest exhibition organised in the country, taking up the entire interior of the indoor Stadium Negara (National Stdium). It was a huge success but Tan Sri Lim recalled how he was given only a few days to come up with a concept and prepare the visuals. He also produced a booklet on the NEP which was printed in four languages and distributed to millions of Malaysians.

"We used a cake to illustrate the point," he said. "We showed how a small cake would not be enough for everybody. And how if you expanded the cake, everyone would have a bigger piece, and there would be more to go around."

The exercise gave Tan Sri Lim his first insight into the thinking of the government. He recalled how he listened to the concept with an open mind because he wanted to help defuse the crisis. He had served in the Red Crescent and experienced the anguish during the May 13 riots, and he never wanted to see a repeat of the incident.

He put in his best efforts to help communicate the significance of the NEP, especially to get the non-Malays to accept the formula.

Tan Sri Lim pointed out that he never thought of himself as 'working on an election campaign'. "I prefer it to be called voter education, because that's what we did."

The 1986 general election, he remembered, "was a difficult one for the ruling party. There was an economic recession. Also the Opposition was vociferous. But the battle lines were clear cut. It was a really solid government dealing with an Opposition that was mostly just making a lot of noise and not seen as a credible alternative."

It was the first professionally orchestrated media campaign by the ruling party. Soon after that, and, no doubt, impressed by Tan Sri Lim's ability to get the work done, Tun Dr Mahathir began to rely more on him to carry out national campaigns.

Tan Sri Lim's former wife Tessie credited this to the fact that Tan Sri Lim was "very acceptable to the establishment".

"They knew he had no hidden intentions," she said. "He had the nation's best interests at heart. In doing the work that he did, I think he also saw up close how many people didn't have the country's best interests at heart, and I know that frustrated him. He really believed that so much more could be done for the country if people wanted the best for it. He's always talking about the bigger picture."

The relationship her former husband shared with Tun Dr Mahathir was built on a solid foundation of trust. "He never betrayed that trust," she added.

The national platform was exactly what Tan Sri Lim relished. He was very passionate about helping Malaysians to build themselves into a nation of quality-conscious people.

"We started to do work on promoting government efforts," he said. "I think Malaysians were warming up to the concept of Malaysia being a leading Third World nation. We were gaining a bigger voice on a lot of platforms including Anti-Drug Abuse, Women's Rights, and Tun Dr Mahathir himself emerged as the spokesman for Third World nations."

When an interviewer asked Tan Sri Lim whether advertising should be used to shape opinions on political and governmental issues, he pointed out that every established democracy – especially in the Western world - was doing just that.

"This has been a very conservative country," he said in that interview, more than two decades ago. "There is nothing wrong with our politicians making use of professional advertising and public relations services, just as a company would do to help it promote a product or service, or help it communicate better, or project its image more effectively."

The government, he added, was no different from a large conglomerate that was involved in the marketing of a wide range of services. It needed professional help to promote its services, and most certainly needed help to overcome public resistance and manage rejection.

In the 1990 elections Tan Sri Lim found the pace comfortable as he had a good story to tell. The strategy was to show a 10-year comparison of how far the country had progressed. This was produced as a newspaper supplement and a booklet for nationwide distribution. By this time the country had a car industry in place with the first car rolled out in style, and a host of amenities as well as facilities related to housing, electricity, water supply, railways and highways had been built or were under construction.

While on one hand the achievements of the ruling party were highlighted, the struggles of the Opposition were delivered through caricatures. These were run as advertisements in the newspapers illustrating the marriage of convenience between the Opposition parties which had totally different, even opposing ideologies. It was not surprising that the ruling party won with a convincing majority.

Of all the elections Tan Sri Lim was involved in, he considered the 1995 voter education exercise as the easiest to strategise and carry out. "The country was on a high. The economy was at its strongest ever, and there was solid political stability. Things were good," he said.

Two years later, that picture was to change dramatically. In July 1997, the Asian financial crisis hit, and another year later, Malaysia was thrown into its darkest period of political instability with the sacking of the then powerful Deputy Prime Minister, Finance Minister and

Campaigns to promote health, education, patriotism are part and parcel of nation-building. It's about building cohesion and confidence. Ultimately all these will influence public opinion of Government and its performance.

Limkokwing

deputy president of Umno, Dato' Seri Anwar Ibrahim. His supporters demonstrated on the streets in Kuala Lumpur, clashing repeatedly with the police. Dato' Seri Anwar was subsequently arrested, charged with abuse of power and sodomy, and jailed. The acrimonious court case divided the nation.

For a country that for much of its 40 years of independence lived peaceably with hardly any political imbroglios, it was a raw emotional time for Malaysians.

Amid the fear, tensions and anger, the country was called to the polls in 1999. For Tan Sri Lim, this was also a turning point. For the first time since his collaboration with the ruling party, his involvement was marginal.

"It was clearly the most difficult campaign to work on, because of the anger that one could feel, and the division that you could see in the country," he said.

"We started work on the campaign as early as the second quarter of 1999. Most of our work was put together for television and, to some degree, billboards."

In addition, 10 voter education videos were produced and all, explained Tan Sri Lim, were about unifying. "It was about getting the public to be rational, with a tone that was a lot more humble than previously."

He also set the record straight about a series of parallel campaigns that were running on television and newspapers at the same time.

"Those were very raw campaigns and we had nothing to do with them," he asserted. "I did not agree with the 'rawness' of the very hard-hitting advertisements that came out the week of the election. I felt what we needed was to unite the people, not divide. But obviously there were others within the political sphere who felt differently," he added regretfully.

"Ours was a polite campaign," he said. "We focused the public on the positive side of things, on the future, on what can be achieved in the next 5 years and we said it with absolute honesty. We didn't tell any lies, embellish anything. We attempted to say it in a very rational way so others would not reject it. To me, that's part of the process of nation-building. That was the mindset.

"The thrust of our campaign was about healing the nation, not to fuel people's anger. Ours was a tone of reconciliation. Of course, there was no admitting mistakes, but we tried to get people to look at the big picture, and to count their blessings when compared to the instability in neighbouring countries."

Mooting A Council for Effective Communication

Just before the general election of 1999 Tan Sri Lim provided Tun Dr Mahathir with an analysis that the Barisan Nasional would suffer inroads into its electorate. It was the result of a survey he had conducted.

Tan Sri Lim carried out surveys from time to time to gauge public reaction to certain issues. "Actually I had to temper my analysis. I could not tell him how bad the incursions would be. The election results confirmed my worst fears," he said.

The results were an eye-opener for the ruling party as it had to concede defeat in Terengganu while it failed to wrest back Kelantan. Both the states in the east coast of Peninsular Malaysia were won by Pan-Malaysia Islamic Party or PAS.

Tan Sri Lim was very much a party to the moves by Barisan Nasional to do a serious self-examination. "There was nothing wrong with the BN fundamentals. The coalition formula was very powerful, very strong. The crux of the problem was complacency and arrogance that had set in over the years."

His strong views led to the formation of a Council for Effective Communication, comprising influential members of industry, government and academia. The members met monthly and issues that affected the country were debated and solutions recommended for implementation.

"You could call it a Think & Do Tank. We looked into various issues. There was the SARS (Severe Acute Respiratory Syndrome, a respiratory disease, outbreak in 2002-03 that began in China and which killed more than 700 people worldwide, causing widespread fears and devastating the travel industry across the Asia Pacific region) and the government's stimulus package to revive business confidence, amongst others. The CEC had a feedback mechanism that had its fingers on the pulse of public opinion. The main agenda was to focus on ideas and how to move forward," he said.

A back to basics proposal

Tan Sri Lim proposed a 'back to basics' strategy to win back support. "Politics is too often seen as a power struggle and there are those who see it as a shortcut to wealth creation. People on the ground feel that it should be about service to society. If that is well communicated and sincerely implemented there is no way the BN will lose in any election," said Tan Sri Lim.

He added that for too long the Barisan Nasional government had assumed the role of a father figure to the nation. "This is a mindset inherited from the founders of the coalition which goes back to the 1950s when people needed to be guided.

"Today the mindset of the people has changed. They are more knowledgeable and they want to participate, to have a say in governance. This is something for the BN to consider very seriously."

He said the Barisan Nasional had introduced policies and projects that had benefited the people. "But often the reasons why there was a need to introduce these policies and projects in the first place were not explained to the people. So there is resistance when new projects come up. This is the flaw in the BN government that the Opposition exploited to paint the government negatively.

"People often do not appreciate the good that has been done for them. If you compare the Malaysian situation with other developing countries you can see how much our living standards have improved. Our roads, healthcare, housing, education, basic amenities are among the best in the world. Yet people still complain and this is because they don't know. They only hear what the Opposition says and the Opposition has nothing good to say about this government even though they themselves benefit from the good infrastructure," he said.

Focused on unity

In 2001, Tan Sri Lim began work on yet another campaign, called the *Unity Campaign.* It was to lay the groundwork to ensure a solid win for the ruling party in the next general elections, scheduled for 2004.

This was another first for him and the ruling party. The first time such an early effort was made. The reason was obvious. The political and social situation in Malaysia at that time was confusing and troubling. The economy had not fully recovered from the 1997-98 Asian financial crisis. In the 1999 elections, the Barisan Nasional maintained its two-third majority in Parliament but suffered erosion in the popular vote. Umno, the party of Prime Minister Tun Dr Mahathir and the most powerful component of the ruling coalition, was rejected by many Malay voters angered by the treatment of Dato' Seri Anwar.

Tan Sri Lim was deeply worried about the possibility of the increased vote for the Opposition in the 1999 elections snowballing into a general voter revolt in the next general election expected in 2004.

He was asked to orchestrate a public information campaign to win back public support. He recommended a three-phase campaign that began in 2001. It was understood that the overall objective of the campaign was to mend the rift between the people and the Barisan Nasional government.

He created short video documentaries about Malay and Malaysian history, the struggle for independence from the British, and the many achievements of the nation over the last four decades. Billboards comparing Malaysia's peace and stability to the chaos in neighbouring countries were prominently displayed. The campaign aimed to foster unity, encourage service and nurture patriotism.

However, Tun Dr Mahathir suddenly announced his intention to resign all his party and political posts at the 2002 Umno General Assembly, shocking the party and the country. He was persuaded to 'retract' the resignation an hour later but, the next day, it was announced that he had agreed to a 16-month transition of power plan.

He finally stepped down on October 31, 2003 and was succeeded as Prime Minister the same day by his deputy Tun Abdullah.

After 22 years in power the departure of Tun Dr Mahathir from the seat of power brought about a huge change for the country. With his friendly personality and consensus style leadership, Tun Abdullah was a great contrast to his predecessor who was authoritarian and impatient with critics. Malaysians warmed to the

In June 2009 Tun Dr Mahathir bin Mohamad was conferred Honorary Doctorate of Humanity by the Limkokwing University

new premier's leadership and the promise of a softer, kinder administration, and awarded the Barisan Nasional its biggest election victory since independence in the 2004 national polls.

However, the Abdullah administration underperformed over the next five years. The economy slowed, ethnic and religious tensions escalated, allegations of corruption increased and the country was widely seen to have been placed on auto pilot mode.

By March 8, 2008 when the 12th general election was held, the damage to the image of the Barisan Nasional government had gone deep and there was a massive loss of public confidence in the leadership of Tun Abdullah. The disillusioned voters rebelled by giving the Opposition parties one third of the seats in the Dewan Rakyat (Parliament's Lower House of Representatives) and erasing the coalition's two-third majority in Parliament for the first time since 1969. The Barisan Nasional was also ousted as the government in four states – Kedah, Penang, Perak and Selangor – in favour of Opposition parties while the Opposition's PAS retained Kelantan state which it first captured in 1990. Perak was re-taken by the Barisan Nasional in February 2009 in the wake of defections by three assembly persons from the Pakatan Rakyat coalition which had governed the state with a slim majority since the 2008 elections.

Tan Sri Lim provided what support he could to mend the political damage done but it was too late.

"People did not vote the Opposition in. They voted the Barisan Nasional out because they were not happy and used the power of the ballot to express their disappointment with the leadership," he said.

Could the huge losses suffered by the ruling party been averted if Tan Sri Lim, with his experience, knowledge and skills, been consulted to plan and implement the Barisan Nasional campaign? The answer to that question will never be known but it is a fact that in all the six general elections in which he played a prominent role in the Barisan Nasional campaign, the coalition emerged the clear victor. He is the most experienced communications strategist in the country and he had been sounding the warning bell to the Barisan Nasional for months before the watershed elections in 2008. He had even proposed solutions by presenting document after document on how to move the coalition ahead but the efforts were in vain.

Shaping Corporate Identity

When Tun Dr Mahathir mooted the Malaysia Incorporated policy – which was anchored upon the concept of a partnership of public and private sectors to promote economic growth – privatisation of a number of government-owned entities was the first step forward. But before privatisation could take place the organisations had to be corporatised. Corporatisation involved a major overhaul of the entities concerned and it began with a new identity.

Designing corporate identity involves a study of every single aspect of a corporation. It is to do with interaction between people who work inside as well as with people that come in contact with the corporation in whatever area – clients, consumers, authorities, investors and the like. Corporate identity also involves what the organisation looks like and this includes its premises – the interior as well as its exterior.

Corporate identity is not simply a graphic design exercise that involves mainly the logo, as people tend to think. It requires shaping the organisation from its corporate philosophy and mission to outlining its objectives. The outcome is a road map that is created in close collaboration with the management of the organisation.

When Tan Sri Lim was asked to assist in this exercise he did not realise the mammoth task that awaited him because these were government agencies that were used to a different work culture. These were agencies that were essential parts of the government machinery. They were fully funded by the government and the concept of bottom line was totally alien to them.

It was a tough task because, as a communications specialist who had been dealing with multinational corporations, he was used to working with people who understood his role. "After dealing with the private sector for so many years I found the public sector to be more challenging. There are many layers of administration. It is bureaucracy at work, if you like, and the government's working style was transferred to the corporatised entities," explained Tan Sri Lim.

"So for my people to get to work and map out the corporate identity took a while because we weighed the choice of spending time to educate the staff of these corporations in the way of the private sector or take the faster route by responding to how they work and adapting along the way.

"As we never had the time to really educate the people concerned we began to adapt. In time we felt the corporations would have to adjust to the new demands and the change to private sector style of management would take place naturally," he added.

So how did he adapt? "In dealing with government officers we faced a perception problem. We were communications consultants. We were not experts in energy, telecommunications, timber, trade or agriculture. We had to be given the information which we then translated into consumer friendly communication. Where necessary we looked at issues and assisted to provide solutions that could be strategically communicated.

"I used to get feedback from my executives who were continuously challenged on their knowledge of the client's business. With our private sector clients we were used to complementing their marketing by doing research and later presenting creative concepts.

"With our government or government-based clients we had to change tack. We had to work that much harder to get all the information and present complete final text on all our recommended advertising or corporate identity proposals even during our initial presentations.

"We had to do it this way. It was tough on my people, especially the creative team because they spent more time on getting the information and less time on the conceptual side. But the communication for the government was less complicated conceptually because the reach was mass audience and the strategies had to be in line with government policies. They were not the same as campaigns for a shampoo, for example. This approach helped our clients to understand the creative

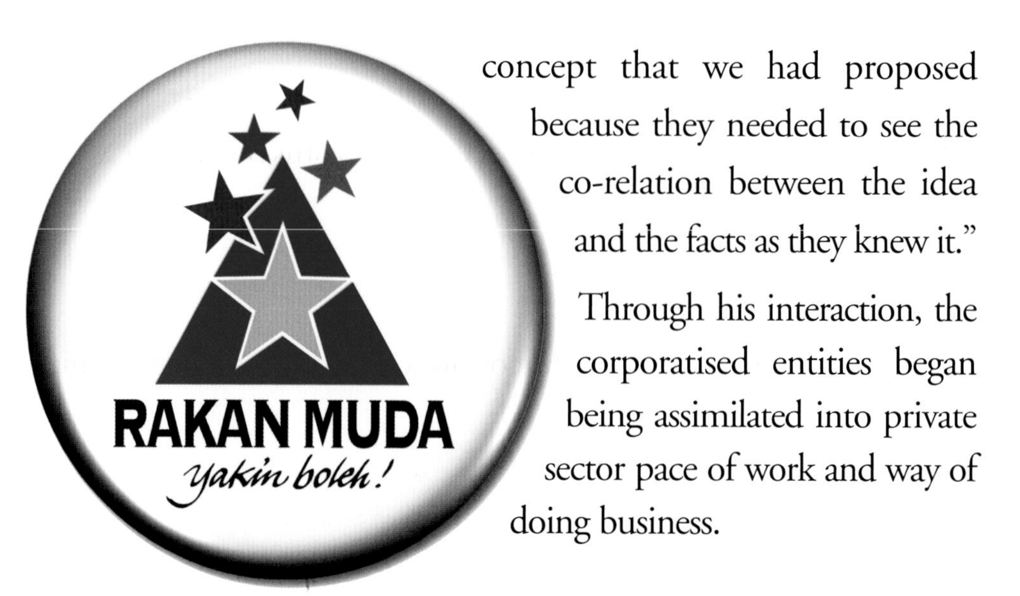

concept that we had proposed because they needed to see the co-relation between the idea and the facts as they knew it."

Through his interaction, the corporatised entities began being assimilated into private sector pace of work and way of doing business.

Malaysia Boleh! Yes, We Can!

In early 1994, national attention was spotlighted on the youth population in Malaysia. In media reports and independent surveys, there appeared to be a lack of motivation amongst many young people. Out of a total population of 18 million in 1990, over 7 million fell into the youth age bracket of 15-29 years. For a fast developing nation like Malaysia, with a keen eye on its economic future and social stability, these were vital statistics indeed.

The country needed to motivate its young people and provide an outlet for their energy and creativity. "The concept was built along a very positive perception in the public – it was not just about sports or recreation, but it was inspirational," said Tan Sri Lim.

First, a strategic mission was devised to turn a national problem into a national pool of human resource. 'A New Vision for Youth' was written to provide support to Vision 2020, Malaysia's set of ideals introduced by Tun Dr Mahathir to achieve fully developed nation status by the year 2020.

Rakan Muda - the blueprint to change mindsets of Malaysia's youths

To initiate a lasting, driving sense of pride, purpose and community spirit in Malaysia's apathetic youth, the concept of *Rakan Muda* or Young Friends, was created to make them the hope of the nation.

The logo developed was based on a concept of 'reach for the stars' because stars are simple and universal devices representing excellence, success and achievement. A spirited, motivational call to action was added – *'Yakin boleh!'* meaning 'Yes, we can!' (Long before President Barack Obama made this slogan globally popular, Malaysian youths were already being inspired by the phrase). This was later modified to *'Malaysia Boleh!'*

As a physical entity, *Rakan Muda* is an all-encompassing, innovative Youth Focal Point – the first and biggest of its kind in the country. The plan was launched in October 1994 by the Prime Minister. Within six months, over half a million young Malaysians had joined the programmes. Confidence was high that the target of recruiting five million youths in five years would be reached.

It was a 100 percent 'Malaysia Inc' effort. A world first, where the resource of every sector of the nation's economy was pooled together for one deserving purpose: the development and strengthening of Malaysian youth.

The NGOs, associations and relevant organisations provided the core infrastructure for carrying out the events and activities. The Ministry of Youth and Sports was the conduit directing applications, with the private sector roped in to underwrite the cost of the various programmes.

But from a high awareness level of 91 percent in December 1994, it dropped to a dismal 30 percent by May 1995. Potential targeted viewership fell from 6.3 million to 0.2 million. Write in or phone-in response dropped from thousands a day to less than 20.

The reason? Media funding came to a complete stop and the media withdrew active support – no promotion on radio, television, newspapers and outdoor advertising.

The government machinery lacked infrastructure and motivational support, and was hazy about the concept, vision and long-term goals. NGOs were poorly equipped and unable to expand quickly to meet the response. There was also lack of proper co-ordination between the ministry and NGOs.

At this time, Tan Sri Lim told the ministry in no uncertain terms that media presence was pivotal to the future development of *Rakan Muda.*

"There were detractors who campaigned against the Minister of Youth and Sports," said Tan Sri Lim. "They also campaigned against me. Half truths were spread, ridiculous numbers were quoted. It was turned into a racial issue. They weakened the programme."

The campaign was attacked by groups within the ruling party. Some questioned why a Chinese company was given the account which they said was worth millions of Ringgit. They did not object to the value of the account but questioned why it didn't go to a Malay company.

"*Rakan Muda* was seen as something effective to deal with social ills. They started something that was really good, but they were not able to cope. It was a short-lived campaign – just 3 or 4 months."

In July 2000, the programme was given a face-lift by the ministry and strengthened to meet current needs.

The new Minister of Youth and Sports, Hishamuddin Hussein said the programme was being 'repackaged' and would emphasise social work and instil social responsibilities among the youth.

But it was an unforgettable lesson for Tan Sri Lim who faced opposition to his ideas for the most ridiculous reasons. It is something he has learned to live with as he continues his quest to change the inner landscape of people.

Mediating a political crisis

Tan Sri Lim is often asked why he has not joined a political party or lobbied for a political position. "They wonder why I never made use of my friendship with the former Prime Minister for political advantage," he said.

The reason is that he finds politics too confining and restrictive for a creative person like himself.

He maintains a cordial relationship with many politicians but the close-up perspective of politics had left him convinced that politics was not to his taste or suited to his temperament. "There are many skilful, charming and very engaging people in politics. But it is too much about keeping control and gaining power," he said.

However, off and on, he was called upon by Tun Dr Mahathir when the latter was the Prime Minister to "see what he could do" about certain sensitive situations. His involvement in mediating a solution to a serious leadership brawl within the Malaysian Chinese Association (MCA), the second largest party in the Barisan Nasional which is headed by the Prime Minister, in 2002-03 was "quite an experience."

Tan Sri Lim was away in Korea on a business trip when he received a summons to return home for a briefing by Tun Dr Mahathir who was leaving for a trip overseas. The then Prime Minister had been approached by the two warring sides in MCA to help resolve the factional struggle that threatened to tear the party apart. The break-up of the MCA, founded in 1949 and which, together with Umno and the Malaysian Indian Congress (MIC), formed the Alliance Party that later expanded into Barisan Nasional, looked imminent. There were allegations of phantom members. Both sides were planning to call their own extraordinary general meeting and the Chinese community was growing increasingly agitated by the infighting.

The central figures in the conflict were the then party president and Minister of Transport Dato' Seri (later Tun) Dr Ling Liong Sik and his deputy Dato' (later Tan Sri) Lim Ah Lek, the Minister of Human Resources. The two factions were divided into Team A led by Dato' Seri Dr Ling and Team B under Dato' Lim.

The root cause of the spat was the appointment of Cabinet ministers from among the MCA leaders after the 1999 general election. Dato' Lim had declined to stand for re-election with the 'understanding' that he would be replaced in the new Cabinet by his protégé Dato' Chan Kong Choy, then a deputy minister. However, Dato' Seri Dr Ling's ally Dato' Ong Ka Ting, also a deputy minister, was promoted to a full minister instead.

Tan Sri Lim knew Tun Dr Mahathir was very anxious to prevent a break-up of MCA, an outcome that would seriously weaken the Barisan Nasional and potentially damage the political balance in the country.

Tun Dr Mahathir asked the two factions to submit two names each as a mediator and Tan Sri Lim's name appeared on both their lists. He was appointed mediator by a letter from the Prime Minister and given a very clear brief: prevent the MCA from breaking apart and get the two sides to agree to a peace plan.

His first task was to ensure the two factions would not take each other to court over allegations of phantom voters among the MCA membership and other alleged wrongdoings.

Second, he had to persuade them not to hold their respective extraordinary general meetings which they were planning to do.

Most important of all was the 'single list' proposed by Tun Dr Mahathir which required the opposing factions to maintain the status quo in the party – meaning that the current list of office bearers, both elected and appointed, as well as at state and divisional levels, who held their positions since the last party elections in 1999 – were to remain unchanged.

The status quo covered the posts of President, Deputy President, Vice-Presidents, Central Committee members and appointed national officials, state liaison chairmen and committee members, Wanita MCA (women's wing) head and committee members, MCA Youth head and committee members, and divisional chairmen and committee members.

And in keeping with the status quo agreement on all party posts, the divisional elections scheduled for the second half of 2002 were to be based on a mutually agreed one 'single list' of candidates for all party positions except for provisions for some youth positions to take account of the age limit of office bearers.

"Everything hinged on that single list that the Prime Minister wanted. I finally understood where he was coming from and it made the negotiations easier to navigate and arrive at a conclusion that was satisfactory to both parties. There had to be some give and take on both sides," said Tan Sri Lim.

However, the MCA's national elections scheduled for 2003 were postponed to enable the party to focus on preparations for the general election due in 2004. Thus, the status quo in the party remained until May 23, 2003 when Dato' Seri Dr Ling stepped down as MCA president and Minister of Transport. Dato' Lim also resigned as deputy president of MCA the same day. Dato' Ong and Dato' Chan were duly elected by the Central Committee as the new president and deputy president respectively, and Dato' Chan was also appointed to the Cabinet to assume Dato' Seri Dr Ling's vacated position.

The Chinese language newspapers had a field day during the crisis while the Opposition parties waited gleefully to see how the fallout would happen so they could make political capital out of it.

Tan Sri Lim's mediation approach was simple enough. He just wanted to get the two opposing parties to talk and agree on a few terms that to him seemed reasonable. The process grew more complex as he realised that he needed to create a conducive environment for the two parties to come together. "There was a need for a 'talking' mechanism," he said.

But he wasn't prepared for the repercussions. He grew appalled when, for the first time, he faced the ferocity of political factional war where his name was bandied about in the Chinese press. He was accused of favouring one faction. "It was not true because I only recommended what appeared to me to be valid requests. I talked to many people both within the party concerned as well as others on the outside.

"As the mediating party I had to weigh all issues and recommend what was right. I also felt the responsibility of giving a fair report to the Prime Minister. I have no regrets over what I had recommended," he said.

"Old friends became quite cool towards me failing to understand the delicate situation I was in. They also did not seem to understand how the press was being used for positioning an argument and undermining the other party," Tan Sri Lim added.

The MCA has been a valuable component to the ruling Barisan Nasional and its state of health was of great concern especially since the disagreement involved two senior members of the party, both of whom were well liked and respected by Tun Dr Mahathir.

In the end the two party leaders agreed to hand in their resignations to help close the ranks of the members and bring back goodwill and unity within the party.

"The best part of a year was spent listening to both sides – separately, never together. It took a while to get Ling and Ah Lek to submit their resignations. I drafted the letter of resignation, which was used by Ah Lek but Ling wrote his own resignation letter," said Tan Sri Lim.

Tun Dr Mahathir instructed the two MCA leaders to hand in their resignation letters through Tan Sri Lim. That was the measure of his commitment to support Tan Sri Lim's mediation effort. It also became very clear that the real power to resolve the MCA tussle and hold the party together was in the hands of the Umno leader.

Tun Dr Mahathir achieved his twin objectives. He headed off a disastrous split in MCA with the assistance of Tan Sri Lim and he enabled Dato' Seri Dr Ling and Dato' Lim's successors to inherit a united party.

As for Tan Sri Lim, it did not matter that he was not given any credit by the MCA leadership or any public acknowledgement of the crucial role he played in the crisis. He was just relieved that he succeeded in doing what the Prime Minister had chosen him to do. "It was a great learning experience," he summed up. And he went back to his own business which he had neglected as he was drawn deeper into the quagmire of MCA politics. He was at it again in 2009 when a new leadership war flared in the MCA, but this time with less success.

Anti-Piracy

The anti-piracy campaign was initiated by the Ministry of Domestic Trade & Consumer Affairs in 2000 in response to Malaysia having gained the 'dubious' honour of being a 'piracy hub' for the region. In fact, as far back as 1985 Malaysia had been identified by the International Intellectual Property Association as having a 'serious' piracy problem. This was followed in 1994 by a "Special Comment" that called for judicial reforms in Malaysia to impose deterrent sentences on copyright pirates. According to the Ministry's 1998 data, it was estimated that piracy cost the country $760 million that year. Between then and 2000, VCD piracy in Malaysia stood at a staggering 90%.

The Ministry wanted a campaign as part of the introduction of newer and tougher legislation, and greater enforcement.

The strategy adopted was for the campaign thrust to show the pirates' true colours – that they are part of the serious crime scene in Malaysia, and that the people who sell pirated items also operate other hardcore activities such as selling and trafficking drugs, prostitution, extortion, gambling and even murder. The campaign was to appeal for public help to wipe out the demand as the source to wipe out the menace. Individual purchase of pirated goods is not an offence in Malaysia.

This skew was chosen because there is no 'pain' or 'shame' associated with the buying of pirated goods. Piracy is not seen as an illegal activity in Malaysia. Pirated goods are sold openly and are easily available and retailers were hardly ever seen to be apprehended by the authorities. When they were, they did not suffer severe penalties.

Still, at the crux of the problem was that original CDs and VCDs are expensive in Malaysia. For example, original computer software can cost RM2,000 compared to RM25 for a pirated version, and so easily available at that.

The campaign was launched and continued to run for a number of years. The media was very supportive and prominently featured stories on raids against pirates and the destruction of pirated goods by the authorities.

Tak Nak - anti-smoking campaign

The campaign was initiated by Tun Dr Mahathir in 2002, a year before his retirement as Prime Minister. He practically planted the campaign on Tan Sri Lim. Such was his confidence in him, making it the latter's responsibility to push for some results after seeing too many of his friends die as a result of smoking.

Tan Sri Lim was put in a dilemma.

The Health Ministry had many campaigns and every one of them was worked out through a tender system. But the order to carry out the anti-smoking campaign came from the top. The first presentation was made to the Health Minister, at that time, Dato' Chua Jui Meng. It was an unusual situation because the normal practice was for the ideas to be discussed with officers directly concerned with anti-smoking measures and arriving at a consensus before presenting the recommendation to the minister.

But Tun Dr Mahathir felt the earlier campaigns created by the ministry had little impact upon the public and wanted something more effective, which was why he turned to Tan Sri Lim.

The anti-smoking movement on the international front was getting stronger and many countries, including Malaysia, had signed agreements to fight tobacco abuse.

In 2003 Malaysia was a signatory to the Framework Convention on Tobacco Control that required the country to adhere to international rules and regulations governing tobacco abuse.

The campaign created by Tan Sri Lim was launched in February 2004. It was meant to be a five-year campaign beginning with a media blitz to build public awareness and primarily to discourage young people from taking up the habit. Being an integrated campaign, the messages were displayed on billboards, community boards, newspapers and television.

For the first time the country had a brand name for anti-smoking, and the media build-up stirred the whole nation to react to the messages. Newspaper features, comics and ordinary Malaysians began to recognise the brand name and use it extensively.

But the campaign came under fire, which was expected knowing how strong the tobacco lobby was in the country.

Critics pointed out that there was no change in the number of people smoking and therefore the campaign was a failure. But an independent research revealed that the awareness level of the campaign was 95 percent.

"The campaign was meant to build people's awareness and alert them to the dangers of smoking. A follow-through campaign would have given the anti-smoking drive a stronger base to cut down on the number of young people smoking," said Tan Sri Lim.

Attempts to derail the campaign were made right from the beginning. For example, the final approval for the campaign to go ahead came two years after it was devised. Another obstacle was financing. There were many hurdles, owing perhaps to the transition process of one Prime Minister to another.

Tan Sri Lim practically carried the entire campaign from start to finish before he received payment. Any other company would have buckled under the huge cost which ran into millions of ringgit that had to be paid upfront to media owners. At one point, he was even contemplating taking ownership of the slogan 'Tak Nak' (Malay for Don't Want) which was already on every one's lips.

Campaigns that took off after that simply lacked lustre and Tan Sri Lim strongly felt that the government lost a golden opportunity to truly address a social ill.

Commonwealth Games - Let's Make it Great!

When Malaysia won the bid to host it in 1998, it was a historic event for the nation, marking global recognition of its advanced social and economic development. The Kuala Lumpur Commonwealth Games was only the second time that the world's second largest multinational

> *I had a mission running the Commonwealth Games and here was someone full of ideas, insight and assistance. He spent a lot of his money on the work he did for the Games. He did it as a national contribution.*
>
> *(Rtd) General Tan Sri Hashim Ali*
> *Executive Chairman Sukom 98, KL 1998 XVI Commonwealth Games, 2000*

sporting event after the Olympiad would be organised by a developing country since the 1966 Kingston Games in Jamaica.

Known as the Friendly Games, this was a huge international event involving over 60 countries that shared a history of having been colonised by Great Britain. The event received international coverage by the media and a television audience of over 300 million viewers. The 14 official games comprised weight-lifting, badminton, netball, gymnastics, field hockey, cricket, lawn bowl, cycling, shooting, athletics, rugby, swimming, squash and boxing. KL '98 saw the largest participation of Commonwealth nations in the Games' history. The efficient management and high technology used in the Games helped strengthen the international image of Malaysia as a modern, progressive and prosperous nation. It was a sort of 'coming-out party' for a country that had made rapid strides in industrialisation but still generally profiled by the international media as a primary commodities producer. It helped that Malaysia won a total of 36 medals including 10 golds – the country's best performance in an international sports event – and came out fourth in the overall medals tally below Australia, England

and Canada. Malaysia's reputation as a country where its systems worked effectively was also greatly enhanced because the Games were held successfully and without disruption despite the 1997-98 Asian financial crisis and an internal political upheaval over the Anwar Ibrahim saga that boiled over into street protests.

"It was a classic case of the kind of low-key involvement we always placed ourselves in," said Tan Sri Lim of his work with Sukom '98 Bhd, the special vehicle company set up to organise and manage the Games.

"We designed the Sukom identity – the mascot (an *Orang Utan* or 'man of the forest', the great ape found only in parts of Malaysia and Indonesia, which was named *Wira* or Hero), the games graphics, the promotional strategies – and organised seminars to promote the Games. We hosted foreign media people for no fee. Nobody was looking into communications in a comprehensive and professional way in harnessing public support. So we went in to do what needed to be done."

General (Rtd) Tan Sri Hashim Ali, the Organising Committee Chairman of the Games, said Tan Sri Lim was "full of ideas, insight and assistance in so many areas.

"Some of the suggestions for the programmes that he wanted to introduce were very ambitious. But he knew the Commonwealth Games would be good for the nation. He spent a lot of his own time and money on the work he did for the Commonwealth Games, but I know it was because he believed in what we were doing. He did it as a national contribution."

Just months before the opening of the Games, Malaysia experienced two major blows – one economic, the other political. First was the Asian financial crisis when the South East Asian economies suffered a devastating meltdown. The Ministry of Youth and Sports was concerned the Games would suffer as people were distracted by the impact of the crisis on their lives. There was a need to touch the hearts and minds of the people to support the Games.

In the weeks running up to the Games, then Deputy Prime Minister and Deputy President of Umno, Dato' Seri Anwar Ibrahim was sacked from the Cabinet by Tun Dr Mahathir and expelled from his party in a bitter break-up between the two most powerful men in the country. It unleashed a storm of protests and confusion inside and outside the country. Thousands of supporters of the deposed deputy premier took to the streets and fought with the police. The capital city of Kuala Lumpur was tense for weeks, and many wondered whether the Games would survive this crisis.

Tan Sri Lim, responding to the situation, quickly weaved together a rousing campaign to whip up public support.

There were songs on the radio, commercials on television; messages appeared on billboards across the land and there were advertisements in newspapers and magazines. The attention of the public shifted back to the Games. He also organised a special carnival in the fashionable suburb of Bangsar in Kuala Lumpur. This was among the events that acted as a bridge between the Games organisers and the people to build up public enthusiasm and support.

Wira, the mascot for the Games developed by Tan Sri Lim, cut through cultural barriers and struck an emotional chord with Malaysians through the image of the gentle and lovable 'man of the forest'. The visual element of friendliness was crucial to evoke the emotion of the 'Friendly Games'.

Preparation for the Games had begun as early as 1995 when Tan Sri Lim presented a comprehensive programme using a three-prong strategy to promote the event to Malaysians and then to Commonwealth member countries before going worldwide. He called for it to be branded a national inspiration and an international showcase of Malaysia as a progressive, developed and friendly nation. The communications mission was to set the foundation for future bids by Malaysia to host high-profile, large-scale events.

Domestic communications were to instil a sense of ownership of the Games to galvanise and mobilise Malaysians. Internationally, it was important that Malaysia must meet, if not exceed, global expectations.

Despite the many contributions Tan Sri Lim made to the Games, and his enthusiasm in doing all he could to help the country to promote the Games, he was never publicly recognised for the work.

Years later he was approached to assist with Malaysia's bid to host the 2006 Asian Games for which he created the logo and promotional items that were needed as part of Malaysia's case to convince the judges that Malaysia had the capability to host the event. Although touted strongly to win the bid, it was the city of Doha that was selected to the great disappointment of Malaysians.

Having been so deeply involved in a number of sports promotions Tan Sri Lim observed the attitude and conduct of Malaysian sports teams. He felt they needed a visual identity that helps to build the competitive team spirit.

Working with his creative team, he used tiger stripes to form the basis for the design of a national jersey. He had earlier used the stripes to design the uniform for youths involved in the National Service Training Programme. He felt the tiger, a national symbol of power and courage, could lend its characteristics to build a sports brand that would identify Malaysian sportsmen and sportswomen to the world.

"The national jersey with the tiger stripes would then become a visual inspiration for children to develop their skills so they may wear the jersey with pride. That was my intention," said Tan Sri Lim. He added that this would, in time, become part of the sports legacy of the country.

Strengthening the branding of Kuala Lumpur

Kuala Lumpur was transforming into a sophisticated world-class city. Tall, sleek skyscrapers share space with brick and mortar reminders of the bygone colonial era. Movement of traffic and people had increased manifold since the city hosted the celebrations of Merdeka

(Independence) for the then Malaya (now Peninsular Malaysia in the larger Federation of Malaysia) from the British in 1957. Tourism had grown dramatically, as had the number of expatriates who represented foreign investors. Vibrant by day and neon-lit by night, Kuala Lumpur was becoming a business and shopping hub in Southeast Asia.

When the biggest projects in the city needed the expert touch, it was to Tan Sri Lim that their promoters turned to.

Kuala Lumpur International Airport

This is one of Asia's largest and most modern airports. It was a RM9 billion architectural wonder that needed a sophisticated, yet user-friendly, signage system in keeping with its clean, spacious interior. The sprawling spaciousness of the airport itself added to its challenge.

Many factors were considered before deciding on the particular signage system. The high percentage of first-time users, the many destinations, the emotional state of the visitors, flow of human traffic through the various checkpoints, practicality, visibility, dual languages and obviously colour were major considerations. They all had to be integrated to ensure smooth flow.

> *Creativity is not about artistry alone but also about economics. Activities that stimulate one's creativity and critical thinking offer prospects of new economic opportunities. They can release untapped potential for economic innovation and enterprise.*
>
> *Limkokwing*
> *2008*

Kuala Lumpur's Light Rail Transit

The introduction of the Putra Light Rail Transit System on September 1, 1998 complemented the mass transit transport service provided by STAR (Sistem Transit Aliran Ringan or Light Rail Transit System) and the two systems played a crucial role in the success of the 16th Commonwealth Games held in Kuala Lumpur from September 11 to 21, 1998. The two LRT systems carried spectators from the city and its suburbs to the Games' venues at the National Sports Complex in Bukit Jalil. The first phase of the STAR system opened on December 16, 1995, the second on July 11, 1998 and the third on December 6, 1998.

Kuala Lumpur Railway Station

Rail transport had been part of Malaysian life since 1885. In 1992, the Malaysian railway underwent a corporatisation exercise and one of the first tasks in the re-engineering process was to upgrade performance. The railways had been suffering dismally for a number of years after modern expressways were built under Tun Dr Mahathir's privatisation policy, greatly reducing inter-city travelling time by road.

KTM Komuter was Malaysia's first electric rail system, heralding a new era in rail transportation. The service was introduced primarily for the congested Klang Valley area, the richest and most urbanised region in the country centred on Kuala Lumpur. It helped tremendously in opening up outlying districts for development. It also encouraged more city commuters to travel between home and workplace by rail, and leaving their cars at home or at parking lots in the suburbs.

Tan Sri Lim's task involved changing the outdated signage and introducing a fresh look in keeping with KTM's new objectives and re-energised entry into the highly competitive public transport sector as a corporatised entity.

Tan Sri Lim was hand-picked by Tun Dr Mahathir to assist Nelson Mandela in educating black South Africans, who had never voted before. Part of the process was to bridge the hatred between the blacks and the whites. He worked with Mandela to begin the reconciliation through the voter education process. He overcame obstacles to create the historic image that helped to position the African National Congress as a peace-loving democratic party.

Tan Sri Lim used South Africa's children to drive home the point that South Africa must focus on its future. The goodwill this historic poster generated not only helped the ANC connect with the people of South Africa but sent a clear message to the international community that South Africa was on the right path to owning its future. The poster shown here carries a personal message penned by Nelson Mandela in appreciation of Tan Sri Lim's effort.

African National Congress

51 Plein Street
Johannesburg 2001
P O Box 61884
Marshalltown 2107

Tel: (011) 330-7273
(011) 330-7052
Fax: (011) 333-7739
Telex: 421252

OFFICE OF THE PRESIDENT

Dato' Lim Kok Wing
Emissary of the Prime Minister
of Malaysia
Kuala Lumpur

12 April 1994

Dear Dato' Lim Kok Wing

It is with great pleasure and deep gratitude that I write to thank you and your team for the tremendous contribution you have given to our election campaign.

Your untiring efforts on our behalf have touched the hearts of us all and you have shown true friendship and solidarity with the people of South Africa in our endeavour to transform South Africa into a free, Just and democratic country. The size and magnitude of your contribution will have a very meaning impact on the outcome of the election and, on behalf of the people of South Africa. I thank you.

We are indebted to Prime Minister Mahathir for commending you to us and I have personally thanked him for doing so.

With warm good wishes,
Your sincerely

NELSON R. MANDELA
President

The People Shall Govern!

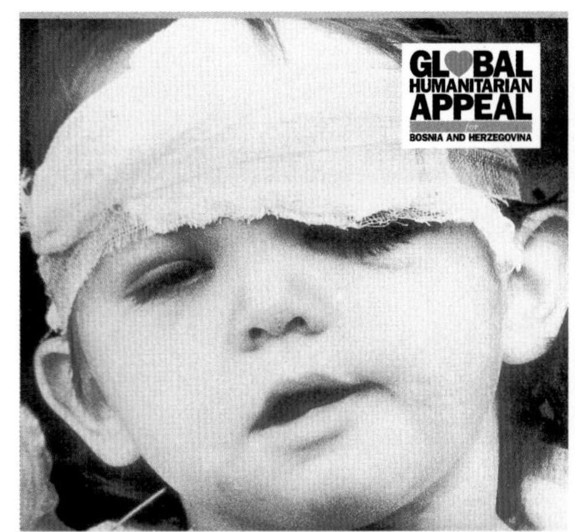

Top: *In 1995 Tan Sri Lim launched a global campaign to raise funds for the rebuilding of Bosnia Herzegovina which had suffered four years of conflict. He began by getting a book written to explain the background of the conflict so people could understand the issue. He followed through with an exhibition which was officiated by Tun Dr Mahathir. A dedicated website brought global attention to the cause.*

Middle: *After the 9/11 terrorist attack on New York in 2001, Tan Sri Lim was disturbed with the association that was being made between terrorism and Muslims. To overcome the perception he organized a global peace conference in 2003. Here you see Prime Minister Tun Dr Mahathir who came to officiate the opening. On his right is Jacob Zuma, who is now President of South Africa.*

Bottom: *Tan Sri Lim never refuses support for peace efforts by others. He lends his time, money and skills to campaign against war and violence. This exhibition called a War Zone Experience was created for Tun Dr Mahathir's Perdana Global Peace Forum in 2005.*

COUNCIL OF MINISTERS OF
BOSNIA AND HEREZEGOVINA
Office of the Co-Chairman
Dr. Haris Silajdžić

Sarajevo, 1st June 1998

Y. Bhg. Tan Sri Dato' (Dr) Lim Kok Wing
LIMKOKWING INSTITUTE OF
CREATIVE TECHNOLOGY
1 Jalan SS26/2, Taman Mayang Jaya
47301, Petaling Jaya
Selangor Darul Ehsan

Honorable Tan Sri Lim Kok Wing,

On behalf of the Council of Ministers of Bosnia and Herzegovina and my own behalf I would like to express our heartfelt gratitude for your support to Bosnia and Herzegovina and its people. Your noble endeavors in promoting the Global Humanitarian Appeal for Bosnia and Herzegovina represent an important contribution to the process of strengthening the peace and stability in Bosnia and Herzegovina
The book " Bosnia, beyond words, beyond tears", co-authored by you and Ms. Faridah Hamed, is a masterful record of suffering and pain of body and soul, inflicted upon the Bosnians by an aggressive force. The book, written with warmth and concern for the plight of fellow human beings, is a strong warning to the world that such tragedy must not be repeated ever again in any part of the world.
Honorable Tan Sri Lim Kok Wing, please accept assurances of my profound regard.

Yours sincerely

Dr. Haris Silajdzić

Address: M. Tita 16, Sarajevo, Tel: (++38771) 664930, Fax: (++38771) 667881

__Top:__ In 2003 the Kuala Lumpur World Peace Award was awarded to French President Jacques Chirac who made a special trip to receive it from Tun Dr Mahathir Mohamad. It was part of the Kuala Lumpur World Peace Conference mooted by Tan Sri Lim.

__Middle:__ Over the past two decades Tan Sri Lim has helped to present the plight of the Palestinians through various media to help people understand the issue. For his endeavours the Palestinian Ambassador to Malaysia H.E. Abdelaziz Aboughosh in 2009 presented him with the award recognizing him as a Distinguished World Citizen of Peace & Humanity.

__Bottom:__ Tan Sri Lim at the 2nd International Muslim Unity held in December 2009, was the only non-Muslim who was recognized with an award for his international contributions in humanity and philanthropy by the Ramadhan Foundation. Here he stands amongst Muslim scholars and leaders from around the world.

Winning Battles Abroad

Building international presence

As Tan Sri Lim began to work on forging an identity for these entities, he became exposed to the enormous task they faced to build a presence not only within the country but also overseas. At about the same time Tun Dr Mahathir was pushing Malaysia aggressively forward.

The Prime Minister, despite heavy criticism, established a steel production company as a prelude to setting up a car production unit, something unheard of in Southeast Asia where car manufacturing meant local assembly of foreign-made automobiles.

The Prime Minister used these two ventures to provide the catalyst for Malaysians to venture into high technology-based manufacturing. The emphasis shifted away from exporting raw materials to manufacturing and exporting Made-in-Malaysia products. His intention was to pull the country out of its dependence on exports of raw primary commodities. He wanted Malaysians to venture into downstream industries and add value to its vast resources of palm oil, cocoa, rubber and timber by processing them inside the country and turning them into finished products.

Tan Sri Lim's role became clearer as he expanded his activities from forging corporate identity for public sector organisations to developing and promoting Malaysian branding to the world. But first he had to build Malaysia's image and position the country.

Image positioning a country

There is a famous saying in Malay – the official language of the country – *Tak Kenal, Tak Cinta*. It translates as Don't Know, Can't Love. What it means is that you won't care for something that you don't know or understand.

That best describes what Tan Sri Lim set out to do. He wanted the world to know about Malaysia. But he needed vehicles to realise his wish. He had experimented with imaging for the country when he handled Malaysian tourism for the Europe market, but that was just a small part of the entire business. He needed something more holistic, more comprehensive that will firmly position the country. He found it when the Prime Minister asked him to present the Malaysia Incorporated policy.

In a publication promoted worldwide he fused together the geographical, economic and historical development of the country. He wooed the corporate sector to support the venture and, working with the public sector, the book was produced in true Malaysia Inc. style.

Every branding campaign Tan Sri Lim worked on was never done in isolation. No international branding campaign was ever developed without a parallel domestic campaign. Synchronising the two was essential to the success of the campaign, for without creating understanding of a policy or initiative at home would weaken the international effort. It would never do for Tan Sri Lim to trumpet the benefits of doing business with Malaysia without educating Malaysians about the need to produce quality goods and services as well as the opportunities to do business with the world.

Promoting Malaysia for investment

One of the most important decisions that played a key role in Malaysia's development was a decision by Tun Dr Mahathir to implement Malaysia Inc.

Though it was not an original idea, its success in redefining Malaysia's public-private sector partnership made it a completely original Malaysian brand.

The Malaysia Inc. concept was adopted from Japan, which had rebuilt itself after the country's devastation in World War 2. It was the close collaboration between the government and the private sector that made Japan's amazing recovery possible.

The reason for Malaysia Inc. was simple: "Public servants were anything but servants of the public," explained Tun Dr Mahathir at the Malaysia Incorporated Summit 2000. "They were not expected to be helpful towards the private sector. A rather negative attitude was adopted. Delays were the general rule and if anything could be rejected, it would be rejected. The slightest mistake or failure to comply with policies or regulations would result in rejection. There was almost a feeling that there was no reason for civil servants to facilitate approval when it meant making some businessmen rich, while the civil servant seemingly gained nothing at all."

Malaysia Inc. became a clarion call to rejuvenate the country's economic and industrial agenda. Essentially, it was a policy that transformed the mindset of the public sector to adopt a private sector-driven attitude.

The best and most efficient country is one where all stakeholders work closely together. The government system must work in tandem with the private sector. We must move forward as a team. It should be Team Malaysia winning for Malaysia.

Limkokwing
2009

When Malaysia Inc. was introduced, Malaysia was not doing well. The country was going through an economic downturn in the first half of the 1980s. There was still too much dependence on the production of commodities such as tin, rubber and palm oil. The petroleum and gas industry was in its infancy, while manufacturing was also a low contributor to the economy.

Just 3 years after Malaysia Inc. was adopted, the country began to turn around. From then on, the economy continued to grow at more than 7 percent per annum. Tun Dr Mahathir's actions within the government and his numerous speeches to the private and public sectors to explain the Malaysia Inc. concept touched a chord in Tan Sri Lim.

"When he was making speeches to get Malaysians to adopt it, and getting people abroad to understand it, and to come and invest in the country, I felt it was necessary to do something to support it," he recalled.

Government policies anywhere in the world are usually enmeshed in bureaucratic verbiage – and often understood by very few apart from the policy makers. As a strategic communicator, Tan Sri Lim knew that the policy needed to be made simple and easily understood by Malaysians as well as foreigners.

He felt it important to have a book that clearly spelled out the policy, how it worked and what were its benefits; a book that could be used as a marketing tool by the government to promote the policy locally and internationally. It was the kind of turbo-charged policy the government needed to attract more foreign investment.

The book, Malaysia Inc., marked Tan Sri Lim's first foray into big-time publishing in Malaysia. Completed in 1995, it firmly established his prowess as a publisher. It also highlighted his close working relationship with Tun Dr Mahathir, a fact that brought him as many supporters as it did detractors.

The book was organised to showcase that the Malaysia Inc. policy had been firmly established and there were many opportunities for investors to tap.

In his introduction to the book, Tun Dr Mahathir said the publication provided the opportunity for Malaysia to reintroduce itself in the next century as a country with a robust, competitive and expanding economy that offered huge investment opportunities but also where the critical parameters for any investment decision existed.

"It was to show the locals that it is up to them to come up with bold ideas and concepts which will help the country leapfrog and to provide windows to the foreigners to look into," he said.

This was the first time that such a book about Malaysia was published, with pictures, data and profiles of companies and people to contact. "It was to help Malaysians as well as foreigners to have a clear idea of what the policy was all about, how it applied to public-private sector partnership, and investment possibilities. Many Malaysian companies were also featured, and it helped Malaysian companies to be known around the world," said Tan Sri Lim.

The book was conceptualised for the international market. It encapsulated Malaysia's emerging confidence as an economic powerhouse.

Tan Sri Lim approached the book the way he always looked at things – to make it simple and easy to understand by every reader. He wanted to focus on the benefits for the common businessmen.

The Malaysia Inc. book was well received and used actively by the Prime Minister's Department, Ministry of Foreign Affairs and the Ministry of International Trade and Industry. An estimated 500,000 copies of the book were distributed, double what was originally planned. It became a potent marketing tool for the country as well as for the corporations featured in its pages.

The book was launched in London, Tokyo, New York and Hong Kong and the launches were attended by top business people, fund managers, bankers and investors. It was distributed to all foreign embassies in Malaysia, as well as in several countries during trade shows and investment road shows.

"It brought together the world's best technicians, some of the world's best ideas, and some of the world's most talented entrepreneurs. And it helped develop our own confidence," said Tan Sri Lim.

Made in Malaysia for the world

The success of the Malaysia Inc. publication brought Tan Sri Lim into discussions with many ministries, among them the Ministry of International Trade and Industry that had set up MATRADE in 1992 as its external trade development and promotion arm. MATRADE's core business was in gathering market intelligence for local manufacturers and at the same time encouraging local producers to consider export as a viable option.

"The establishment of MATRADE was an important move by the ministry because exports were gaining ground as the country's engine of growth," said Tan Sri Lim. "It was primarily the result of the Prime Minister's push. In just over a decade, the profile of Malaysian exports had changed. We were the leading exporter of electronic semiconductors, room air-conditioners, audio-visual equipment and value-added products."

The GATT International Trade Report in 1994 placed Malaysia as the 18th largest exporter and importer in the world. Malaysia's total exports and imports had increased by 15.7 percent and 14.2 percent, respectively, to US$47 billion and US$46 billion, respectively.

Tan Sri Lim's task was to build the brand image of Malaysia as a nation that exported quality products. "The intention was to inspire confidence in Malaysia as an international trading partner. We needed to not just produce quality, we needed to look and talk quality."

He created the catch phrase Made In Malaysia For The World and developed international as well as domestic campaigns for MATRADE. The campaigns signalled Malaysia's global assault on overseas markets. It also marked a sharply focused and more determined effort to enhance Malaysia's standing and image as an exporter.

"I think Malaysia has improved tremendously in this area. Today, despite all the problems faced by the world, Malaysia is still among the top

20 largest exporting nations. In 2007 we exported more than RM605 billion worth of goods. Compare this with the RM147 billion in 1995 and you can see that we have done pretty well," said Tan Sri Lim.

He pointed out that Malaysian branding did not suffer the poor quality image that many Taiwanese products had to go through when they began to export. "I think the credit has to be given to Tun Dr Mahathir because he was the country's best salesman. Our export figures are good because it was his strategy to move into non-traditional markets."

More recently Tan Sri Lim has been working with MATRADE to push Malaysian branding. "There is a strong need for SMIs (Small and Medium Industries) especially to understand the power of branding," he says. He pointed out that there are currently more than 100,000 manufacturing establishments in the country. "Of these, 91 percent are SMIs. They form the backbone of the manufacturing community. And they need to understand that the market is fast evolving with new trends and many new players. They need to build brands because it has been shown that more than just products, it is brands that survive and retain consumer loyalty."

Promoting Malaysia as a tourist destination

When the brief came to Tan Sri Lim and his team for a campaign to sell Malaysia as a tourism destination to the world, it came with research that the 'world' wasn't quite sure *what* it was Malaysia was selling. Compared to Thailand and Singapore, tourists were less sure about what *exactly* Malaysia had to offer that was different from these two countries that share borders with Malaysia.

Instead of trying to sell the tired line of Asia all rolled into one (a claim already touted by various Asian countries), a strategy of promoting 8 destinations was adopted by Tan Sri Lim and his creative team. These 8 destinations would cover 3 different kinds of holidays to appeal to the key categories of holiday-makers – nature lovers; sun, sea and sand pleasure seekers; and history and culture enthusiasts.

At all times it would be clear that all these destinations could be found in Malaysia. The word *Fascinating* would be retained as a consistent proposition in keeping with the advertising of previous years. A consistent visual identity was maintained, dominated by large photographs.

"We were very strategic about the branding of Malaysia where tourism was concerned," explained Tan Sri Lim. "When we were doing the campaign, we had big photographs of fishes and butterflies on huge double-decker buses in London. Our research showed people recognised them immediately as Malaysia. We worked really hard at branding and creating an image that would benefit Malaysians in the long-term as a unique tourist destination."

Unfortunately, he said, Malaysia's tourism branding was still lagging

Above: Tan Sri Lim mooted the KL Festival 2006, designing the logo and its signature line "Where the arts come alive". He felt the city should develop its identity as a centre for art and culture.

behind famous destinations like Bali, Thailand and Singapore. Part of the problem, he said, was that every time a new minister was appointed to the tourism portfolio, the campaign skew changed so there was no consistency and continuity.

"The biggest problem is that we do not have, in one place, a decision-making process that helps us formulate an overall strategy to sell or market Malaysia in totality and to orchestrate it right down the line – which is what a good campaign is all about," said Tan Sri Lim.

"Tourism is related to trade, to the people, to the culture, to how people in this country live their lives. You can't sell that in bits and pieces. People must know Malaysia as a complete entity. In the case of Malaysian tourism – one day it is nature, next day it is shopping, another day it is friendly people, another day it is the airport. There is no consistency, there is no complete or clear concept on how to market and promote Malaysia as a whole."

Defending Malaysia's rainforest management

Malaysia is a tropical country located at the edge of the Equator. It rains a great deal in the country and temperatures vary from 20 degrees Celsius to 30 degrees Celsius, with the exception of the highlands which are cool throughout the year.

The climate has produced one of the biggest and oldest tropical rainforests in the world.

In the mid-1990s, the Malaysian rainforests became embroiled in accusations that there was uncontrolled logging and deforestation, and the government was not doing enough to manage timber harvesting. It was ironical that the very countries who had logged their own forests for development were now pointing an accusing finger at Malaysia as well as other developing countries, insisting they stop cutting down the forest to reduce global warming.

Tropical forests are particularly under the spotlight in the 'green' fight because more than half of the world's bio-diversity is found in tropical rainforests.

Malaysia was at the losing end of the attack on rainforest management. The country was lumped together with other developing economies that were cutting down their forests at an alarming rate.

So distorted were the reports coming out of the Western media that one actually pointed out that there would be no rainforest in Malaysia by the year 2000. A government in Europe even went so far as to introduce legislation forbidding the import of timber from Malaysia. If they had bothered to do their research, they would have discovered that Malaysia was one of the greenest countries in the world and a leader in the management of tropical forests.

Former Malaysian Timber Council (MTC) CEO Tan Sri Wong Kam Choon recalled: "In 1995, a major thrust of the UN Conference on Environment and Development was actually on the issue of forest and forest management. We had to deal with this growing international awareness and concerns about how forests were being managed. There was also concern whether the timber that was getting into the trade came from poorly managed forests."

(The Malaysian Timber Council was established in January 1992 to promote the development of the timber-based industry in Malaysia and the marketing of timber products. Formed on the initiative of the timber industry and incorporated under the Companies Act 1965 as a company limited by guarantee, MTC was governed by a Board of Trustees appointed by the Minister of Primary Industries.)

Malaysia is a major player in the tropical timber trade, and one of the leading countries in terms of the sizeable areas of forests. It was the world's leading exporter of tropical sawn timber, the second biggest exporter of tropical plywood next to Indonesia, and the leading exporter of tropical timber wood mouldings.

It was, recounted Tan Sri Wong, the perfect target for Western environmentalists bent on shifting the blame on global warming to developing nations. It was also a convenient issue to divert attention away from domestic ills arising from having to control pollution within their own countries due to the kind of lifestyle that Western countries were used to.

"When they started putting pressure on European governments, in particular, to enact rules and regulations to boycott the use of tropical timber, of course this affected Malaysia very seriously," said Tan Sri Wong.

"But at the same time, we knew that our forest management policies have in place a long time – well before all these concerns about tropical forest management problems."

Tan Sri Wong said the tropical timber issues included "a certain amount of vested interests to protect the interests of temperate timber which actually is a competitor to tropical timber".

"It was a complex issue with a lot of underlying interests and motivations by different groups," he pointed out.

Malaysia, he said, in an effort to correct the distortion and unfair accusations, was placed in the forefront to face this issue "not only to safeguard its own position and interests but also for the other tropical forest countries who were also subject to all these pressures".

When Malaysia decided it was time to fight back with facts and figures, Tan Sri Wong turned to Tan Sri Lim for recommendations on how best to get Malaysia's side of the story to the world media.

The two had met when both were members of government delegations to foreign countries. Tan Sri Wong reckoned that their first meeting was when he (Wong) was Secretary-General of the Primary Industries Ministry in the late 1980s and early 1990s.

"My first impression of him was that he was a very composed person," said Tan Sri Wong. "He was able to articulate his thinking very clearly and chose his words carefully. Because I'm one of those people who was always conscious of how people communicate when they talk to me, that stood out for me."

Tan Sri Wong also felt that Tan Sri Lim is a man who thinks ahead. "He was able to relate the various aspects of the goings-on in not only Malaysia but also how the outside world is moving along and how Malaysia interacts with their interests. He seemed to have a very good feel."

Tan Sri Lim, he added, also showed a great deal of pride in having Tun Dr Mahathir as the leader who was spearheading the establishment of symbiotic South-South partnerships.

He added: "I think Tan Sri Lim found this all very much his cup of tea."

As their association progressed, he found Tan Sri Lim to be someone "who acts in earnest to play his part as a corporate citizen".

At informal discussions on how the timber issue could be handled, he said Tan Sri Lim "was very much taken up because I think he could grasp that this issue was being used by so-called environmental activists for their own ends – although of course some might do it with quite genuine intentions".

Still, Tan Sri Wong said, the reality was that a lot of NGOs were using this issue to popularise their own organisations and building a platform to get public donations for their cause. This was then capitalised by politicians who took on this green issue for political mileage in their own countries, particularly in Europe.

These actions negated decisions taken at the Rio Earth Summit, he said. "It was actually decided at the Rio Earth Summit that for forest management to be improved - particularly in Third World countries - what is needed is greater understanding, more assistance, more transfer of technology and that trade itself is not really the cause of tropical deforestation.

"But these environmental activists were harping on this and instigating all these negative actions on the market and restricting the importation and use of tropical timber.

"If the tropical timber trade is unfairly jeopardised, then it could lead to diverting the land under forests into other areas – the value of the forest is very much reduced because the timber is not accepted in the international market. We need proceeds from the export to be reinvested in redeveloping our forest areas. We also need it for R & D efforts and providing the forest service – to keep track of development and to help maintain forest areas that have been logged."

Many other environmental issues like the emission of greenhouse gases and pollution – of which the biggest perpetrators are the developed countries –took a backseat.

"People were picking on trade as a way of resolving the tropical forest management issue whilst the real problems of deforestation in tropical forest countries are poverty, under-development, the need to service foreign debt and the like."

It was, said Tan Sri Wong, "like throwing all the problems into the backyard of Third World countries".

Tan Sri Lim's company was asked to come up with a campaign to counter the anti-Malaysia campaign on the international stage.

Working with MTC, Tan Sri Lim and his creative team prepared a comprehensive strategy that was largely aimed at the international audience. There were advertisements for newspapers and trade publications as well as a book and a series of calendars featuring Malaysian plants that had medicinal and commercial uses. While retaliatory in spirit, the strategy was designed to be meaningful, and to present the facts in a clear and common sense manner.

He is a person who is mindful of the affairs of the country. He is someone who thinks deeply and is able to articulate his thinking and his visions clearly. He feels he has a lot to contribute because there is so much lack of knowledge.

Tan Sri Wong Kum Choon
Chairman, Malaysia Rubber Export Promotion Council, 2000

This was the first time a cohesive campaign had been put in place.

"I made several trips to Europe to meet the media people and I came away feeling that they really had no idea about the country. They only read about how many tons of logs and how many trees had been felled – very dramatic presentation of facts.

"It was all stacked against us – making us look very ugly – and ignoring the fact that 70 percent of the country was still under forest cover," said Tan Sri Lim.

His strategy was to attack the 'over-simplified' and 'illogical' information provided by mainly European NGOs about the situation.

In the communications proposal to counter the claims, Tan Sri Lim pointed out that there was a need for one body to speak with authority on rainforest/tropical timber foreign management. It had to be a voice, he added, that was authoritative and credible to the NGOs. Many of the NGOs, he noted, had sophisticated communications skills and networks that were extremely well funded.

He told MTC that a clear 'corporate vision' was crucial to carry out an integrated campaign. Response over the last decade, he noted, had been reactive and defensive.

He recommended that MTC be established as a 'leading voice' in the advocacy of sustainable forest management, and that Malaysia must be established as a leading nation in the overall management of tropical forests.

For this, he recommended MTC adopt a positioning statement: *Malaysia. Leading in Tropical Forest Management.*

Tan Sri Lim laid out a five-year communications campaign for international and domestic target audiences, streamlining all public relations and promotional efforts. It would shift MTC from a fire-fighting position to a broader-based, pro-active one.

It called for the broadening of the information base of Malaysia's rainforest management and conservation through advertising, promotional materials and events. It also required expanding international and domestic perspectives on the influence of commercial logging upon deforestation, targeting information to relevant country audiences to educate them on important issues including Sustainable Forest Management and Certification.

Tan Sri Lim also called for the integration of the information base with other authorities such as the Ministry of Primary Industries, Forestry Department and the Science, Technology and Environment Ministry.

Based on feedback and research by his team, Tan Sri Lim was convinced that while MTC should continue to send out facts and figures to foreign media, what was needed was something they can hold in their hands and look at and know that we are proud of our green heritage.

"We needed to tell them that this forest is ours, and we will protect it;

that we know how to protect it, because they were talking about it as if it was theirs. So the book *Green Horizon* was produced.

"It wasn't a defensive tool. It introduced Malaysia through this green passage, but through reading it you will know that this much of the country is covered by rainforests.

"You know that selective logging is being done and you will know that there are still a lot of people who live in the jungle. These are nomadic people who go from place to place. " said Tan Sri Lim.

Green Horizon was published by Limkokwing Integrated. It provided a photographic walk-through of the Malaysian rainforest. It was just one item in an orchestrated campaign to provide Malaysian and international consumers and government representatives with data on Malaysia.

The book was distributed through embassies, trade missions and through the Timber Council and Primary Industries Ministry.

Still, both Tan Sri Wong and Tan Sri Lim admitted that it was an uphill battle for developing nations to fight the anti-tropical timber lobbying mounted by Western NGOs and other special interest groups.

In the final analysis, said Tan Sri Lim, the campaign was a success in that Malaysia did something to counter the unfair reports.

"It was one more step in our effort to make our position known to the world, and to refuse to take these attacks sitting down."

The currency crisis

In July 1997, the Asian Financial Crisis hit Malaysia like a typhoon. I use the word typhoon to describe it because in Malaysia, we have no experience of this natural disaster. So, when it hit us, we were shocked by its ferocity. The Ringgit came under relentless attacks by speculators and was devalued to half of what it used to trade before the crisis hit – at around 2.50 to the US dollar. The inflation rate climbed to double-digit levels, people lost their jobs overnight, and large corporations went bankrupt.

Also in July of 1997, the Australian Broadcasting Corporation (ABC) ran a story on its documentary series programme *Four Corners* called *Mahathir: Wounded Tiger.*

"I remember the conversation I had with the PM. That was before I saw the videotape of the programme. I had been thinking about how we should respond to the very bad media coverage of our country. We talked about our concerns on this negative media coverage. And he asked if I had seen the video of the Australian programme *Four Corners.* I hadn't, and he said I should. On retrospect, I wondered how he could be so calm about it. All he said to me was I should take a look at this programme. He did not tell me what was on the tape."

It was a damning piece, said Tan Sri Lim, who viewed a videotape of the programme and came away feeling 'extremely frustrated' at the broad swipes taken at the Prime Minister of Malaysia and the country.

"It was a total lie," he recounted. "It was written to destroy the PM's reputation. They stitched together snippets from everywhere...from events that took place many years ago, and made them look like they all happened yesterday."

Tan Sri Lim also felt ABC was completely arrogant and had no business commenting on what it felt was right for Malaysia.

"They showed the (Petronas) Twin Towers and said this is something the country could not afford," he related. "Who are they to say if we can or cannot afford it? They said this was Tun Dr Mahathir's two fingers to the world. They intersperse these with scenes of the poorer, rural countryside."

The producer's agenda, Tan Sri Lim said, was clear. "There could only be one conclusion after viewing the whole programme. That this was a very corrupt country, this was a very corrupt leader."

Interestingly enough, on its website *Four Corners* was described as Australia's longest running current affairs programme, and was often referred to as the "flagship" of the government-funded ABC. It was a programme that supposedly brought analysis and insight to Australians about world events.

It was after the viewing of this tape, that Tan Sri Lim decided something needed to be done to tell Malaysia's side of the story. It was the culmination of severe beating from the Asian Financial Crisis, earlier discussions he had with Tun Dr Mahathir about the Western media's portrayal of the country, and specifically that of the former Prime Minister.

The result was the book ***Hidden Agenda*** *In The Eyes of The Tiger* pub-

His faith in my ideas never diminished even when the whole world's media condemned my tirade against the currency traders. He was up front fighting my battles.

Tun Dr Mahathir bin Mohamad
Prime Minister of Malaysia, June 2000

lished by Tan Sri Lim's company Limkokwing Integrated in 1998. It featured writings and thinking by prominent leaders and financial analysts about how the Asian Financial Crisis really came about. At that time, Malaysia had foreign investors from more than 40 countries, companies that had established multiple manufacturing operations and progressed rapidly from producing simple assembly products to producing high value-added and high-tech products for regional and global markets.

The opening chapters set the tone, briefly outlining Western interests in Asia from the spice trade to the new global scenario. An argument was presented for a possible conspiracy to stop East Asia in its development tracks. The chapters highlight the Malaysian Prime Minister's early warnings on neo-colonialism and his concern regarding the damage that currency speculation could do to the economy.

"I didn't plan a book at that time," Tan Sri Lim explained how *Hidden Agenda* came to be. "I had thought about a video, but if it wasn't played, no one would see it. But a book could reach anyone. So a team was gathered to work on it, because there was a lot of research to be done. The strategy was, basically, to inform the audience what the truth really was. Whatever the audience, whoever was prepared to listen."

Said Tan Sri Lim: "The book was an Asian perspective of the economic situation in Malaysia and the region. It was a no-holds-barred questioning of the West's intentions. Some in Asia believed that the West engineered the currency crisis to forcibly open the Tiger markets (the newly industrialising economies of East Asia outside Japan) that were closed. Its purpose was to give a more balanced view on that theory which the Western media and Western leaders had taken note of but were quick to dismiss as untrue."

In his introduction entitled *Is There a Hidden Agenda?* Tan Sri Lim wondered about the conspiracy theory espoused by Tun Dr Mahathir that led to the currency crisis and recession that hit Malaysia and East Asia with such ferocity. The conspiracy theory questioned whether the West could be using the economy – instead of gunboat diplomacy – to dictate unfair and unequal treaties.

Hidden Agenda, he said, "may appear to be extreme in its arguments... but it was unavoidable, solely because much of the Western media view had been extreme in blaming all on East Asia's 'reckless growth'."

In many ways, this book provided the two-pronged platform to address the endless economic and political tirades against Malaysia by the Western media.

Still, Tan Sri Lim did not see the possibility of any clear improvement in the Western media's reporting of Asia anytime soon for obvious reasons.

One is the lack of media might in Asia.

"With their colossal size, globe-girdling reach and financial muscle, these companies effectively control what we hear and see on the airwaves everyday," Tan Sri Lim contended in an article *Malaysia: A More Confident Voice in the 21st Century.*

"Asia has been getting a raw deal where coverage of its news, views and issues are concerned. Asian content was largely being reported within a framework of Western news values and agendas, which limit the issues covered. Often, these are rooted in colonial and snobbish perceptions of Asia."

The other is that Western media had vested economic and political interests to maintain the economic and social divide between the West and the East.

The Western media were largely ignorant of what was going on in this part of the world and there was a natural bias against Asia, he asserted. "Anything normal or good – like the building of roads and schools is not reported."

There was support for this view from veteran Western journalists. In a paper entitled *What Are Journalists For*, correspondent for *Sky News* and *The Independent* of London, Jake Lynch presented a case for Western journalists having created the hype about the Asian Miracle economies, as much as they were responsible for the Asian Financial Crisis.

News organisations, wrote Lynch, had invested heavily in business coverage of Asia as the perception spread that it was the place to invest. The region's business publications became valuable prizes. Dow Jones purchased the *Far Eastern Economic Review* (Dow Jones announced in September 2009 that it closed the magazine). The now defunct *Asiaweek* became part of the then Time Warner empire, and CNN, CNBC and Star TV all set up operations in the region with much of their programming devoted to business news.

Lynch quoted an important critic of this version of events, Walden Bello, who said these channels became "critical interpreters of the news in Asia to investors all over the world". They "highlighted the boom, glorified the high growth rates and reported uncritically on so-called success stories, mainly because their own success was tied to the perpetuation of the psychology of boom".

When the meltdown began, noted Lynch, there was no shortage of political and economic experts laying the blame on the very culture that they once credited for being 'miraculous'.

The following quote provides another way of looking at it.

"Examined for how things come to be, rather than how they are, it appears, if anything, (the Asian Financial Crisis was actually) a Western Financial Crisis with Asian victims," wrote Lynch.

"In the Asian case, undiscriminating inward capital flows to the region, hyped by Western or Western-owned news organisations, inflated a souffle of bank lending against soaring property values. This, along with Western speculation against fixed currencies pegged to the US dollar, as a way for Asian countries to develop economies within the Western created global system they confronted, were the very factors which fuelled the boom and also transformed downturn into collapse."

In his foreword to *Hidden Agenda*, Tan Sri Lim presented the East Asian dilemma as "to speak out and be damned or to remain silent and be damned". The havoc caused to the region's economies and the destruction had long-lasting ramifications. Chief among them, said Tan Sri Lim, was that it set the development clock back 20 years.

"The relentless Western media attacks on East Asia with reports that were negative, damaging and destructive further eroded confidence in the region," he said. "Never mind that they may be distorted half truths and lies. What was clear was that the relentless attacks had left a damning impression of the region generally, and Malaysia specifically."

A paper by Canadian public policy analyst Gerald Caplan at the *Open Markets, Open Media?* forum in November 1997 said: "It is useful to remind ourselves that free expression is threatened not just blatantly by authoritarian governments and all those in the private sector who fear public exposure, but much more subtly by the handful of global media conglomerates that have reduced meaningful diversity of expression in much of the globe.

"Towards the end of the 1990s, even the mainstream media's reporting on the global financial crisis can warrant criticism. Their phrases used (an *Asian* financial crisis, *crony* capitalism which was the fault of the people in the affected countries and so on) and their angles portrayed, the influences of Western corporations, etc, all resulted in coverage that tended to implicitly, sometimes explicitly, blame others. It came over as though excuses and other explanations had to be provided so as not to let us imagine that some of the root causes would ever come from home-grown 'prescriptions'."

Malaysia's selective exchange control regime implemented in September 1998 helped Malaysia to regain control of the economy from currency speculators and manipulators. By 1999, Malaysia was back on its feet, reawakened from its financial slump faster than most of its neighbours.

For Tan Sri Lim, there was a real need for a book like *Hidden Agenda* even though he knew that it would not become an international best-seller. It was an important psychological step. A step – albeit a small one – to point out that there was another side to the story; one that countered the blatant and unfair assumption that the crisis was caused solely by corruption and cronyism.

Even as Tan Sri Lim was planning *Hidden Agenda*, he was already looking ahead. Next on his own agenda was a magazine called *Voice of Asia*.

The magazine would carry on the work of *Hidden Agenda* by providing ongoing information and analyses of events in Asia and around the world. Its strength would be as a source of alternative interpretations of Asian events. The publication was targeted at an intellectual readership – covering academia as well as business and corporate leaders.

The inaugural issue was dedicated to articles on the crisis. It was, he said, "to bridge the chasm between what was really happening and what had been depicted by the majority of the media controlled by Western interests".

While Tan Sri Lim felt strongly about the need for Asia to have a voice in the world media, he acknowledged that it wasn't going to happen anytime soon.

"If you want to continually provide someone with what you consider to be an accurate report, you have to do it daily," he pointed out bluntly. "That's beyond a lot of Asian countries. Even in Malaysia we're in no position to do that."

Increased and fairer Asian content in the international media, said Tan Sri Lim, was a numbers game. "It will only happen when Asia becomes a major media space buyer," he said. "That's the only way to balance up the perspective. I'm sure that will change things. How long will that take? At least 10-20 years for countries like Malaysia. Maybe 50 years for poorer countries."

Bosnia: Beyond Words, Beyond Tears

Bosnia-Herzegovina, prior to the 1990s, was unknown to the average Malaysian. Malaysians knew of Yugoslavia but few, if any, beyond the diplomatic circles, had ever heard of Bosnia-Herzegovina.

Then, in the early 1990s, when civil war broke out in the Balkans, Bosnia was no longer a strange land. Pictures of terror and atrocities became standard fare on national prime time news, horrifying Malaysians – as well as the world.

In February of 1996 Tan Sri Lim published the pictorial essay of the

Bosnian tragedy. Entitled *Bosnia: Beyond Words, Beyond Tears,* the book – in black and white – presented pictures sourced from the government of Bosnia-Herzegovina and the Sygma agency.

The book was a key component of the Global Humanitarian Appeal for Bosnia-Herzegovina, a non-profit international campaign spearheaded by Tan Sri Lim's company Limkokwing Integrated. It contained names, addresses and phone numbers for Bosnian government agencies as well as the Permanent Mission of Bosnia-Herzegovina at the United Nations where donors could forward various kinds of assistance needed in the rebuilding of the war-torn country.

It was the first such international campaign run by one country for another aimed at heightening awareness of the tragedy and raise funds to support medical and rehabilitation aid efforts as well as to help rebuild the country. The cost of reconstruction was estimated at US$5.1 billion.

Tan Sri Lim's penchant for doing things in a big way resulted in not just developing a book. From the single idea to do a book, he envisioned a global appeal – one that would help Malaysians as well as other donors from around the world to give directly to the Government of Bosnia-Herzegovina in their national reconstruction efforts.

With the book, Tan Sri Lim planned a video as well as an exhibition. The book was launched in February 1996 in Kuala Lumpur by Tun Dr Mahathir Mohamad during the Muslim fast of Ramadhan.

"The willingness of the private sector to mobilise their resources in support not only of the country's economic policies and growth, but also its diplomatic initiatives and international role is commendable," said Tun Dr Mahathir.

"This horror could have been stopped earlier. Certainly it must never be allowed to happen again. This is the underlying message of *Bosnia: Beyond Words, Beyond Tears.*"

The book launch was held simultaneously with the launch of an international video and exhibition with the same title. The video received great support from Malaysian television stations and was aired over a period of a few months. Tan Sri Lim also arranged for it to be sent to several television stations around the world, mainly the Middle Eastern countries, and the International Red Cross and Red Crescent networks.

A year later, the Global Humanitarian Appeal won a national honour when it was named the inaugural Krystal Award recipient for the Most Outstanding Public Relations Campaign.

South Africa

In 1960, Malaysia's relationship with South Africa took a dramatic turn. A very young nation then – having achieved independence from the British only three years earlier, Malaysia was so horrified by the Sharpeville massacre that it initiated an international campaign in the United Nations that led to Pretoria's isolation by the international community.

The massacre – in which police fired on a crowd of unarmed protestors, killing 69 and wounding over 180 – resulted in the proclamation of a state of emergency and the banning of the African National Congress (ANC) and the Pan Africanist Congress (PAC) which organised the protest. The ANC did not dissolve but went underground.

Malaysia – through its first Prime Minister Tunku Abdul Rahman – was among the world's most vocal opponents against South Africa's policy of Apartheid, severing its diplomatic relations with South Africa. South Africa responded by making it clear that Malaysians were unwelcome in South Africa. Classified as 'coloured' under Apartheid's vile racial laws, they were discouraged from entering the country.

Yet, time and again, this small multi-racial nation in the South China Sea spoke out vehemently at every opportunity it had on the world stage to renounce the Apartheid regime. It was a small voice of dissent, but an important one, when the silence of giant nations reverberated with apathy.

At the London Commonwealth Heads of Government Meeting (CHOGM) of 1961, the Tunku – along with the premiers of India,

Ceylon (now Sri Lanka), Australia, Pakistan, Nigeria, New Zealand and Canada – successfully pressed for the expulsion of South Africa from the Commonwealth.

Malaysia also joined in an international trade embargo against South Africa.

Then Deputy Prime Minister Tun Abdul Razak Hussein said Malaysia decided to accept the consequent loss in Malaysia's foreign trade in order to uphold a principle.

Tun Dr Mahathir, at the1985 CHOGM, said one of Malaysia's priorities was to galvanise support from fellow Commonwealth leaders to pressure South Africa to dismantle its Apartheid laws.

In 1986, at the UN General Assembly in New York, Tun Dr Mahathir expressed Malaysia's outrage that despite its efforts to bring an end to Apartheid, it still existed. He called again to the world community to embark "seriously on sanctions".

In 1990, South Africa took its first significant step towards ending Apartheid and handing power back to the majority black Africans by freeing ANC leader Nelson Mandela – at that time the world's most famous political prisoner – who had been locked away for 27 years.

A historic election

When the African National Congress (ANC) began to put in place its election campaign for the country's first democratic elections, it was to Malaysia that ANC leader Nelson Mandela turned for assistance.

The ANC, after all, was in the business of fighting for liberation, not campaigning for elections.

Mandela in his autobiography *Long Walk to Freedom* explained that despite the fact that pre-poll surveys showed the ANC enjoyed a healthy lead, "we never took victory for granted".

In 1990, when Mandela came to Kuala Lumpur after his release from prison, he described Malaysia as a "loyal friend of the people of South Africa and one of the ANC's strongest allies" as it has been an "important and most consistent" opponent of the Pretoria regime.

Though the ANC had made its mark by fighting for freedom, they now wanted to look to forging a future of peace and prosperity for South Africa.

"Some in the ANC wanted to make the campaign simply a liberation election, and ask the people to vote for the ANC because we set them free," said Mandela in his autobiography. "We decided instead to offer a vision of the South Africa we hoped to create. We wanted people to vote for the ANC not simply because we fought against Apartheid for 80 years, but because we were best qualified to bring about the kind of South Africa they hoped to live in. I felt that our campaign should be about the future, not the past."

The ANC had drafted a 150-page document known as the Reconstruction and Development Programme which outlined its plan to create jobs through public works; build a million new homes equipped with electricity and flush toilets; extend primary health care and provide 10 years of free education to all South Africans; redistribute land through a land claims court; and end the value-added tax on basic foodstuffs.

"We were also committed to extensive affirmative action measures in both the private and public sectors," he said.

This document was translated into a simple manifesto called *'A Better Life for All'*, which in turn became the ANC's campaign slogan.

Reconciliation

An estimated 20 million people would vote for the first time in the South African elections. Many were illiterate and likely to be intimidated by the mere idea of voting.

Though assured of victory, the ANC wanted to ensure no stone was left unturned in rallying all-round support that would appeal to both blacks and whites; a call of reconciliation and hope that would bridge a nation divided by racial prejudice for three centuries.

Mandela, who was fascinated by Malaysia's policies that had maintained ethnic harmony in a multi-racial nation for more than 30 years, turned to Tun Dr Mahathir for advice.

Tun Dr Mahathir offered the skills and expertise of Tan Sri Lim, and the ANC engaged him in December 1993 to put together its election campaign strategy.

"When you first get into South Africa, you are struck by the great divide in wealth between the blacks and the whites," Tan Sri Lim recalled of his first trip there to familiarise himself with the country.

"The palatial houses in the whites-only suburbs contrasted starkly with the poverty and deprivation in the shanty towns. You really have to see it to believe it because you cannot imagine that people were living like this in this day and age in what most of us considered a free world. It struck you then that there was no way this divide could be bridged."

Despite his initial misgiving, Tan Sri Lim said he also "couldn't help but realise that the best thing for them to do was to reconcile".

"Politically, they had to reconcile and the whites were needed to stay on to help continue building the country," he said.

The political reality that existed in South Africa at that time, said Tan Sri Lim, was also different from the Malaysian situation. "Firstly, they were full-time politicians. They were incredible communicators. Though many of them had been imprisoned in a very cruel and unjust system, they didn't condemn the whites or were extreme in their views."

Tan Sri Lim remembered that he himself was moved by the process – which he noted was often taken for granted by people living in democratic nations.

"This was the beginning of their struggle as a free country," he said. "There was still a lot of emotional pain and suffering. But there was a great deal of hope for the future.

"At election rallies, they talked of the sun shining tomorrow. They talked about warm water, hot food on the table for their children. These were basic things that most of us take for granted. They spoke about the injustice of the political system and about a future in which everyone had the same opportunity. But they also reminded the people not to

> *Tan Sri Lim was one of those who came here, not to seek fame, or other benefits, but in a very humble way to work with us to make sure that the people who sacrificed so much for the freedom of this country would usher in a new government led by Nelson Mandela.*
>
> *Dr Popo Molefe*
> *Former Premier of Northwest Province, South Africa, June 2008*

forget leaders who had sacrificed their lives for their cause such as Steve Biko (a leader of the black resistance to the Apartheid regime who died from injuries suffered while under detention).

"They made incredibly inspiring speeches – speeches that could even move an observing foreigner to tears."

Tan Sri Lim said he was struck by the magnitude of the rallies. There were huge rallies everywhere, each easily numbering 100,000 or more people. People would stand on top of cars and trucks to speak.

"If Mandela were to speak, 500,000 people would show up. It was amazing because there was also hardly any security control.

"But there was such hope and energy, and it struck me that these were a people prepared to sacrifice themselves for their beliefs and their rights. Their issues were so basic and their rallies so heartfelt and so 'raw' in the power and devotion they evoked that I couldn't help but compare them with the rallies in Malaysia.

"Standing there in South Africa observing a rally made me realise here was a scene that had none of the coziness and comfort of election rallies back home," he said.

Putting pictures to words

In his autobiography Mandela explained how the campaign slogan came to be. It was a slogan, Tan Sri Lim said, that he wanted to tweak to *'A Better Future for All'*.

"They had already decided on that by the time I was engaged. I wanted to change it to *'A Better Future for All'* because a better future was a more long-term goal. I felt *'A Better Life…'* was too definitive and would have to be delivered soon after the election."

He didn't succeed.

"I couldn't convince them and I gave up on it because they gave in, in a lot of other areas," he said. "For instance, in the main campaign photograph, I wanted it to be very inclusive of all the different races. We discussed way into the night how many white children, versus black children, versus coloured children were to be in that photograph. Often the arguments went on for a long time and they were very emotional."

'A Better Life for All' posters and billboards – featuring a smiling Mandela surrounded by children of various races – sent a direct and immensely powerful message not only to South Africans but to a world watching with great interest.

"It is a profile that will appeal to the cross-section of the public," Tan Sri Lim was quoted as saying in 1994.

The posters proved so popular that many ended up on the walls of black shanty town huts. That perhaps was the greatest accolade to Tan Sri

Lim's genius in capturing the heart of a campaign that transcended geographic boundaries, cultures and lifestyles.

That picture in the poster that defined the ANC campaign, said Tan Sri Lim, also had its many sticky moments during discussion with the ANC's election committee.

"They felt that the picture was too 'Kellogs', too wholesome," he remembered with a wry grin. "They felt it was too conciliatory, giving away too much."

But Tan Sri Lim did not back down because experience told him it was the right way to go.

"I told them they already had all the black votes and we needed some white votes. Of course they were concerned that there were other black nationalist parties campaigning and they were worried about losing votes to them.

"It took me a while to convince them that they were not fighting for freedom anymore but for recognition.

"They were fighting for all round support, respect and trust because they did not need the whites to leave South Africa in droves. That was why I was insistent that the tone had to be inclusive and conciliatory."

Finally, it took Mandela to step in to resolve the impasse.

"He said he knew I had the experience and he believed I was being objective and it was for good reason," Tan Sri Lim said. "After that, things moved forward much more smoothly."

Though details of Tan Sri Lim's scope of work for the ANC campaign are sketchy and limited, an article in Malaysia's English daily *New Straits Times* in April 1994 revealed his company produced 60 tonnes of ANC billboards and posters that were put up mostly by his own staff throughout South Africa.

His company helped organise election rallies, and further strengthened the ANC's theme and image. They also organised transport and enlisted volunteers to help voters at polling stations.

These were crucial as the ANC – consisting of former liberation fighters – had never organised an election campaign before.

That Tan Sri Lim himself has tremendous respect for Mandela is obvious.

"When I first met him, I was struck by how tall he was," he said. "Politically, he was like a god to the black South Africans, and the white South Africans had a healthy respect for him. He's a very clever communicator and a rousing orator. He could move quickly from one level to the next. You would see him dancing with young ladies and then he's talking with footballers.

"He reads his game very well in any situation, in front of any audience. His eyes and his mind are very sharp. He has a magnetic personality."

Mandela, said Tan Sri Lim, was the leader of South Africa even before the election. "He was not the president yet but he was undoubtedly the leader. And he carried himself that way, without being pompous."

In June 2008, Limkokwing University conferred an Honorary

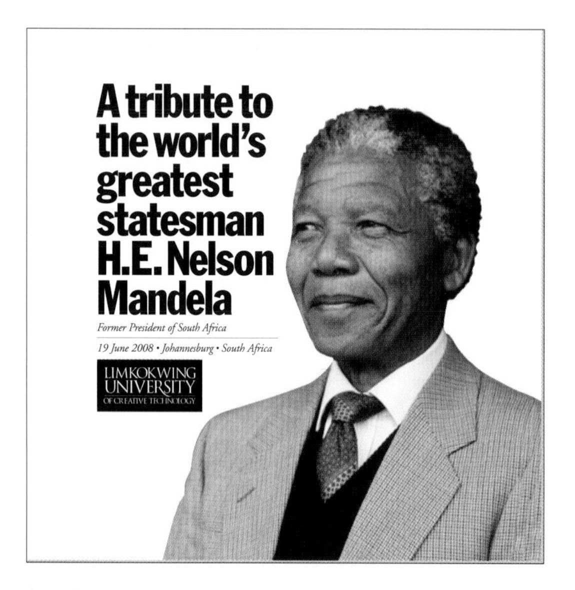

Doctorate of Humanity on Mandela who celebrated his 90th birthday the following month.

In his speech at the award presentation held at Mandela House, Johannesburg in South Africa, Tan Sri Lim said Mandela "exemplifies the best qualities attainable by humanity. A man respected, admired, loved by peoples across the world as a role model of a moral leader.

"A statesman who rose above hate and vengeance to embrace peace and reconciliation, a man whose courage, wisdom, visionary leadership and almost unhuman-like capacity to forgive continue to inspire people far beyond South Africa.

"Without doubt, His Excellency Nelson Mandela's willingness to walk the road of sacrifice distinguishes him as one of the greatest symbols of resilience, tolerance, non-violence and moral integrity of our age. Perhaps of all ages.

"He has redefined the concept of leadership. He has proved through his own example that faith, hope and charity are qualities not beyond the attainment by humanity. Because of him, the world is a better place. Because of him, the world is working to be a kinder place."

Above: On June 2008 the Limkokwing University conferred the Honorary Doctorate of Humanity upon Mandela in a special ceremony in Johannesburg.

Among the one hundred over awards Mandela received from around the world included the Nobel Peace Prize in 1993 which he shared with the last Apartheid-era President Frederik Willem de Klerk for their work in ending Apartheid and for laying the foundation for a new democratic South Africa.

Tan Sri Lim's sojourn in South Africa made him many important friends, among them Thabo Mbeki, who succeeded Mandela as President of South Africa in June 1999. (Mbeki resigned on September 21, 2008 after losing a power struggle in ANC to his deputy Jacob Zuma who went on to become the next President of South Africa.)

Asked about his observation of Mbeki and his difference and similarity to Mandela, Tan Sri Lim said theirs was a relationship "like father and son".

"Mbeki was a very senior person in the ANC, and clearly the person assisting him, the person implementing."

Inaugurating a new era

In May of 1994, the ANC's historic win put an end to 300 years of minority white rule, restoring dignity and rights to South Africa's 30 million blacks.

For Malaysia, that had been among the few nations that refused to have anything to do with the Apartheid regime, the ANC's victory was a resounding validation of its 34-year-long steadfast denunciation of white-minority rule.

Malaysia, which had been a member of the Commonwealth Observer Group to monitor the election process, was represented at Mandela's inauguration by a Malaysian delegation led by then Foreign Affairs Minister Tun Abdullah Badawi who later became Malaysia's fifth Prime Minister.

The whole world was in South Africa, said Tan Sri Lim, who recounted how things had moved so quickly that telling remnants of Apartheid still prevailed at their arrival.

"All the delegations were picked up at the airport," he said, "and we couldn't help but notice that all the big cars were used to pick up the European delegations. We, among others, were assigned smaller cars. The Apartheid bureaucracy had yet to be dismantled then and it was very noticeable."

Since then, Tan Sri Lim has led several Malaysian business delegations to South Africa on behalf of the Malaysian government.

"I was sent to help forge business links between Malaysian businessmen and the South Africans," said Tan Sri Lim.

He himself though does not have any business interests in South Africa today.

"I was there to do a job," he said by way of explanation. "I stayed away from doing my own business because it was a question of doing what I was sent to do and not deviate from that trust given to me."

"Let me introduce you to a South African..."

In Tan Sri Lim's office today is a giant ANC election poster, one of the many 'mementoes" of campaigns that grace the walls.

Alongside is a copy of a letter that ANC president Nelson Mandela wrote to thank him for his efforts. It reads:

It is with great pleasure and gratitude that I write to thank you and your team for the tremendous contribution you have given our election campaign.

Your untiring efforts on our behalf have touched the hearts of us all and you have shown true friendship and solidarity with the people of South Africa in our endeavour to transform South Africa into a free, just and democratic country. The size and magnitude of your contribution will have a very meaningful impact on the outcome of the election and, on behalf of the people of South Africa, I thank you."

That Tan Sri Lim made an impact with Mandela and the ANC is without doubt. The friendship and trust he enjoys with the revered leader is perhaps best exemplified by this story - one of the few tales he is willing to tell about the whole affair.

When news of the ANC's win reached Tun Dr Mahathir, who was leading a Malaysian delegation (that included Tan Sri Lim) in Zimbabwe, it was Tan Sri Lim who arranged a private meeting between the two friends for Tun Dr Mahathir to offer his congratulations in person.

The meeting was to have a special and definitive recognition for Tan Sri Lim from Mandela. Introducing the Malaysian delegation to Mandela, Tun Dr Mahathir was stopped by Mandela just as he was about to introduce Tan Sri Lim.

"Mandela told the former PM: 'Stop, let me introduce you to a South African', when they came to me," remembered Tan Sri Lim with a smile.

Championing Malaysia as a voice for world peace

Peace is something Tan Sri Lim values above everything else. Perhaps it is because he was born a year after the end of the Second World War. It was a time of healing and the world had had enough of violence.

He detests confrontations in his personal dealings. He always finds ways to avoid it. The escalating violence around the world made him want to do something to make things better. He settled on creating something permanent that would attract peacemakers from around the world. He wanted to provide a forum for peace issues to be discussed. He wanted an Asian viewpoint on these issues. Most of all he wanted to change global association of the word Muslims with terrorism – the repercussions of the September 11, 2001 terrorist attacks on the United States.

In 2003, just months after the United States launched its war on Iraq, he mooted and organised the Kuala Lumpur World Peace Conference. World leaders and other prominent figures participated in the conference that was planned to become an annual affair. The two-day conference ended with a nine-point declaration. A month earlier the inaugural Kuala Lumpur World Peace Award was given to then French President Jacques Chirac for his dedication to peaceful resolution of international conflict.

Tan Sri Lim in his message in a brochure outlining the intentions of the peace conference said:

"Kuala Lumpur will serve as a point of rally for those who would sue for peace. Kuala Lumpur will provide new impetus to thoughts and actions that will trigger chain reactions and result in peace."

He pointed out that despite this being the Information Age, there is a great deal of misinformation about the common ground all religions share – that of humanity, forgiveness, compassion and tolerance. "These noble values are being drowned out by the extremist elements that are destroying the peace, trust and understanding between peoples and nations. That is why it is critical that peace advocates – both from peace organisations as well as from the great faiths of the world – gather together to help heal the hurt and allay the mistrust," he said.

He pointed out that Kuala Lumpur was uniquely qualified to host the conference. "Malaysia has built over four decades of development on a formula of collaboration and co-operation. It has worked well to move the nation forward.

"The country is no stranger to violent conflicts. Over many centuries it had suffered wars and foreign occupation. It defeated a savage communist terrorist insurgency.

"Through it all, Malaysians have held firm to their belief that war is not a solution; that winning hearts and minds offers the only true path to achieving lasting peace."

Tan Sri Lim, however, faced an uphill task in getting the second conference organised because of the change of government leadership. In 2003, just months after the conference Tun Dr Mahathir handed over the reigns of power to his deputy Tun Abdullah Ahmad Badawi.

Tun Abdullah was preoccupied with putting his mark on the country and his priorities were placed elsewhere. He had his own ideas about changing global perception about Muslims through his *Islam Hadhari* concept. Loosely translated as 'Civilisational Islam', *Islam Hadhari* sought to change mindset, break the shackles of dogma and rigidity that limited the progress and development of Muslims, and enable Muslims to engage with the wider world.

For Tan Sri Lim there was little point in pursuing the matter of organising another world peace conference although he tried very hard to interest Tun Abdullah in hosting it.

And the frustration for Tan Sri Lim was that a conference of this magnitude and nature needed government support as invitations had to be made on a government-to-government basis.

Instead, he lent support to the peace endeavour initiated by Tun Dr Mahathir through the Perdana Leadership Foundation that organised conferences on a yearly basis.

Part 2

Engaging The Present

The lessons that we pick up from the past serve as the template to build the present. It is all we have to plan what the future can be. Tan Sri Lim learnt many lessons from his dynamic involvement with society, industry and government. But the responses he received were often not to his satisfaction. He decided to tackle issues from a different stand-point. He saw very clearly that change can only take place if he was directly involved in shaping the mind and the character of the country's next generation.

He made the decision to set up an institution for higher education, one that would be different from the normal expectations.

- ***Designing the individual***
- ***Designing the environment***
- ***Establishing the brand***
- ***Creating the architecture***
- ***Inventing the experience***
- ***Inviting the world***

Designing The Individual

When you set out to design something there is a process, a method used to create a product that is beautiful to look at and that is useful to others. It starts with identifying the use and defining its purpose. And then we begin to explore. The imagination takes flight – searching, considering, judging, discarding and searching again. In that great wonderland of the human mind we will discover the ideas that we seek, then shape them until we arrive at a design that is moulded into a prototype. The prototype is the model that takes the full impact of all the problems that can arise with its use. From the prototype emerges the actual product, moulded to perform.

Now imagine applying that process to an individual.

That's what Tan Sri Lim did when he decided to create the school which he named after himself – Limkokwing Institute of Creative Technology – in 1991. He was 45 years old and already a well-respected individual, well-established in the advertising business, a philanthropist, a titled person carrying the rank of Dato' which is an Order of Chivalry awarded by the Malaysian King, a happily married man with a beautiful wife and two young children.

The future of a country is always shaped and defined by people who have the passion and the drive to push beyond the ordinary, beyond limits and boundaries; by people with big ideas and even bigger, bolder commitment to accomplish what may now seem impossible.

Limkokwing
2005

Most people that age would be basking in their success and moving their business further up the value chain.

Instead, Tan Sri Lim plunged into a new field where he had no track record. He had never been to university but he decided to invest his energy, his time and his money into education. He designed, shaped and moulded it.

The Institute served as the 'factory' to design this individual that he had in his mind. He wanted his graduates to be confident, smart, tech-savvy, well-dressed, well-spoken, well-connected and well-skilled individuals.

He then set about putting his road map together to achieve this outcome. He began his school not with bricks and mortar but in the mists of the future. He visualised it. He imagined what it was going to be like and how it was going to achieve his vision.

In the following pages you will find the road map he used to shape and mould the institution from a small organisation catering to just

Top: *The first campus established in Jalan Tun Razak in 1991 gave indications of its non-traditional approach to education, taking away the formality and injecting inspiration in learning.*

Middle: *In 1997 the campus found new premises in Taman Mayang in Petaling Jaya where it occupied an entire complex to house its growing number of students and expansion into new faculties. The non-traditional approach became a strong feature of the institution.*

Bottom: *In 2004 the Limkokwing University moved into its own premises. It completely changed the whole idea of what a university should be, from both the outside as well as the inside.*

The Limkokwing University campus in Cyberjaya stimulates the imagination from the first glance. The use of a wrap was innovative. The "skin" which is a giant wrap of the exterior provides opportunity to renew its image from time to time

As much as it can the University has carried its concept of a new approach to education in all its campuses across the world. The top picture shows the campus in Botswana, which is the largest to accommodate over 10,000 students. The London campus, shown in the middle picture, has a more sedate exterior because it is a historical building which does not allow for experimentation. The bottom picture shows the campus in Lesotho where the brightly coloured exterior has been attracting attention in the capital city of Maseru.

The interior of the Cyberjaya campus is designed with the creative student in mind. The Limkokwing Creativity and Innovation Research Centre is three floors that capture a three decade journey of Tan Sri Lim. How creativity is applied in various situations – from crisis management, trade promotion, international relations, brand management, investor relations, youth development to peace promotion, voter education and many more issues are presented.

The Limkokwing Creativity and Innovation Research Centre showcases hundreds of panels of actual campaigns that Tan Sri Lim had been involved in. Every panel has a story of strategic communication to address an issue or a challenge.

The Cyberjaya campus houses a branding innovation gallery which was established at a cost of RM1 million. Improving the branding of local products has always been a priority for Tan Sri Lim. He had begun the first phase of the branding gallery at the Mayang campus which developed into a dedicated showcase by 2004. He used it to explain what he had been advocating for a long time to the government.

Fitofly, Wings Coffee, Oneworld Club, Makanlah are a few of the unique brands developed on campus. They provide valuable lessons where students learn how different skills are needed to build a business.

The campus reflects the lifestyle of today's generation. From a place to design hair, stay fit, indulge in some recreational activities, surf the net or chat with friends over a cup of coffee, the business units on campus began as experiments that grew into commercial entities.

The campus is self-sustaining in terms of producing all its creative content. It has professional units that come together to lend support to the University to produce its printed literature, advertising, video production, 3D animation, event management, public relations, web communications and music composition among others.

Top: *In 2005 the then Deputy Prime Minister Dato' Sri Mohd Najib Tun Abdul Razak (in the middle wearing a blue tie) came to launch a special project to empower youths from the rural heartland with digital skills.*

Middle: *The campus was ablaze with Malaysian flags as the country celebrated its 48th year of Independence in August 2005.*

Bottom:*From royalty, heads of government to movie stars the University always welcomes its visitors with pomp and pageantry. This was a visit by the Duchess of Gloucester to the Mayang campus in 2002 during her 3-day visit to Malaysia.*

The University is characterized by its youthful personality which attracts students from all over the world. It is a place that celebrates creativity and encourages young people to build their talent while they pursue their degrees. The picture at the bottom shows Hollywood movie star, producer and director Mel Gibson surrounded by Limkokwing students. He was amazed with the vibrancy of the campus when he visited in September 2007.

LIMKOKWING world's first

One in a million in Malaysia, one in 75 million in the world.

The surname Lim was first bestowed by the King of the Zhou dynasty three thousand years ago to honour a Chinese called Jian whose father – Bi Gan – was renowned for his loyalty and kindness. Today there are some 75 million Lims dispersed around the world with an estimated 900,000 here in Malaysia. But only one Lim has established a university that also carries the surname Lim. On 24 May 2010 Tan Sri Dato' Sri Dr Limkokwing was formally presented with a recognition by the Federation of Lim Associations of Malaysia for founding the world's first university by a Lim.

Standing next to YB Datuk Seri Liow Tiong Lai, Minister of Health (fourth from left), a beaming Tan Sri Dato' Sri Dr Limkokwing holds up the award presented to him by Dr Robert Lim from the Federation of Lim Associations of Malaysia witnessed by Tan Sri Dato' Sri Lim Gait Tong, Honorary President of the World Federation of Lims among others from the Federation and the Limkokwing University.

university founded by a Lim

"The milestones that this University keeps creating, primarily comes from the fact that at the helm stands an extraordinary man that is Tan Sri Dato' Sri Dr Limkokwing. He was recently described as the Father of Innovation in Creative Education. Congratulations Tan Sri, our country needs creativity and innovation for breakthrough to the next level. To many it is unbelievable that a Malaysian has set up campuses in so many countries across the world, from Africa to Europe and across Asia. And in every country he has brought his philosophy of bridging gaps in human capital development to assist in expanding economies, especially in the developing world."

YB Datuk Seri Liow Tiong Lai
Minister of Health, Malaysia, 24 May 2010

"Limkokwing University was founded by Tan Sri Limkokwing in 1991. The brainchild of Tan Sri Lim has become a full-fledged entity, not only in Malaysia but in the world. This is truly a great achievement. Such a feat could not have been thought possible. We were always of the view that education was something special only to the West. Tan Sri's brilliant leadership, and his generosity and kindness in contributing to the country should be a role model to all of us."

YBhg Tan Sri Dato' Sri Lim Gait Tong
Honorary Advisor to the Federation
Honorary President, World Federation of Lims, 24 May 2010

"All Malaysians, particularly the Lim families are very proud of this achievement because it is the one and only globalised university founded by a Lim. And also the fact that the university itself carries the brand name of Lim. We are very proud of the achievement by Tan Sri Limkokwing and we wish to appoint him as National Life President of the Federation."

Dr Robert Lim
President, Lim Federation of Malaysia, 24 May 2010

"In the spirit of 1Malaysia, I do hope this sense of accomplishment will also be shared by all in all the other communities. I certainly did not plan to be the first Lim in the world to establish a university. But it is good to know that we are ahead of the millions of Lims in China and across the world."

YBhg Tan Sri Dato' Sri Dr Limkokwing
President, Limkokwing University of Creative Technology Worldwide, 24 May 2010

Tan Sri Lim only recently discovered that out of 75 million Lims in the world he was the only one to have established a global university and carrying the surname Lim. Through the Federation of Lim Associations of Malaysia he also was able to trace back the origin of the name Lim to China in the fourth century.

The University has maintained a consistency in its communications. It has a distinctive style that has sustained its branding over the years. It always seeks to excite and to inspire which are elements needed to sustain the interest and cultivate the passion of the young.

Designing the future

"The future of a country is always shaped and defined by people who have the passion and the drive to push beyond the ordinary, beyond limits and boundaries; by people with big ideas and even bigger, bolder commitment to accomplish what may now seem impossible; by people who would move mountains if the mountains are getting in the way. These are people who would simply not take things as they are and would never choose to take the easy way out. In reaching beyond the ordinary, they achieve extraordinary success. In doing what they do, they transform societies and influence the way of life of many across the world. In doing what they do they build the most successful enterprises and brands the world has known. The future will always be about making the impossible possible."

Tan Sri Dato' Sri Dr Limkokwing
Speaking at National Mark & Brand Entrepreneur Conference, 2 March 2009

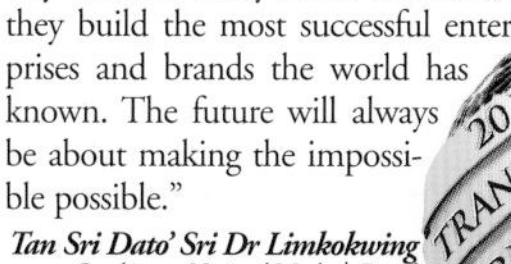

Empowering a smart web generation

"Innovation has its genesis in places where there is encouragement for new ideas. It survives best when it becomes part of a country's culture and is woven into its educational system, its industrial infrastructure and its political leadership. Malaysia must be rebranded to stand for innovation if we are to remain a credible force in global competition.

For our country to succeed in the long term, we must make our national competitiveness a mission for the whole country, involving every Malaysian and every strata of our society. We must make a concerted effort to take the country to where we aim to be – a country known to the world as an innovation nation by 2020. To succeed the whole nation must be on board, from farmers to teachers, taxi drivers to bankers, business leaders to political leaders. Everyone from every walk of life must feel ownership of the need for quality and embrace it every step of the way. Everyone must be prepared, new systems must be built, out-dated mindsets must be changed.

We must make that transformation happen quickly and successfully. The Prime Minister's call for 2010 to be the Year of Creativity and Innovation is, therefore, most timely."

Tan Sri Dato' Sri Dr Limkokwing
Speaking at a seminar organized by the Branding Association of Malaysia, 17 December 2009

• 30,000 students from 150 countries • Off-shore campuses in United Kingdom, China, Cambodia, Indonesia, Botswana and Lesotho • Limkokwing degrees & diplomas delivered in 20 countries • Global network of 282 university partners from 77 countries • 100 million hits from 190 countries every year accessing the University website • Cited by World Bank and UNESCO for innovation in global education • Recognised by QS APPLE as "University of the Future"

www.limkokwing.net +603 8317 8888 +603 8317 8988

An advertisement that appeared in January 2010 a twin celebration of the University's 20 years anniversary as well as the year being declared by the Prime Minister as the year of creativity and innovation. Tan Sri Lim felt vindicated after two decades of pushing the two vital building blocks of progress.

Events are the lifeblood of the University. Every event brings together a cross-section of skills and students who participate and learn more in one event than in a year listening to lectures. Every Limkokwing event pulls the crowd and stimulates the students performing on stage.

Events bring out the best in young people. Many discover latent talents from modeling to dancing, singing, presenting, producing to art direction and choreography. These add to their confidence and their ability to multi-task.

The Limkokwing campus is always abuzz with people visiting, training being conducted, foreign students celebrating their national days, student clubs holding events and a variety of exhibitions featuring creative work. The plaza has a feel of the outside which is inside and allows thousands to congregate.

Graduation is always a day of celebration when success is greeted with inspiring songs that congratulate the students and thank the parents. There is pomp and pageantry but none of the stodginess associated with traditional graduations of other institutions of higher education.

The University's Hall of Fame where all formal events are held projects the international personality of the institution where the ceiling is covered in flags of all nations.

The special ceremony to confer an Honorary Doctorate upon Tun Dr Mahathir Mohamad in June 2009, turned into a huge celebration as students from over 100 countries dressed in their national costumes gathered to honour a man who had inspired millions across the developing world.

Graduates from the University's rural next generation programme showed their appreciation to Prime Minister Dato' Sri Mohd Najib Tun Abdul Razak when he came with his wife Datin Seri Rosmah Abu Mansor to applaud their success in 2008.

Tiffanee Marie Lim, Tan Sri Lim's daughter has taken on the role of representing him at many functions held both within Malaysia as well as abroad.

Top: *In October 2009 Tiffanee was selected as Malaysia's Most Promising Female in the under 40 category of a nationwide competition organized by Prestige Magazine.*

Middle: *Tiffanee was in New York to receive the 2010 Global Innovation Leadership Award in Education on behalf of the University.*

Bottom: *Receiving the "Most Popular Brand" award in June 2010 on behalf of the University from Dato' Mukhriz Mahathir, Deputy Minister of International Trade and Industry, Malaysia.*

Inspiration
personified

The second volume of thoughts and memories of national and international leaders, diplomats, industry peers and Limkokwing students and alumni, whose 100 voices pay tribute to a truly inspiring figure:

Tan Sri Dato' Dr Lim Kok Wing

Top: *Tiffanee Marie Lim receiving the Technology Business Review's Excellence in ASEAN Education Management award for 2008 on behalf of the University.*

Tiffanee helped to host the visit of the Duke of York, Prince Andrew when he came to officially open the Malaysia Britain: Partners in Innovation exhibition at the University campus in 2004.

Middle: *Tan Sri Lim has inspired and empowered thousands of young people who pass through the University. The responses of 100 of them are captured in these publications.*

Bottom: *The launch of Magic was a mesmerising event in itself with Limkokwing students lending their talents that made for a memorable evening.*

The visiting Minister of Education and Training from Lesotho, Dr Mamphono Khaketla (in pink) officiated the launch of Magic. She said: "In every language we have words that define Magic. It is something you cannot touch, you cannot see, you cannot hold in your hand, but you can just feel it. This book is really about magic. There are no boundaries in this world. This is what Limkokwing is teaching us."

300 students to a global university within 16 years. By 2009 he had established campuses in seven countries where more than 30,000 students from 150 countries were enrolled to pursue their higher education. It started by designing the environment.

Designing The Environment

In his mind's eye Tan Sri Lim saw very clearly what his school would look like. He first visualised the kind of graduates he would produce and worked backwards to shape the environment. What would he call his great new adventure? What would he teach? How would his students learn? As a person who had built his reputation in branding he set out to develop the identity of his new journey. He knew shaping the environment was an important exercise and it involved everything from establishing the brand name and creating the architecture to inventing the experience.

The university has a presence in the heart of Kuala Lumpur for promotional activities and to build its brand.

Establishing The Brand

Having spent two decades in the communications industry Tan Sri Lim knew he needed to build the brand giving his venture an identity and a personality. Today people often ask the reasons why he decided to lend his name to his university. Was it pride, an ego trip? It was neither. It was a practical decision that was strategic because at that point of time he was managing a successful communications business. He was at the crossroads of his life when he broke away from a merger he had with a global conglomerate called BBDO with which he ran a successful advertising business at the top rung of the industry. He dissolved the union to set up Limkokwing Integrated because he was moving into a new level with his business, one that was more nationalistic and wide-reaching. In setting up Limkokwing Integrated he began to use his name. He had built value into it. The industry and the government knew the quality of his work while the public knew him as a philanthropist.

Limkokwing Integrated stayed in the background because of the nature of its work which did not require a public face. However, with his Institute, he needed to build a brand that was consumer-oriented. It needed a strong image and powerful positioning.

Laying the foundation

He decided that this would be a school unlike any other – not just in the country but also internationally. It would be a school that would offer the highest quality art, design and creative education.

"All through my working years I had held a desire close to my heart. It took me a long time to visualise what it was exactly. My experience of working for other people helped. I saw the struggles of local talent trying to penetrate a market dominated by foreigners," said Tan Sri Lim.

At that time, only the government-run Mara Institute of Technology offered programmes in these areas, but Mara was open only to Malay and other bumiputera (indigenous people) students. For non-Malays, it was either small-time 'art schools' or, if they could afford it, an overseas education. And many of those who went overseas seldom came back. For Malaysia it was a talent-drain.

Private education was considered small game but Tan Sri Lim had big ideas and big plans. It was not an impulsive decision to invest his time, skills, knowledge and money in education. He pondered over it for a considerable time.

To understand what he had to do, he travelled the world, talking to professors, university administrators and other professionals; appraising ideas and absorbing the lessons from the experiences of renowned educators. He adapted the knowledge he had gathered to create his institute's own programmes, designed for industry in Malaysia. No 'one-size-fits-all' approach for him.

"You don't want to just learn what others learn because educational programmes are designed to meet the needs of the local industry," he explained.

At the time, private education was not well regarded. There was a stigma attached to it. "Private education in those days meant tuition centres which catered mainly for school dropouts," said Tan Sri Lim. "It was certainly nothing near the mainstream industry it is today."

Then as it is now, private education in Malaysia has been driven by non-Malays, simply because it catered largely to non-Malays.

Tan Sri Lim took another major step by going against the prevailing tide of offering 'twinning programmes'.

Twinning programmes were the preferred route taken by the mushrooming private educational institutions in the country at that time. Essentially, twinning means a foreign university programme is done partly here (usually for two of four years) and the final part completed overseas in the university that originated the programme. It is a popular choice for most private tertiary institutions in Malaysia as it helps students save costs while the college offering it also benefits as it does not have to develop any syllabus on its own.

Instead, Tan Sri Lim offered degree programmes jointly with foreign institutions, and diplomas under the Limkokwing name. He created strategic links with rep-

> *It took British universities quite a long time to grasp the importance of what Tan Sri was achieving here in Malaysia. Certainly I think he has been the benchmark for innovation in education.*
>
> *Maurice Dimmock*
> *CEO, Accreditation Service for International Colleges, UK, 2010*

utable and well-established universities and colleges in the United Kingdom, United States, Canada, Australia and New Zealand. At the same time, the college created strong industry collaborations that enabled students to get real work experience while they learned.

Limkokwing: institutionalising personal qualities

Registering the name was the first step.

Tan Sri Lim admitted that it was a gamble to go with his name as the institute's brand name but it was one forced on him.

"Market research results came back consistently that my name was the most recognisable. Because the name was known, it came out on top whether it was recognition, credibility, quality or creativity. In advertising you are very conscious of the need to put something in place that consumers would have no difficulty accepting. That is the first thing."

Yet he was also clearly aware of the risk. A Chinese name to front a regulated business was rare where a Malay name was almost always the favoured choice to enhance its national 'acceptability' – otherwise known as political correctness.

He said many people he spoke to believed a Chinese name in this market could not sell because it was local. They were afraid the Malay market would not accept it. It was actually going against the trend, especially 15 years ago, when names with Malay words such as Majujaya or Muhibbah or generic types like Asia Pacific were popular.

But he pointed out that in the West "whenever someone starts a business, his first choice is always to use his name because there is pride in that".

"The Americans used their names, the names of their founders. Very seldom do they use generic names unless it is a merger or it is a new technology, like Microsoft. You look at the Japanese and Koreans. Of course, they also created generic names like Goldstar and so on, but they also have Toshiba, Sanyo, Seiko and Hyundai."

He stood firm on his decision, refusing to be swayed by the prevalent herd mentality, and went ahead to name the school Limkokwing Institute of Creative Technology.

"I consciously set it up as a test case," he said. "Not just on the basis of it being an obvious Chinese Malaysian-owned establishment but also the bias against local products compared to imports. I wanted people to change their mindset. People should accept that a Malaysian Chinese name is a Malaysian name."

Recalled a friend, Dato' Dr Ian Chia: "He once asked me if he should retain the name of Limkokwing Institute. I told him that the institute bears not only his name but also his personal qualities: his enterprise, his diligence and his striving for excellence, particularly in design. Because of this, I advised that he should not change the name."

Tan Sri Lim came up the victor. His name turned out to be the biggest selling point for the school. Success was immediate. There was a full enrolment of 300 students for the first semester, confirming that he had been right all along on just about everything connected with the concept of the college.

The word 'Wings' in the name of his advertising business, Wings

Creative Consultants, was also inspired by his name. "You don't go out of your way and create something that is not you. You have to come back to you, somewhere. There must be linkage," he explained.

'Wings' led to the adoption of a bird in flight as his corporate logo. "From the first bird I used in 1975, I never left the concept of flight. Since then it has been a building process – 35 years. That is brand building."

Shaping the delivery

In a newspaper interview in 1995, Tan Sri Lim said, "We were serious in building a brand known for its commitment and dedication to producing capable human resources who were highly creative and well-versed in the use of new media technology."

Moving away from the often stodgy mainstream education philosophy, Tan Sri Lim created a unique yardstick for the institute – making industry requirements and global trends the benchmark for developing new programmes. He has never deviated from this commitment. In fact, as the institute grew to become a university college and then a full-fledged university, he built upon the industry platform, evolving it to new practices that were to attract the interest of the developing world's governments to shape their development of human resources.

At the outset, instead of just offering Graphic Design like many of the local institutes did, he expanded it to include Electronic, Product, Fashion, Industrial, Interior, Multimedia, Information, Communication and Animation. He had his finger on the pulse of the changing times, and tapped into a market hungry for such skills.

> *As a university of the 21st century we are compelled to look forward and attempt to visualize what the future will look like. We must develop the ecosystem that will produce the graduate able to manage the challenges of the future.*
>
> *Limkokwing*
> *2007*

In his mind's eye he kept his focus on the outcome that he wanted to create. He had to grapple with the regulations involved in getting his programmes approved by the authorities. He had to deal with a market and legislature entrenched in tradition and control. His ideas went against the tide. As a businessman he knew the needs of industry but he was now involved in a sector that treated education as a sanctified pursuit, almost totally separated from the reality of the work place where the needs were different.

This rigid mindset is still present today and the battle is an ongoing one with each success being hard won after a long struggle. But Tan Sri Lim is never one to give up. There are signs of policy makers beginning to grasp his ideas. They are forced to look at what he has achieved because world events and trends are demanding new approaches.

The focus on creative technology

Creativity is a process of thought that comes naturally to everyone. This process of thought and free expression is stifled as people grow up and are told to do things in ways that fit in with the current norms. There are less and less opportunities for experimenting and exploration. Creativity in a person then becomes dormant.

Tan Sri Limkokwing has built an exciting, interesting, refreshing, energetic university. And he identifies the university with innovation and creativity. It's like his laboratory, his building, his ideas about creativity and innovation. I think the likes of Tan Sri Limkokwing should be encouraged and given the support to help the government and industry to build a new Malaysia strongly based upon creativity and innovation.

Dato' Dr Syed Ahmad Hussein
CEO, Malaysia Qualifications Agency (MQA), 2010

Tan Sri Lim is able to appreciate the frustrations of people whose creativity is stifled and has dedicated his life to providing the outlet for creative talent to grow.

From the time he set out on his own with his advertising company – Wings Creative Consultants – he had always given local talent a route to express their creativity, an opportunity to build a meaningful career. Many in the industry today owe him their start in the business.

As his business grew, he felt compelled to do something about widening the pool of talent. He also saw a need to champion creative careers and give them the dignity they deserved. The best way he could do this was by providing training and education right up to degree levels.

Tan Sri Lim's quest to start a school that taught creativity took many by surprise. He was already a tycoon and highly successful in the advertising and communications industries. He had money and respectability, and was closely aligned with those in the corridors of power in the country. He was flying high and didn't need a school to achieve more success.

But it was one of the best decisions he had ever made in his life. It had many plus points. Not only was it a boost to education – in that it introduced young people to new career pathways – its arrival was uncannily timely.

The then Prime Minister, Tun Dr Mahathir, was fast forwarding the country into the Information era. There was a dearth of talents needed by rapidly growing industries in the automotive, telecommunications, broadcasting and multimedia fields.

The first batch of students actually signed on without seeing an actual school building. People signed on because they trusted him and his reputation.

The media blitz began to stress the importance of creativity and how it gave a competitive edge. The institute didn't start as a business, said Tan Sri Lim. Instead, its focus was that the programmes were important to the country's future.

"The information technology boom – though relatively young in Malaysia at that time – was sending out signals that every industry would be affected by it," he remembered.

"Then the Multimedia Super Corridor project was launched, and the demand for human capital in this area became more urgent. We had to make people see that creativity was not about a job – but about a thinking process and problem-solving abilities."

The emphasis on creative thinking is crucial, explained Tan Sri Lim, because of the country's drive to achieve fully developed status, as well as the reality of living and competing in a globalising economy.

"The global playing field is much more level, so competition in trade and market share is very stiff," he said. "Sustainable competitive advantage occurs only if there is innovation. Innovation only happens if you nurture it through continual improvement."

In those early days, Tan Sri Lim had creative luminaries on his International Advisory Council such as Arthur Sturgess, Chairman of BBDO Asia Pacific, Ken Cato, Chairman of Cato Design which was the largest design studio in the southern hemisphere based in Melbourne, and Vinit Suraphongchai, Managing Director of a leading Thai advertising agency Damask Advertising.

Also, as a forceful proponent of Asian creativity, Tan Sri Lim ensured top guns in the local advertising and communications fraternity were included in his line-up of advisors. Among the Malaysian figures that made up his Industry Advisory Council were George Chen – President of the Association of Accredited Advertising Agencies, K. Haridas – President of the Institute of Public Relations Malaysia, Michael Tang – joint Managing Director of Ogilvy & Mather, and Shahreen Kamaluddin – Managing Director of Shahreen Corporate Communications.

The institute opened in 1991. Its aim was articulated in the first booklet – "to specialise in the business of making creativity a productive national resource…and to produce the finest creative minds in the region".

A tall order, some might say, but few would dispute it was vintage Lim Kok Wing.

Challenges excite him. The more difficult it is the more intense he becomes. He would appear to do foolhardy things but in the long term his seemingly 'crazy' ideas would be understood and valued. From the name for the institute to the groundbreaking creative programmes and the emphasis on technological mastery, the many decisions he had to make about the school were difficult, but they were the kind he relished.

"There was no hesitation in deciding on focusing on creativity. All my life I had seen the value of creativity. It made a difference to people's lives. And I knew our Malaysian youths sorely needed this added value. There is no point in pursuing learning without being able to take the thinking process a step further to innovate and to create.

"The challenge then was to communicate this fact to parents and employers. All along they had seen it only from the point of view of designers and artists. The value to other careers was not understood," he said.

Today there are a number of institutions of higher education that are using creativity as a marketing platform to promote their programmes. But it takes experience in the use of creativity and understanding of how it is applied in learning that can evoke creative thinking in students.

For Tan Sri Lim, it was the only way he knew to enable learning. The whole environment at his campus is soaked in creativity – from the design of the place to the way that learning is inspired in the individual.

Creating The Architecture

In designing the individual you have to create the environment that will appeal to young people. These are teenagers keen to escape the confines of their classrooms where they had followed a regime of intense study for all of their school years. They are not going to like jumping into another prison-like atmosphere with rigid rules and regulations.

Tan Sri Lim set out to change all that. "Certainly you have to have some rules to look after the safety, security and the well-being of the students. But not so much that the creativity of these young people is stifled."

Capturing the spirit of creativity

Curiosity and exploration are part of the creative journey and Tan Sri Lim wanted to encourage it. He also wanted to project youth and vitality in the brand.

Even after two decades he has kept up with the times, evolving the university to reflect the tastes and lifestyle of the young. From the beginning he made sure that the brand personality was well-anchored. All communications were given a sophistication that had never been applied to education in Malaysia. He gave it a lift through the language used and the entire presentation of the institution was well-orchestrated.

"I needed to do that because creativity was relegated to the arts and creative careers were not seen in the same light as medicine, engineering and law. I needed to change the perception held by parents that a creative career was not worth pursuing," said Tan Sri Lim.

"Traditionally, the best students would take up medicine, law or architecture. Or parents advise their children to take up business studies. Nobody wanted their son or daughter to be an 'advertising person' or an artist. So for years, people sort of stumbled into it. People would say, 'you're a friendly person, why don't you try PR or advertising?' and the industry had been fumbling for people of quality. And we are still battling that problem."

He did not want the institute to look like a formal institution. He understood the impact the architecture would play on the people working or studying within. This was a place that young people, after emerging from long years of school, needed something more refreshing, more stimulating, more motivational.

When he opened his institute at Tun Razak Road, in Kuala Lumpur, he used the key elements of design – the square, triangle and circle – to form a unique identity. In fact many people were not aware that it was a place for learning. He spent RM1.5 million to renovate the premises that he had leased from a company for a period of three years. It was a pleasant cluster of bungalows that he converted into classrooms, studios and laboratories. The tiny campus had a rustic environment that Tan Sri Lim felt gave it character.

It was in this setting that he set out to produce a corps of creative minds trained to bring new thinking, new knowledge and the skills greatly in demand by industry.

The education sector was unprepared for the manner in which he burst onto the scene. He became the talk of the town in the way he set up the institute and the forcefulness with which he promoted the programmes. It was invigorating and excited public imagination. The most excited were of course young people.

As the institute expanded, he had to establish another campus in Barat Road in the suburbs of the capital city. He used the Tun Razak Road campus to house the faculty for business communication while the Barat Road facility accommodated his design students. Within five years, Tan Sri Lim had to move to new, larger premises as his student enrolment had expanded to 3,000.

The Atrium – centralising activities

He moved his campus to Mayang in Petaling Jaya, a satellite city of Kuala Lumpur, taking up an entire building originally meant to house a shopping complex. It had an atrium in the middle and the complex was just right for him to house all his businesses under one roof. Previously, the institute and his communications business were located in three separate places. The faculty of art and design was in Tun Razak, the faculty of architecture was in

Imbi while Limkokwing Integrated occupied a distinctive heritage bungalow in Medan Tuanku in the very heart of the capital where he had also housed Artiquarium, a novel centre for artefacts and antiques.

The atrium at the Mayang campus was to have a strong influence on the way the institute – which had by now become a university college, the first private college to be accorded the status – was to evolve.

Tan Sri Lim liked the manner in which the atrium played a central role in all of the college's activities. In fact, the atrium was one of the reasons why he chose to move his campus into this complex. With classes and businesses surrounding the atrium, no event went by unnoticed with students and staff lining the balconies of three floors to watch the action taking place below.

The atrium was the centre of campus activities – ranging from fashion shows and cultural events to exhibitions and workshops.

With this new campus he was able to pay equal attention to his communications business as well as the college, both of which were booming. The presence of industry in the heart of the campus was a strong influence as he saw how the two merged to result in interesting outcomes. This was the time when Kuala Lumpur was playing host to the 16th Commonwealth Games. This was also the time when the currency crisis that melted East Asian markets made its impact. Malaysia reacted by imposing sweeping controls of capital outflows and pegged the Ringgit to the US dollar. The decisions were universally condemned by conventional economists but later acknowledged to have been successful in arresting the free fall of the Malaysian economy and enabling Malaysia to recover from the turmoil quicker than most East Asian economies.

Tan Sri Lim was deeply involved in communications that addressed these and other developments. While he worked on countering the negative effects of the crisis, he also created pathways for his students to participate in the planning, production and staging of some events related to the developments.

Industry integration became part of a Limkokwing education. Tan Sri Lim had planned from the start for the integration of industry into the curriculum. As a newcomer to education he did not want to push his method too strongly but as the college grew and he became more confident of his ideas, he knew it was the best thing to do.

By the turn of the new millennium the student numbers had reached a critical point. He was bursting at the seams. He needed new premises again. But he was not keen to lease another complex. He wanted to design a new one that had all the features he wanted to put in to make it one of the most distinctive and outstanding campuses in the country.

The Plaza – where the outside is inside

He found it in Cyberjaya, the twin 'intelligent city' to the new federal government administrative centre of Putrajaya which was designed to take the Malaysian government into the 21st century by incorporating features that embraced technology in its operations.

Both the townships were revolutionary in their concept. It was in Cyberjaya

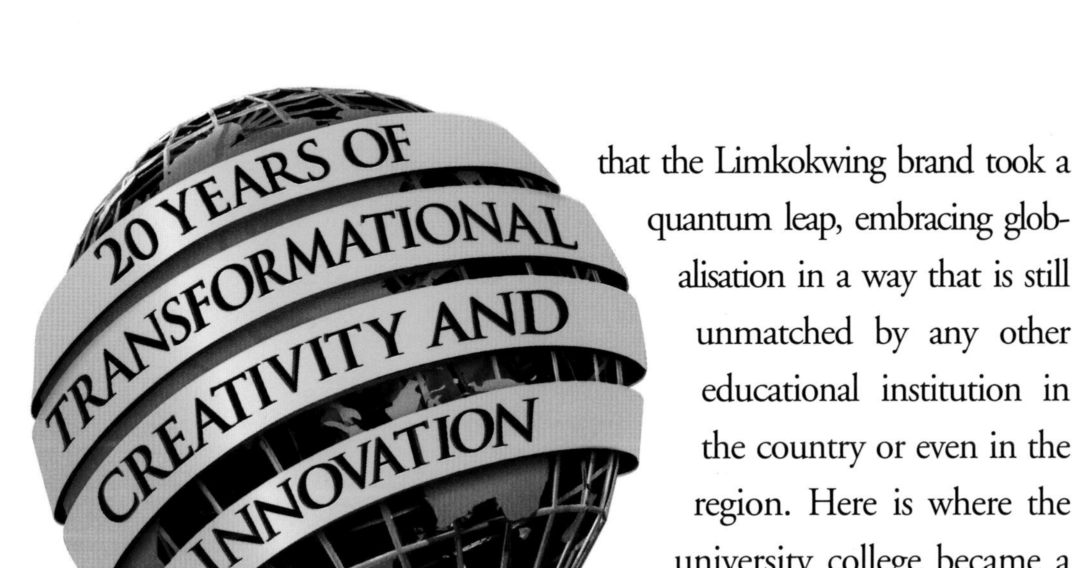

that the Limkokwing brand took a quantum leap, embracing globalisation in a way that is still unmatched by any other educational institution in the country or even in the region. Here is where the university college became a full-fledged university.

At Cyberjaya Tan Sri Lim designed the campus to be inspiring and unusual. The atrium of the Mayang complex was expanded into the Wings Plaza at Cyberjaya which is bigger, resembling a mini-stadium, to accommodate the envisaged activities of 10,000 students.

After a decade immersed in education Tan Sri Lim was acutely aware that the built environment was in itself a form of education, especially in the effects on the senses. It is called transformational creativity. He was keenly aware that a stimulating environment can motivate a person to do more and better.

He set about tackling the mammoth task of designing the new campus to provide that stimulation. The campus in Cyberjaya comes in two parts – one is where the academic process is set in motion. Here is where the library, the architectural materials resource centre, the lecture theatres, and the various workshops for design and fashion are located. The other is the Plaza which houses the business centres, galleries and professional units that provide the activity to attract students and staff to spend most of their time there.

The Plaza, with its high roof, is a huge open space. Here you can engage in sports activities, browse through an exhibition on creativity and branding, get your hair designed, sip coffee at a stylish café, have a hearty meal from a choice of Asian, Middle-Eastern and Western cuisines, buy consumer items you need from a convenience store, stop at the Art Shop for some resource materials, get your stuff printed in a professional manner at the Print Shop, hang out with friends to play snooker at the OneWorld Club, surf the net at the cybercafé, visit a doctor if unwell, hit the gym for an hour to work out and, if so inclined, pick up a few dance steps at the dance centre.

"The Plaza is the most important place in this campus for students to meet each other. A shy person becomes not so shy and learns to make friends; a bold person becomes a really outstanding person," said Tan Sri Lim.

The campus is designed to kindle responses from students to engage their minds and develop their personalities. Tan Sri Lim designed the environment to make the students feel they belonged, that they are cared for. He wanted to inspire in every way. And he is proven right every time because the mediocre students who come to him blossom into high achievers.

Visually exciting

The Cyberjaya campus is noted for its distinctive wrap-around which Tan Sri Lim refers to as the 'skin'. It is the first time that such a large-scale screen was attempted and when it was mounted in 2004 it generated a lot of interest. The wrap is made of a see-through plastic sourced from South Korea. The whole idea of the 'skin' was described as "outrageous, bordering on the impossible" by one newspaper writer.

"It gives me the opportunity to explore various designs to convey the philosophy and the objectives of the university," Tan Sri Lim said.

The first wrap had a fusion of exquisite designs that also used students in fashion wear to create focal points that communicated design and lifestyle. Since then he has changed the screen several times to reflect the theme of senses. The design covers elements related to sight and sound with a strong techno feel.

Tan Sri Lim loves the impact of the 'skin' on both visitors and new students. "It creates a sense of pride among the kids and they also have a sense of belonging. It reflects their lifestyle very strongly."

Inventing the experience

From the very start Tan Sri Lim set out to create learning experiences that would challenge students to apply thinking into everything that they do. He set out to evoke creative thinking and insisted that every student acquires technical skills to translate their ideas into tangible products that express their thoughts and which prepare them for a satisfying career in the future. Most of all he wanted them to be able to contribute to the industries that employ them, the communities where they live and the nations they call their own.

Into this equation he brought industry experience to help them make a seamless transition from classroom to the real world.

He also made certain that the qualifications they would receive were internationally recognised. He did not subscribe to the twinning programmes with foreign institutions that were prevalent at the time in the early 1990s when he started his institute.

Instead, the syllabus at the institute was the same delivered by the Auckland Institute of Technology. This meant that the students need not go to New Zealand to become fully qualified. They received the same standard of instruction as the New Zealand Institute. He evolved the concept as his institute expanded.

This was the concept that was to develop later into the innovative 3+0 programme that enabled students to complete their foreign degrees in Malaysia.

The emphasis on technology

Tan Sri Lim invested millions of Ringgit on computers and multimedia and animation software to ensure his students were trained to use the latest tools. In fact, the common feedback from Limkokwing graduates was that they had been schooled so well in the latest high-technology tools and skills within the university environment that when they entered the 'real world', they found that most employers did not have state-of-the-art facilities and they had to advise them on the software they needed.

"Our increasing dependence on computer technology presents unparalleled opportunities for the young to meet the challenges of designing systems and applications," said Tan Sri Lim, adding that the long-term goal was to train a pool of people skilled in 3D animation and designing, digital imaging and broadcasting. He had not only achieved what he set out to do but also extended the technology emphasis to all the campuses he set up overseas. "Traditional approaches to higher education will take a back seat. New technologies will surge forward. You can be in business but you will have to be technically driven, and must have specialised skills," he said in a newspaper interview back in 1996.

Tan Sri Lim is aware that technology advances rapidly and he make sure the university keeps pace with the changes. "We prepare students for jobs that are not available today but in the future," he said, explaining the difficulty he sometimes faced in obtaining enough students for some of the new courses that he introduced. But he carries on knowing that it is his responsibility to ensure that the qualifications obtained at his university must always be relevant in the future when his students graduate.

Many have wondered about Tan Sri Lim's zealous push for tertiary education when he himself only had formal education up to Form 5, the equivalent of high school.

"This is a very different world from when I started out," he countered. "Many people who are tycoons today learned through working in the real world, and we learned our lessons very well. It is not a surprise to me that many people who returned with Masters or PhDs were unable to solve problems and provide leadership. They were unable and unprepared to take on a challenge."

That is why, said Tan Sri Lim, the type of tertiary education provided by the university stresses academic rigour, technological skills, industry relevance, personality development and leadership training.

"We ignite the passion that makes them want to be the best and we train them in a global perspective," he said. That makes them much more marketable and gets them to think beyond borders.

"We worked very hard to put these in place. You need to have skills to make things happen and to get things done. Knowing the right answer is one thing, but being able to get things done to get to this right answer is a completely different process."

Tan Sri Lim has always been a vocal proponent of the need for Malaysians to be creators rather than being mere consumers of technology. He has urged Malaysians to be more creative in the way they think and more innovative in the way they do things. He has encouraged them to believe in their own ability, to think outside of the box. He has challenged them to break down the norms and push the boundaries.

Bridging rural-urban divide

Tan Sri Lim said there was a digital divide right here within the country. "Rural students are not performing as well as those in the urban centres. Their priorities lie elsewhere. Education has to address and bridge this gap. Rural students have problems grasping new concepts related to new media and new technologies. There are highly intelligent and very creative minds that the country will not be able to use if these students lose out."

He said Malaysia is a small country and it needs to build up its intellectual capital in order to be competitive. "We cannot deny the opportunity to our rural citizens. They must be able to participate in schemes that build up our human capital."

He created a programme in 2005 called *Generasi Baru* which means Next Generation in Malay. It had the core intention to provide an exclusive pathway to young people from the rural heartland to gain skills in the use of new technology. The programme was officially launched by then Deputy Prime Minister Dato' Sri Najib Tun Abdul Razak who said the University provided the ideal environment for the rural next generation to be transformed into creative and innovative thinkers.

The University forged a collaboration with FELDA (Federal Land Development Agency) a world-renowned conglomerate that had about a million beneficiaries in the rural heartland of Malaysia.

The endorsement by Dato' Sri Najib was important because FELDA was created by his father, Malaysia's second Prime Minister the late Tun Abdul Razak in 1956. It had an agenda to redress poverty and overcome landlessness among the rural poor. The philosophy of the scheme was to create a prosperous farming community. After five decades FELDA had evolved to be the most successful land development agency in the world, giving nearly a million people a better future. It has become a conglomerate supplying about eight percent of the world's palm oil.

In 2006 as part of its celebration of 50 years of success, FELDA has embarked on a five-point strategy to take the conglomerate to the next level. A priority within the five-point development plan is to develop the second and third generations of the FELDA settler community.

Tan Sri Lim believed that change would not come to the rural heartland without the empowerment of its young citizens. He not only provided an avenue for them to pick up new skills and knowledge. He sent some of them to his Piccadilly campus in London to make a point.

"We sent 19 students from the Generasi Baru group to London to spend a semester at the Limkokwing's Piccadilly campus. These students learnt to converse fluently in English, intermingled with students from other countries who were studying there and used the facilities in London, like the Tube and the bus services, with curiosity and with confidence.

"They visited the world's most outstanding retail outlets and saw creative thinking at its most active. They tutored with English professors and managed the culture shock admirably. They came back with renewed energy, a more global mindset and personal pride," he said.

Tan Sri Lim's point was that given the opportunity young people will shine, no matter what kind of background they come from. He said their passion for excellence must be aroused and they will succeed in any task.

In a graduation message to the University in 2009, Prime Minister Dato' Sri Najib Tun Abdul Razak said. "We live in unpredictable times. We all need to be well prepared as a people and alert as a nation so we can respond rapidly and accurately to the challenges that often come from beyond our shores. The capability of people, to not just cope but, to thrive in these conditions is tied to the right kind of education and training that builds resourcefulness, intelligence, creativity and, very importantly, the ability to innovate.

"In this respect the Generasi Baru programme has to be lauded as it seeks to equip young Bumiputeras in a manner that will bring change and bridge the urban-rural divide.

"What has contributed to the success of this programme is the ability of this university to provide knowledge of the inner workings of industry through the provision of internship with private sector companies as well as the professional units on campus.

"Of particular interest to me is the participation of some of the students in the Global Classroom programme encouraged by the University.

"This is the kind of support these young people need to build their ability to cope with a changing world."

"The Generasi Baru programme is in its fifth year and already graduates from the programme are doing sterling work with industry while a number of them have moved on to become entrepreneurs.

Raising the bar

In the early years of establishing the university Tan Sri Lim found himself moving ahead of other institutions of higher education while at the same time moving in tandem with the thinking of the Malaysian government.

Malaysia was pushing to get its goods on the world market. He felt strongly – like the then Prime Minister Tun Dr Mahathir – that the time was right for Asian talent to come into its own.

"If we want to be export-oriented," observed Tan Sri Lim pointedly, "we need people to engineer and design things. We need people to stop copying and stealing design ideas from Japan or somewhere else, then simply making the products cheaper here. We must create our own quality and identity in design, and the university is training people who can do that."

He passionately pushed for his students to come up with original designs and encouraged them to take part in competitions – not just at the national but also international levels. He also got them to compete with industry by participating in industry-organised competitions. His students won award after award – and the university soon gained yet another unique branding – a Culture of Nurturing Winners and Whizkids.

Gail Phung, who is the university's Senior Vice-President and who has

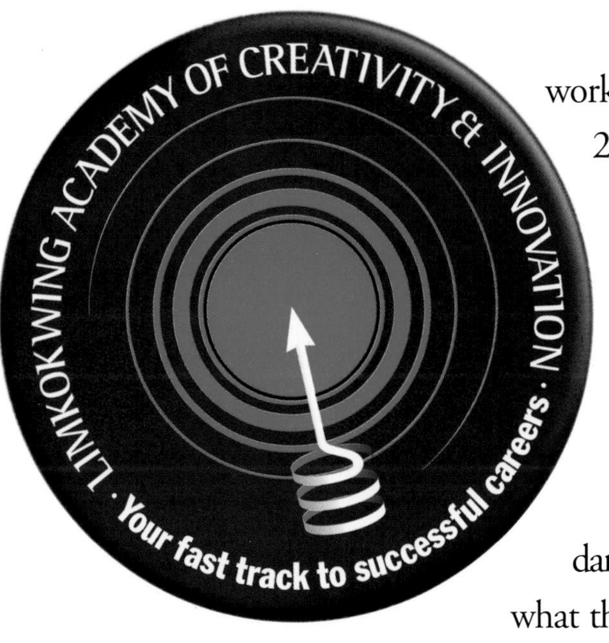

worked with Tan Sri Lim for over 20 years, said he created a very competitive school environment from the beginning.

"I remember when we first started, he would review students' work and he would evaluate them from his standard," she said. "Can you imagine what that meant? He is such a creative person, an icon, and then he looks at the students' work and he said it's not good enough. There is a certain growth curve but he expects that curve to be very short."

Still, she said, the way Tan Sri Lim drove his staff and students was the very factor that enabled the school to develop its winning culture. "If he hadn't pushed us so hard and insisted on the highest quality of work, we wouldn't have the world-class reputation we have today."

The university grew to become the most recognised and respected among educational institutions in the region for its highly professional and industry-related programmes in creative education. It was the first private university to offer degrees in Design, Mass Communications and Architecture.

It was the first private university in the country to be granted MSC Malaysia status by the government. The status, which comes with a host of

Above: This is a new initiative begun in July 2010 to empower anyone with the desire to learn a skill, especially in the use of digital technology.

privileges and financial incentives, is awarded to both local and foreign companies that develop or use multimedia technologies to produce or enhance their products and services. In Limkokwing's case, it is an endorsement of the university's high input of multimedia in its facilities and teaching.

The stress on creativity

The basis of creativity is about achieving something from nothing, breaking down established patterns and seeing things in new ways.

But why is creativity so important to Tan Sri Lim that he has devoted all his life to practising it or teaching it to others? To most people, creativity is an obscure characteristic that seems to be in abundance among artists, entertainers and musicians. But it is, perhaps, the single most important building block that a person needs to develop so that his or her life will mean something. Nothing is more revealing of this importance than the exhibition *Cultures of Creativity* developed by The Nobel Museum showcasing the mind map of a selection from over 700 Nobel laureates. Creativity is the common bond that connects this bewildering mix of chemists, astronomers, physicists, mathematicians, biochemists, physiologists, peace activists, freedom fighters, priests, economists, bankers, poets, writers and many others who come from all over the world.

Creativity is locked within a person and it is unlocked through the application of strong emotion. It can be anger, curiosity, love, anything. However, what is needed is intensity. One has to be obsessed or passionate about the subject that they push forward, ignoring personal pain or personal needs. It is the intensity of the application that enables a person to achieve something extraordinary.

This is something that Tan Sri Lim believes in passionately. It is how he applies himself to every task. He knows the value of the outcome. He has built his success upon it. It is what he wishes to pass on to others.

Almost every one begins his or her early life using creative thinking to understand the complexities of growing up. Learning takes a leap in the young when they grasp so many things – from language to motor and social skills – within days, weeks and months. The intensity of concentration in the young becomes a lost ability in the older child as he or she loses the spontaneity of thought and is influenced by society or their peers to react in predictable ways. In other words, to conform.

Children spend their time honing their skills in using their critical thinking to understand issues and solve problems. Some are able to strike a balance between creative and critical thinking. These are the ones who, most probably, excel in language, music and art-based subjects because they require a heavy dose of creative thinking to be able to conceptualise ideas and express them through mediums such as art, music, design and writing.

Critical thinking is important in making deductions based on reason and logic. Creative thinking is important to take a thought across to new realms of conceptualisation and innovative thinking.

Students who arrive at Limkokwing University struggle in their first semester. At orientation they are taken through exercises that challenge their assumptions. They are encouraged to think of solutions and work in teams to build leadership skills through ice-breaking sessions that are disguised as fun exercises to start the thinking process.

"With creative thinking there are no wrong answers. Every answer is simply a different approach," said Tan Sri Lim.

The tireless efforts by the university to promote creativity and design have improved awareness to an extent where it has led to the set-up of other design schools. "People are now more aware of creativity and its importance. Creativity has currency and relevancy to the knowledge economy. What has worked for us is our pioneering spirit. We have always stayed in front. We don't have a competitor. Our pioneering has opened the eyes of the government as well as the public."

But, he lamented, there was too little pioneering in this country and part of the reason for this was the lack of a mechanism to encourage this. He had tried to remedy the lack by stitching together a programme that could be used to teach young children.

In the late 1990s he attempted to interest the government in introducing a special programme that would benefit primary school children by awakening their creative thinking. The university first devised a course that was tested on 12-year-olds from a selected school in Damansara Jaya, Petaling Jaya. The children responded well and the experiment was videotaped and documented.

Tan Sri Lim then followed up with a train-the-trainer seminar where teachers could be educated to conduct the process. His idea was to empower 10 teachers who would then go on to train five others each, cascading downwards until all teachers would have been trained within a short time.

He had taken all the relevant steps to influence the teaching of school children in the same way he developed programmes for the older students who joined the university.

"We conducted a pilot programme in the late 1990s on this concept. We later held a seminar to brief teachers. They were very sceptical at first but after the briefing and after watching the pilot programme which we had videotaped and documented, they were convinced. They said it was very good. The students did exceptionally well," he said.

He then presented the results to Tun Dr Mahathir and at the same time he started to engage the Ministry of Education to work the programme through but, unfortunately, his proposal was rejected by the ministry. Their reason was that they were busy implementing the smart school concept and computer programmes so the creativity programme could not be done.

"I was not surprised by this because bureaucracy is set up this way. There is no mechanism in our bureaucracy to be able to absorb this," he said.

The creative mindset

In every meeting that he holds Tan Sri Lim never dismisses an idea as absurd. He will pause to think about it no matter how ridiculous it may sound. He will only use the solution that works best.

A former staff member who is a practising architect recalls the early days when they were planning the design of the Cyberjaya campus. "I put forward an idea that I thought would be laughed at. But he actually took a moment to consider it. His reaction even made me stop and think about the idea a little seriously."

Alumni of the university often talk about how different they are to those who graduate from other universities. Tan Sri Lim regularly receives messages from many foreign graduates of his university, typically thanking him for "making it happen for me".

One writer wrote, "When I entered the university, I had no idea of what to expect. I was expecting something to happen to me from outside. But you have taught me to make things happen to me from inside. I am now in control of my life."

Tan Sri Lim's reasoning for insisting that every student engages in creative thinking is to create the graduate who can survive the enormous changes that are influencing the world. "The world is constantly changing. With new inventions and innovation the change is happening very rapidly. To be able to think creatively is to be equipped with a survival tool that will help every graduate who has grasped the concept well to adapt and progress. Without the ability to think creatively and critically, the graduate can become irrelevant and obsolete," he said.

He is attempting to create graduates who are well-equipped to dictate changes in the future and not just follow directions set by others.

The accent on industry

Technology is leaping into new advancement that will see industry moving completely away from traditional methods and adopting new infrastructure for global computing. The next generation networks are already predicting gigabit-per-second and terabit-per-second access capacity. This roughly translates to 100 times the speed of current scientific connections for the Internet.

"This is the world that students who enrol now will graduate into. I have to analyse the trend and translate the implications. To do that well I must move with industry closely," said Tan Sri Lim.

The changes on the technological front are penetrating into traditional industries that have previously shied away from automating their operations. This could mean a dramatic change is heading in our direction as new product development becomes easier to manage and innovation will be the competitive edge, more than it is now.

It has been speculated that the organisations of the future will rely on global collaboration networks of creation and production. They will replace bureaucratic systems. To put it simply, the world will go flatter and faster once it recovers from the economic recession of 2008 and 2009.

As an educationist Tan Sri Lim feels it is his responsibility to know the terrain that his students will graduate into. "The future is not totally unpredictable. We can make some intelligent guesses." He thinks industry will have far better ideas of what will change and who will be most affected by the change.

Tan Sri Lim has always attempted to stay ahead and it is this canny ability to plan and strategise that has kept his ventures afloat in downturns. He moved into private education after more than a decade in advertising and it was the right move at the right time. Advertising had become a fragmented industry with many of its component parts becoming obsolete in the past 10 years while private education has been growing from strength to strength.

Through his close collaborations with industry he has been able to anticipate what will have currency in the future. For example, when he began his institute in the early 1990s, before the explosion of multimedia, he introduced computer design as a subject to his students which later morphed to become electronic design and multimedia design. Graduates from his institute were already well-versed with the new tools that their absorption into industry helped many fledgling companies make that transition into the era of the Internet.

In the new millennium he established a department at the university and called it Indusity by merging the words university and industry. He never saw education purely for education's sake because he believed every pursuit must have purpose and value. But in the early days when he had to submit his programmes to the scrutiny of accreditation authorities he had a tough time trying to make them understand the need to build the right kind of human capital for the country.

Tan Sri Lim said he is very concerned that the education system is still not relevant to today's world. He pointed out that the world is moving very fast and the country has to respond. He said he keeps submitting new programmes to the accreditation authorities for approval. "If these programmes were business disciplines we would face no delays in the ministry assessing them. But we faced difficulties with programmes like computer games, web technology and virtual design. The more innovation we put in the programmes the longer we have to wait for approval," he said.

He knows the difficulties industry faces in getting trained talent able to take business to new fields of enterprise. But he has made some progress with the authorities who are beginning to understand what he us trying to do.

If he had his way he would allow everyone who wants to enrol in his university to do so. "The benchmark that has been created to categorise the achievements of students is outdated. It is regimented and forces young people with all kinds of talent and capability to fit into something that does not recognise their unique individuality.

"I have always believed that every person is born with a talent for something. They must be given the opportunity to find out what that talent is and develop it to its full potential. I want to help young people excel in whatever they do best. There should be no unsuccessful graduates.

"I don't see anyone as a failure unless they are lazy and indifferent," he said.

An album produced by Limkokwing university graduates promoting peace and celebrating culture.

Inviting the world

In 1997 when the Asian financial crisis hit the region many businesses in Malaysia tumbled or stumbled but not the education sector. On the contrary, it swarmed with opportunities. When it became too expensive to send Malaysians abroad to study because of the devaluation of the Ringgit, the government liberalised the sector allowing private educational institutions the right to award degrees. The immediate response was to import British, Australian and American degrees that could be completed entirely in Malaysia. It was innovative and the 3+0 programme, as it was called, completely transformed higher education in Malaysia.

The novelty of obtaining a Western education in Malaysia at a fraction of its cost appealed to many governments that were in search of alternative routes to build their human capital.

The simple amendment made to the law turned a sector that took up the single largest portion of its annual budget into a foreign exchange earner. The government soon after announced its intention to turn the country into a regional education hub.

For Tan Sri Lim, the liberalisation of the private education sector opened up prospects to tap into the global market. He was excited by the possibilities and immediately expanded his marketing department by employing his own graduates to begin the global push. At the same time, he consulted with his university partners and added new programmes that would be needed a few years down the road.

He began by marketing his university to developing countries. By the year 2000, about 25 percent of the student population was foreign. He doubled that figure to around 40 percent by 2005. By 2009, foreign students made up more than 65 percent of the university's worldwide enrolment.

His choice of the countries to market the university's programmes was easy. After more than two decades of being a leading participant in the branding of Malaysia, and being intimately acquainted with the human resource needs of emerging economies, he knew what Third World countries would need to drive their future development.

"Look at the state of development in those countries, and you can see they need the very skills that we train our students to acquire," he explained. "The minute they know that they can get these skills from us, they will come. And because it costs a quarter of what they need to pay a university in a developed country it makes good sense for them to be here."

Tan Sri Lim never fails to point out the many advantages working in Malaysia's favour to attract foreign students.

In an article he posted on his blog, he elaborated on these advantages.

"We have excellent infrastructure offering good amenities and facilities comparable with those in the developed countries. English is widely spoken and used, and the learning of other languages is encouraged.

"We are a middle income economy working towards developed nation status and a role model nation for the developing world. The standard of living is much more affordable than in many advanced countries.

"Foreign students, especially from developing countries, come here seeking degrees awarded by internationally recognised English-medium universities through local partner colleges. They want to learn English, get a lower-priced education than that available in the developed countries, and study in a cultural environment that they feel more comfortable in.

"Many countries in the developing world look to our experiences to learn and create similar outcomes. These are the countries that are sending their citizens to study in Malaysia.

"Malaysia, being a developing country in transformation, offers a more suitable model for education to other developing countries. When their students study here, the chances are they will be able to practise what they learn when they go home. When they study in a highly industrialised country, they may not be able to apply some of the systems and theories they learn on their return home to a developing country environment.

"The delivery of education by people in any particular university is based on their experience and surroundings. And the Western world, as we know, is a very expensive place and uses many tools not easily or cheaply available in developing countries."

He also reminded developing countries that they are creating their own brain drain by sending their best talents to study in the developed world. Many of these students eventually stay back in the developed countries after completing their studies because the quality of life, level of income and opportunities there, are all more attractive than in their home countries.

Tan Sri Lim was also a great believer in reversing the flow of students that had, for centuries, moved only in one direction – from East to West. A two-way traffic in education between Asia and the rest of the world was a goal he set for his university from the outset.

He explained why an education with a Western bias is no longer sufficient in the world today in another article in his blog.

"In today's reality with Eastern economies such as Japan, China, South Korea and India challenging the Western economies for global leadership, a strictly Western-centric education is no longer sufficient even for people living in the West.

"If you know only one side of the world but not the other, you will spend your lives knowing only half the story, seeing only half the picture and missing out on half the opportunities.

"The people in the West must want to know why the East is rising so rapidly and how this shift in the balance of economic power is going to impact on their countries and their future. To those living in the East, the ways of the West are very important because this region is home to the world's richest nations and the world's most innovative economies. These countries dictate whether economies around the world expand or decline.

"The increasing connectivity of economies and the convergence of ways of life across the world is the clearest result of the globalisation phenomenon. Our presence in three continents, is part of this advancing globalisation."

With each passing year his grasp of the global state of education helped him to see clearly where the problems were, and he knew he must re-think the road ahead for education. He felt very strongly that he needed to do this because the development divide between countries was growing wider. While the developing countries needed the new skills, the developed world needed to know more about the side of the world where most of the people lived. Most of the countries in the developing world had fallen into a pattern that emulated Western standards. This did not fit into their culture or answer their needs. What they were left with was a high number of young people schooled in knowledge they did not need or skills learnt in an advanced country which they could not apply in a developing country's environment.

Strengthening Africa

He is particularly concerned about Africa. "In Africa, the current state of education is plagued by a lack of funds, teachers, textbooks and all kinds of shortages. The result is that primary school enrolments and literacy rates in Africa are among the lowest in the world. Some 42 million schoolchildren in sub-Saharan Africa are out of school. Many children cannot afford to go to primary school or stay in school after they are enrolled."

According to UNESCO, Africa has the lowest primary education completion ratios in the world. In 19 African countries at least every second child does not complete primary school. In another 25 percent of countries, only one in three pupils at the end of primary school moves on to secondary education. The low level of education is aggravated by an alarming rate in the 'brain drain' from Africa.

"Since 1990 Africa has been losing 20,000 professionals annually. There are more African scientists and engineers working in the United States than in the entire African continent. The brain drain has placed Africa at risk of becoming home to even greater mass poverty," said Tan Sri Lim.

Since education in Africa is not well developed, the focus on eradicating poverty must involve a strategy that will get as many people as possible into work to earn an income. There must be a massive effort to create jobs by making use of knowledge and skills that are indigenous to the rural population.

Training, innovation and marketing are key components in the development of the indigenous craft industry. These are areas where partnerships could be forged between institutions of higher learning and national governments.

"We could help develop new and better designs, enhance the appeal of products, expand the range of products, research the use of new materials and find ways to produce crafts cheaper and in larger quantities for export," he said.

He added that a partnership between government and industry would encourage investors to supply machines and bring in the most sophisticated technologies that would increase productivity, add value and enhance quality.

Working with national governments, universities could help set up training centres to improve existing skills of crafts people, expose them to the use of modern production methods and educate them in marketing skills that enhance the value of their work.

"If developed as an integrated platform, the crafts industry could create large-scale employment, increase exports of value-added products and produce human capital that will be able to create more and more wealth, year after year," he said.

Building Botswana human capital

Tan Sri Lim likes to talk about his mission to bring a new education formula to Africa, starting with the Republic of Botswana. "Limkokwing University is working with Africans to liberate the vast store of African talents. We have been putting into practice the Smart Partnership principles adopted at the Langkawi International Dialogue (a regular informal gathering of heads of government from developing countries) in Malaysia and its spin-off Southern Africa International Dialogue."

In all the places in Africa where the university has set up campuses Tan Sri Lim said he worked closely with the national governments under the Smart Partnership concept.

The university adopts a participatory model in operating its campuses. "We work with the local population and share our experiences, knowledge and skills. Most of our staff in the local campus is alumni of the university."

He explained that through his investment in campuses in the developing countries he was helping to save millions of foreign exchange which

LIMKOKWING BOTSWANA

Building a regional innovative education hub for Africa

Since 1999 Limkokwing has been working with the Botswana Government to equip its best and brightest students with skills and knowledge in creative technology as well as ICT and business management. Currently there are over 700 Botswana students at the Limkokwing campus in Cyberjaya. In 2007 this collaboration has turned into a serious partnership to transform Gaborone, the capital city of Botswana, into an education hub that will serve the whole of Africa.

First Asian university to establish a campus in Africa

Limkokwing, in establishing a campus in Gaborone, is building human capital to fuel a new wave of progress that will help Africa integrate with the rapidly advancing global economy. Africa needs to tap the energy and talent of its young citizens to move forward. Botswana, being the most progressive nation and economically stable economy within the African continent, has the potential to provide the leadership Africa needs to address challenges with African solutions.

Building skills and knowledge to fuel Africa's transformation

Limkokwing, in 16 years, has built an innovative education hub for Asia that has benefited many countries in developing their human capital as they struggled to make that transition into k-economy status. We will attempt to do the same for Africa. Africa is in the process of rebuilding itself to rejoin the global economy with dignity. It will need a highly skilled and knowledgeable next generation to pull itself out of the problems that it faces. Limkokwing is pledged to lend its expertise in building this human capital.

In doing so we are also building a global reputation for Malaysia's quality of education.

LIMKOKWING UNIVERSITY OF CREATIVE TECHNOLOGY

BOTSWANA

Plot 28562, Fairgrounds Mall, Samora Machel Drive, Gaborone, Botswana

+(267)395 1830 +(267)395 1838 www.limkokwing.edu.my

An arresting advertisement to communicate the University's presence in Africa and presenting the core intentions in doing so.

In commemmoration of the 1st anniversary of Limkokwing University of Creative Technology

Inspire to empower

The credo to arouse passion, stir enthusiasm and fire imagination to transform an entire generation to adopt a creative and innovative mindset.

Our journey to empower young Batswana with skills and knowledge to build a new future for their country began in 1999. But it was only in 2007 that we truly engaged in the task. It was the year that we connected with thousands more Batswana because we made the landmark decision to base a new university right here in Gaborone. It has been a year since we plunged our roots into Botswana soil and what a year it has been. Today we celebrate this momentous journey.

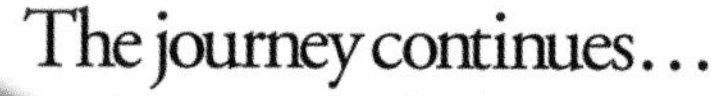

The journey continues...

We set up our first off-shore university in Botswana because we understood the challenges facing this nation. They were the same challenges that Malaysia faced almost two decades ago.

True enough when we opened for registration there were queues so long that we had no choice but to turn away thousands because we did not have the space to accommodate them. We had to open a second campus just so we could absorb the large numbers of young people seeking to enrol. Such is the hunger of Batswana seeking the empowerment to shape their future.

LIMKOKWING UNIVERSITY · CELEBRATING CREATIVITY & INNOVATION ·

1 year

Empowering a smart next global generation

After one year in Botswana this supplement traced the journey of the University as it crossed the oceans and overcame obstacles to bring a new kind of education to empower the continent's next generation.

The thirst for a new kind of education is clearly evident. They came by the thousands, young Batswana (as the people of Botswana are called) eager to gain the skills that would get them into careers. The top picture shows the huge turnout in their coloured clothes that came to register. The picture at the bottom shows them in T-shirts carrying the University's dominant black trademark colour when they became its students.

In both Botswana and Lesotho where the University set up its campuses the enthusiasm of young Africans were unbelievable. Leaders from both countries have acknowledged that the University has changed the landscape of education.

Tan Sri Lim has superstar status with the young people at all his campuses. First year student Kefilwe Monorwa said: "We all wanted to touch him because he made us proud by establishing a school here in Botswana that we wanted to go to in Malaysia."

In setting up a University in Botswana Tan Sri Lim had a larger intention to create an education hub that will provide Africans from neighbouring countries an alternative route to build their skills. Tan Sri Lim had a lot to learn about working with Africans who operated differently from Asians. But he has persevered and brought change through African youths who have embraced his philosophy.

Top: *"Our young people here are so inspired it is impressive," said Botswana President Festus G. Mogae when he came to officiate the opening of the University campus in May 2007.*

Middle: *Timothy Limkokwing Jr is all smiles when Lesotho Prime Minister Pakalitha Bethuel Mosisili said, "right here in Maseru we have the best University in the entire world."*

Bottom: *The Lesotho Prime Minister and other government leaders are intent on the explanation given by a student. The Lesotho campus provided the University's Botswana faculty the opportunity to build new skills in campus development and management.*

Building 21st century skills means equipping every campus with facilities that ensure students are able to use the latest in computer software. The investments have been high especially when you find that the major brands do not have outlets in these countries.

All the investments, the blood, sweat and tears become worth the effort when faces shine with the joy of the success achieved. The future of these countries are being altered. Skilled human capital is the vital building block for nations that seek progress.

Today Botswana is that much richer with skilled human capital empowered to fuel its progress to the next level. These are graduates with the skills to expand the creative sector of the economy in the areas of publishing, music, ICT, film and television, fashion and web, among many others.

would otherwise flow out of the countries, as well as generating jobs and increasing business opportunities for the local people. By keeping their students at home, the university is also helping to reduce the brain drain of precious human capital to other countries.

The Limkokwing African connection

The Limkokwing African journey cannot be fully understood without tracing the role Tan Sri Lim played in the Langkawi Dialogue series that began on the Malaysian tourist island during Tun Dr Mahathir's premiership. Leaders from mainly African countries converged to discuss ways to collaborate to spur social and economic development on the continent through Smart Partnerships with other countries.

In 2007 Tan Sri Lim presented his view about Africa to an audience of African leaders who were initially taken aback by what he said. He told them that he found Africa to be a puzzle. He wondered why the world believed this to be a continent with a high rate of poverty.

"A puzzle because this is a continent that is enormously wealthy. It has natural resources of minerals like diamonds, gold, copper, iron ore and huge reserves of oil and gas.

Above: In January 2008 the Limkokwing University conferred the Honorary Doctorate in Humanity upon the former President of Botswana, Festus G. Mogae.

"This is a continent that is enormously wealthy in unique wildlife. Exotic animals not found anywhere else on Earth. A tourist paradise. This is a continent that is enormously wealthy in history, the cradle of mankind where the rest of the world traces its DNA to. This is a continent that is enormously wealthy in the arts, the crafts, the music and dance. Africa is vibrant. Africa is exotic. Africa is rich. Tell me why everyone is saying that Africa is poor?" he asked as Africa's leaders applauded enthusiastically.

He told them that they must teach the world to see the continent from this point of view. "With the right planning and dedicated commitment of the various governments in Africa and the world at large, these gifts which are the natural resources of the African people, can be converted into income.

"With the right marketing systems and distribution networks, Africans can very easily climb out of the poverty circle and into a productive, meaningful and dignified existence. It all starts with a vision. A vision with timelines that gives everyone a sense of purpose and a sense of urgency," he said.

What followed were invitations from countries such as Swaziland, Lesotho, Malawi, Kenya and others for Tan Sri Lim to visit with the idea of setting up a campus of his university in each of them.

Designing Limkokwing University Botswana

Before Tan Sri Lim set out to establish his first African campus in Botswana, he already had hosted hundreds of African students at his main campus in Malaysia. Many of the African students were sponsored by their governments to study in Malaysia largely because of the respect they had for Tun Dr Mahathir and what he had achieved for Malaysia.

"There's a lot of admiration for this country, especially for Tun Dr Mahathir, in Africa. These governments feel there is much to be learnt from Malaysia. For instance, the Botswana government sends its students here to learn Asian cultures and values and to understand how Asians have been so successful in developing their countries and economies," Tan Sri Lim said.

But it was only in 2005 that he developed the idea of exporting his education formula to Africa. His rapport with the Botswana government made it possible for him to present his vision for Africa.

Botswana, inspired by Tun Dr Mahathir's Vision 2020, had introduced its own version called Vision 2016. Diamond mining forms the backbone of the economy of Botswana which is the world's largest producer of diamonds. The World Bank has cited Botswana as one of the world's great development success stories.

Tourism is also a strong foreign exchange earner for the country. Its Okavango Delta is a big draw for scientists as well as tourists seeking to view the region's Big Five – a collective term for lions, elephants, giraffes, rhinos and zebras.

Most of the country, which has a population of less than 2 million people, is covered by the Kalahari Desert. Life expectancy has been severely shortened by the spread of AIDS. But the government has been very protective of its people, using the money earned from diamond exports and tourism to fight the disease as well as build the country's infrastructure and human capital.

Developing human capital is a pillar of the country's Vision 2016 blueprint. However, the going has been slow because the Botswana leaders, like most Africans, tend to debate an issue for some time before implementing it. For instance, they had been talking about setting up a second public university for a number of years. After five years of planning, the Botswana International University of Science and Technology is expected to enrol its first students in 2010, to complement the University of Botswana established in 1982.

It has been a long wait for the country's tens of thousands of young people who wanted a tertiary education while only the best were selected by the government to be sent to institutions of higher learning abroad.

Tan Sri Lim stepped in and offered to speed up the establishment of a campus of his private university. And he was as good as his word. What amazed the Batswana (as the people are called collectively) leaders was his speed in putting together a programme to set up a university in Gaborone, the capital city of Botswana. He did it in six months. He had made his proposal in 2005 and by September 2006 he was ready to recruit.

What the Batswana people or authorities did not know was that Tan Sri Lim comes from a country that gives top priority to education and, after 50 years of independence, has established 20 public universities, 36 private universities, 21 polytechnics, 37 community colleges and 485 private colleges.

In Botswana, in true Lim Kok Wing style, he booked full-page advertisements in the local newspapers and changed perceptions in that small country about how effective advertising could be if it is well-designed, carefully strategised and innovatively presented.

"I was concerned that the country was struggling to organise its educational infrastructure that needed to cater to an increasing number of students who were looking to build their skills. My own experience with young people and my understanding of the world, especially industry, made me design the programmes most suited to a country like Botswana. It needed programmes aimed at building the capacity that is needed to transform the country," said Tan Sri Lim.

It was an eye-opener for Batswana leaders to see the enthusiasm of young people who turned up to register when Limkokwing University advertised to recruit.

"The university had places for only 1,500 students but 5,000 turned up, queuing up from the early hours of the morning to sign on. It was an astonishing sight and became the talk of the town. The radio stations even sent reporters to investigate," said Gail Phung, Senior Vice-President of Limkokwing University who was entrusted with the responsibility of overseeing the establishment of the Botswana campus.

By 2007 the one campus, which was located in a renovated shopping centre in the middle of Gaborone, was no longer adequate as more students applied for placement. So a bigger campus was secured in another part of the city which could accommodate 6,000 but even this was not enough as the number of young people who wanted an education that they could relate to kept increasing.

So Tan Sri Lim established one that was big enough to take in as many students as were keen to build their future in creative industries. By

then he had 12,000 young people pursuing their higher education at his university, saving their country millions in foreign exchange that would otherwise have flowed abroad. More importantly, the university enabled those with no prospects of studying in the only public university to obtain a tertiary education, without which there was no possibility of them getting the skills they needed to improve their lives.

"We were literally taking kids who would have ended up on the streets, without skills and without hope," said Tan Sri Lim.

But his time in Botswana has not been without issues and the university often found itself caught in the political crossfire between rival parties. "The way we had recruited has been open. Students with a certain level of credits can apply and obtain scholarships from the government. They have the freedom to choose where they want to study. That so many of them want to take up programmes offered by this university was because no one was providing them the options to take up studies in the creative arts and business.

"The Africans are predominantly creative people with strengths in oratory, dance, music, poetry, design and writing. By setting up a campus

Above: The University has helped budding writers by publishing their work, like this book by a Limkokwing student.

in their capital city, we gave them alternative career pathways, something that they have lacked for a long time."

A campus in Lesotho

In 2008 at the invitation of the Prime Minister of the Kingdom of Lesotho, Pakalitha Bethuel Mosisili, Tan Sri Lim visited this African mountainous land-locked country entirely surrounded by South Africa. Sometimes referred to as the Switzerland of Africa, Lesotho has snow-covered mountains that yield water – the country's main export. Basotho, as the people of Lesotho are called, refer to their water as 'white gold'.

Lesotho ranks among the world's poorest 50 countries. The bulk of the government's revenue is derived from royalties from the sale of water to South Africa, remittances from Basotho men employed in the mines in South Africa and customs duties from the Southern Africa Customs Union. However the Lesotho government is attempting to expand manufacturing to improve its GDP.

Manufacturing is driven in recent years by the textile sub-sector whose products enjoy duty-free access to the United States provided under the African Growth and Opportunities Act. Tertiary industries also provide growth, principally in the areas of wholesale and repairs, hotels and restaurants and education.

Compared to Botswana, the Kingdom of Lesotho has a high incidence of poverty with the United Nations estimating 40 percent of the population as 'ultra-poor'. Lesotho also has one of the world's highest rates of HIV-AIDS infection.

Lesotho, inspired by the vision of Tun Dr Mahathir, has formulated its own roadmap to achieve economic and social progress, called Vision 2020, the same name as Malaysia's.

By now, Tan Sri Lim and his team are quite adept at setting up campuses overseas and, despite the many obstacles, he opened one in Lesotho's capital city of Maseru. The Botswana campus provides vital support in terms of administrative and academic staff to run the Maseru campus.

Best of East and West

Tan Sri Lim took the concept of "The Best of Both Worlds" and put an educational spin to it. "The world is two sides of the same coin. If we remain in our own sphere we will see only one side of the story. It will never be complete. By creating the opportunity for young people to see the other side of the world, they will develop a better understanding of other cultures. They will see issues from new perspectives," he explained.

He devised a pathway to enable his students to cross borders easily to acquire better understanding of other countries.

Leaping continents – from Africa to Europe

From the early days of its inception the university had forged strategic connections with the Western world to provide avenues for its students to gain entry into universities in Australia, New Zealand, United Kingdom and the United States. Some of its collaborations included programmes to complete a Western degree in Malaysia.

In 2006, Tan Sri Lim was presented with an opportunity to take up a building that one of his partners, International House that specialises in the teaching of languages, was giving up. It was bold. It was unprecedented and it was vintage Lim Kok Wing. Certainly it is expensive to be at this prestigious address but he understood its value.

106 Piccadilly in London was no ordinary building.

A heritage building in the heart of London

Steeped in history, the mansion of 18th century architecture with English art decorations prompted the United Kingdom government to preserve it as a heritage building. It was originally built for Sir Hugh Hunlock and bought over by the Earl of Coventry in 1764. For a while it was known as the Coventry House which became the Coventry Club, a sort of Bohemian institution, where there was free supper and gambling for the diplomats who gathered there. The mansion reportedly had an underground passage running below Piccadilly Street and emerging at Green Park where the Lady of Coventry supposedly had her garden. In 1860, the house was acquired by the Comte de Flahaut, the French Ambassador, who was once an aide to Napoleon. After the Count's death and that of his wife, the lease was bought by the St. James Club in 1869 and it expired in 1999. In its heydays, the club was frequented by diplomats – "27 members of Her Britannic Majesty's foreign services" as writer Charles Graves described the club in his book *Leather Armchairs – the Chivas Regal book of London Clubs.*

The establishment of Limkokwing in London marked the university's pioneering endeavour to integrate Asian, African and Western values, traditions, creativity and technology in education; one that would broaden the cultural and intellectual learning experience of the student, and open minds to new ideas and perception.

From music, architecture and design to fashion and communications, London is a trendsetter. Tan Sri Lim loves to roam its streets and shops, invigorated by its creativity and vibrant lifestyle. He admits to feeling more at home in London then he does in Kuala Lumpur. Establishing a campus in Piccadilly was not a coup, as some would say, but quite a natural progression for a man given his mindset.

He is never a man to sit back and enjoy his accomplishments. He is always planning ahead and positioning the brand, keeping it relevant and current.

In many ways, he broke the mould for education when he opened in Piccadilly. The British were of course quite taken aback. It never crossed their mind that someone from this small little former colony called Malaysia that they had ruled for 150 years would be now sitting in their front yard offering a Malaysian education with a Western slant.

It made them view education from a different point of view.

The official opening of the campus was a strange affair. To see British Lords and Ladies sitting side by side with Malaysian dignitaries was unusual, especially when you reflect upon the timing of the opening which coincided with the celebration of 50 years of independence from British rule by Malaysia. It was not purposefully planned. It simply turned out that way.

Tan Sri Lim did not realize what he had unleashed. *The Times Higher Education* supplement of December 8, 2006 saw the opening of the Malaysian campus as a "wake-up call for UK about the harsh realities of globalisation."

The Guardian newspaper reported that the campus was an example of the many new challenges that British higher education was facing. It quoted John Hearn, deputy vice-chancellor (international) at the University of Sydney that they now " have to reinvent universities, reinvent academics and reinvent the students."

The Independent newspaper even headlined the story as - *From Malaysia to Mayfair: The foreign university that is sending out shivers in the higher education world.*

The Malaysians were ecstatic of course. The Prime Minister Tun Abdullah Badawi who officiated at the launch said:

"Indeed, 50 years after independence, education in Malaysia can be said to have gone full circle. While we used to send most of our students to study abroad, and still do so for quite a number, more and more foreign students are now coming to Malaysia to study. Today, Malaysia is among the most important providers of international education, together with other countries like the UK, Australia, Canada and New Zealand."

The Deputy Prime Minister, at that time, Dato' Sri Najib Tun Abdul Razak, who later became Prime Minister, wrote a letter to Tan Sri to say:

"I applaud this achievement by the Limkokwing University of Creative

Technology. This certainly raises the benchmark of Malaysian education to a higher level, one that is able to compete with the best of the world."

But it was Maurice Dimmock, from the Accreditation Services of International Colleges (ASIC) of UK, who summed it all up when he said:

"It takes a certain kind of courage to venture into the United Kingdom, the bastion of global education and position an institution of higher learning right under the noses of some of the world's most respected universities."

Mr Dimmock in conducting a study for the purpose of accreditation of the Limkokwing campuses in London, Cambodia, Cyberjaya and Botswana said that " it takes a certain kind of vision to awaken British educationists, entrenched in pomp and tradition, to the harsh realities of globalisation, that the world is, indeed, going flat."

He later presented Tan Sri Lim with the ASIC award for Innovative Leadership in Globalised Education. In his citation he related that the opening of the London campus was a wake-up moment. "Since then some of us in the UK have made the effort to understand what had moved this man, from a small nation in Southeast Asia, to take over one of London's prestigious heritage buildings in Piccadilly and convert it into a global learning centre."

He said he was especially intrigued with Tan Sri Lim's philosophy of Merging the Best of East and West. "We agree whole-heartedly that there needs a two-way traffic between both sides of the world. And we understand the logic that knowing only one side of the world is akin to seeing only half the picture."

West to East – Beijing and Phnom Penh

China had always held a fascination for Tan Sri Lim. He found its history of creativity and innovation to be very inspiring. Its economic resurgence compelled him to seek out collaborations to include China in his fast expanding global network.

The year 2008 was a watershed year for Limkokwing University. In that one year he forged strategic agreements with two of China's elite institutions of higher education – Beijing University and Tsinghua University. Limkokwing set up its campus within Tsinghua University which, like almost everything in China, is huge and sprawling. The Beijing campus is an important part of the university's global expansion especially in fulfilling his philosophy of merging the best of East and West.

That same year he also set up a campus in Phnom Penh, Cambodia. This bewildered many people who were closely following his moves. Why Cambodia?

> *Anywhere in the world it is creative people who create new business, new products, new media, new markets, new lifestyles, new trends, new standards, new heroes. It is creative people who build economies around the world.*
>
> *Limkokwing*
> *2000*

"I went to Cambodia with Tun Dr Mahathir a long time ago. I got to know the city and met some of its people. A lot of Malaysians have established businesses there so it is a familiar place to us. More recently when it was

The story of a university as unusual as Limkokwing University is both wide-ranging and multi-layered. Yet, through it a simple message shines like a beacon – a message of hope for the oppressed and disadvantaged – among whom may be counted almost the entire populations of many of the developing nations of the world.

Lawrence Watson
Accreditation Service for International Colleges, UK, 2009

suggested that I should set up a campus there I found the city to have evolved. It is ready for the kind of programmes I can bring to the country which is eager to transform itself. It will need human capital well trained to take the economy to the next level," said Tan Sri Lim.

He added that the university will make a meaningful difference and help speed up the transition.

Phnom Penh is a chaotic city bustling with activity. But it has a changing landscape with new buildings sprouting, an indication of an expanding middle-class. Tourism is the biggest draw, especially to the city of Siem Reap where the famous Angkor Wat is located.

The Limkokwing University campus has already become the most hi-tech campus in the country offering programmes that have attracted eager young Cambodians. Eventually, the Phnom Penh campus will serve as a regional hub for students all over Indo-China.

In Asia, the university is fast expanding as it establishes itself in Kuching, in the east Malaysian state of Sarawak, and Jakarta and Bali in Indonesia. There are also plans to set up another base in the Middle-East as well as in New York in the United States.

Part 3

Designing The Future

The Present is in our grasp. Every second gives us the opportunity to decide our next action. The Present is all we have to develop the Future. The Future blossoms in our minds but it takes courage, willpower, perseverance and determination to transform what lies hidden in the coils of our brains into something that people can touch, feel and experience. There is much Tan Sri Lim has done in the Present to influence the Future. He has been able to do that because of the kind of person that he is. The power of the individual to influence the future is determined by the kind of responses he or she makes to challenges faced. The kind of people we are ultimately decides the kind of future we will create.

- ***The future is in the mind***
- ***The mind of Limkokwing***
- ***Mind-mapping the future***
- ***The future is with the empowered collective***
- ***The empowered generation***

Top: *Tan Sri Lim with Tun Abdullah Badawi when he came to open the Cyberjaya campus in 2005.*
Tan Sri with King Mswati II of Swaziland who invited him to set up a campus in his country.

Middle: *Tan Sri Lim with Dato Hishamuddin, Minister of Youth and Sports when he came to officiate Tujuh Interior Design 2002.*

Tan Sri with Popane Labesa, Minister of Trade, Industry, Co-operatives and Marketing of Lesotho when he visited in June 2010.

Bottom: *Professor Doctor of Science Viacheslav V. Gorlopanov of the Moscow Academy of State and Municipal Management presents Tan Sri Lim with the Russian Federation's full Professorship, the first Malaysian to receive the honour.*

Tan Sri Lim with Ahmad Kathrada, Chairman of the Nelson Mandela Foundation and Dr Popo Molefe, former Premier of the Northwest Province at the conferment of Honorary Doctorate on Nelson Mandela in Johannesburg in June 2008.

Top: *Tan Sri Lim with Maldives Minister of Human Resource, Youth & Sports Hassan Latheef who visited in May 2009.*

M.M. Musthapa, Deputy Minister of Higher Education, Sri Lanka paid Tan Sri Lim a visit in June 2009.

Middle: *Indonesia's Minister of Culture and Tourism Jero Wacik and his wife Triesna visited in November 2009.*

Tanzania's Minister of Infrastructure Development Dr Shukuru Kawamba was on campus in January 2009.

Bottom: *Prime Minister of St. Vincent and Grenadines Ralph E. Gonsalves was impressed with the campus when he visited in March 2006.*

Tan Sri Lim met with Prime Minister Hun Sen of the Kingdom of Cambodia in May 2010.

The future is in the mind

The mind. It is the one place where we are able to travel to the past while staying in the present and attempt to design the future – all at the same time. Those who believe that the mind is the most powerful thing on earth are absolutely correct. The most beautiful works of art, architecture, music, design and literature as well as the most ingenious innovations co-exist alongside the most monstrous inventions that cause death and destruction. Both are the results of minds engaged creatively in translating ideas into physical reality.

The mind is a limitless sphere of possibilities. The brain and the body are merely tools to carry out the grand dreams of the mind. Through every age of Man's history we have conquered the impossible and crossed into new realms of existence. The momentum has picked up with new discoveries and innovations happening in such rapid succession that our lives and environment keep getting transformed in ever decreasing time cycles – from years to months to days and minutes. What the future will look like is locked within the minds of the world's youngest inhabitants.

How they are nurtured will decide in what shape the future will form. Will we overcome our differences and create a brave new world of peace and prosperity or will we shatter violently apart and in the process endanger the continued survival of human kind on Planet Earth?

These are challenges that those involved in the education of the next generation must concern themselves – very urgently.

If we are able to converge as a collective mind or a collective consciousness for the good of mankind, we can establish a quality of life that will be akin to creating a heaven on earth. But there are many divides and serious kinks in the relationships between regimes which slow down the global convergence taking place.

Tan Sri Lim has put his mind to the issue and the solution he chose to apply is to expand his university and spread education across the world. He has gathered young minds from all over the globe to see the future through his eyes and close the divide and dismantle the barriers that keep people from taking the world to greater heights of achievements.

The earlier portion captured the journey of Tan Sri Lim as he honed his skills, built his business, crystallised his intentions, chapter by chapter, fusing his experiences to this moment in time when he is ready to launch his ambitions for the future.

He has arrived at the position where he has the means to reach out to – and influence – a generation of young people from every corner of the globe. His present campuses already have more than 30,000 students who come from over 150 countries while the university's website registers over a 100 million hits from 190 countries per year.

Tan Sri Lim is today where he wants to be, where he had planned to be. In 2002, long before he built his first overseas campus, he sketched his vision to his staff with these prophetic words: "This is not just another private college. This is an international endeavour – an effort with far-reaching international dimension. We are well on our way to becoming a world centre for inventive and innovative thinking – a world campus for education, incubation and exploration."

Since then, he has quickened the pace as he worked on shaping that future he envisaged in his mind long ago. He has come very far but he is keenly aware that any attempt to change the way things are will be met by resistance. But he has resilience and perseverance to weather the opposition.

In a published interview, Tan Sri Lim spoke of the effort he made to convince others to see things his way. "You spend time to get the right mindset in place, change the thinking of people, reduce the resistance, pre-empt the questions and at the same time keep pushing forward, keep implementing so that people can see how you translate an idea into reality, how you bring into existence something that was never there before. You will need a lot of determination to do what has never been done before."

But first it is worthwhile to understand the mind of Tan Sri Lim for herein lies the design, the template for the future, as he envisions it.

The mind of Limkokwing

The mind of Tan Sri Lim is focused, sharp and reflective. It is a restless space filled with ideas, dreams and hopes. He has devoted his entire life to his work, taking no breaks as he turned ideas into reality, tackling one challenge after another. His mind is well primed to think deep, think far and think with clarity.

Pioneering is something that comes naturally to him. Look back at the journey he has travelled and you can see that the trail he blazed was not something that he strived to create for selfish reasons. This is a man who simply immerses himself completely in an endeavour and does what comes naturally to him. He creates. He innovates. He tries to stay ahead of the game. He likes to take a peek at what lies ahead and he makes intelligent guesses that have guided his moves. He creates new actions, often in fearless, unprecedented ways that those attempting to compete with him find that they cannot keep pace. By doing what he does he influences the future through every action that he takes.

His mindset is vastly different from many other individuals who have succeeded. His wealth is spent carefully, meaningfully. Global financial crises have not impoverished him because the investments he has made are not on material things but on people. While others wind down their businesses, he globalises. While others retract, he re-invents.

Those who attempt to predict his next move find him to be a puzzle, an enigma. But he said there is nothing eccentric or mysterious about what he does or the way he works. He attributes his actions to the state of being positive. Even in the face of enormous challenges he keeps his faith in what he does. He has built his life using the golden principles of perseverance and determination and they have never failed him. They remain his constant assistants. His resilience in times of adversity or in the face of resistance comes from his ability to think with purpose and implement with tenacity.

Tan Sri Lim's life journey illustrates how the power within an individual provides the energy, the stimulus and the motivation to direct one's life. But it begins with goal-setting and having a purpose for doing anything. He has no time for frivolity. You won't see him at the golf course, horse-riding or yachting, the usual leisure pursuits of the rich and famous. He allows himself the occasional trip to scout for antiques. His mind is always engaged in mind-mapping something or other. It comes automatically to him.

He is an asset to his country as he easily maps the way forward when approached by bureaucrats, politicians, academicians and industry professionals. He is included in high-level discussions to plan the country's economic well-being. He is a familiar figure in Malaysia, quoted and featured regularly in the media. Yet, there is little that people know about the impact this man has been making behind the scenes, in both the business and the political worlds.

In political circles he maintains a neutral stand that invites all parties to consult with him. He is actively engaged in mediating between disputing parties to seek amicable settlements. There are many deals he has helped broker quietly to sustain the fragile stability that the country is facing these days after so many decades of peace and harmony.

However, his efforts are rarely acknowledged as it is the nature of politicians to claim credit for success without looking back to thank those that helped them overcome issues that impeded their progress. Asked why he still bothers to help when he knows it is a thankless task, his simple answer is that he cannot refuse those who seek his advice and intervention. As party infighting and leadership crises continue to roil the political landscape in Malaysia after the watershed 2008 general election, he is sought by many politicians for advice. His neutrality and the known fact that he does not ask for favours in return are his greatest strengths.

He is convinced that the future of this country depends on the acceptance of the different races to see themselves first as Malaysians. He pointed out that he himself has gained great benefits from being a Malaysian because Malaysians possess a give-and-take attitude that has helped him venture confidently into the most unexpected overseas markets, like Africa. Malaysians, he said, have the advantage of knowing both sides of the world.

In the business world, he is a highly respected entrepreneur, sometimes considered a radical player who takes enormous but calculated risks.

The advertising industry would not have built the foundation that enabled Malaysian talents and Malaysian entrepreneurship to take the lead if not for Tan Sri Lim's groundbreaking initiatives. His determination and passion to push past obstacles and succeed as the creator of the first home-grown advertising agency in a highly competitive market paved the way for others to follow.

His perseverance, discipline and talent changed the future of the advertising industry in Malaysia and his involvement during the two decades that he devoted his energy to the industry saw it flourish. Malaysian talents gained recognition and a new generation of Malaysians came to dominate the field. Today, Malaysians are recognised worldwide for their originality and creativity.

In a study of a person's life you often look for trigger points that reveal a shift in the mindset which signals a change of direction. In Tan Sri Lim's life, there were several trigger points. Every shift not only influenced the flow of his life but also influenced the character and the growth of the industry that he was involved in. Even though he was born into a poor family and did not go beyond secondary school, he rose up rapidly to position himself as a rare thinker in a country where there are few such individuals. He succeeded in almost every business he invested in. He survived financial crises that destroyed many businesses. He re-invents and re-engineers constantly. He is never complacent with his achievements. He is always moving, planning, thinking ahead, and working his way to reach the future that he envisions.

In 1983 Malaysia's fourth Prime Minister Tun Dr Mahathir Mohamad introduced the Malaysia Incorporated policy to strengthen national competitiveness through a strategic collaboration between the public and private sectors. In 1991 he introduced Vision 2020 as an ideal to inspire the nation to strive for fully developed nation status within 30 years. Malaysia Incorporated evolved to become the main vehicle to carry the country through to its aspiration.

Within the Malaysia Incorporated policy, there were mechanisms for the private sector to approach the government with proposals to diversify or strengthen the economy.

The spirit of Malaysia Incorporated provided Tan Sri Lim the impetus to create ways to help drive the economy up the value chain.

He found great satisfaction in this role and immersed himself in the issues facing the country. He studied the strategies the government had put together in its 5-year national development plans. At high-level discussions he put forward ideas – and he had plenty – on what he thought should be done to improve economic performance and shared his views on how national issues could be tackled with positive results.

Always a 'big picture' man, he provided the perspective that helped ministries that he was collaborating with to see beyond the narrow confines of their responsibilities and political agendas. He wrote papers mapping the way forward for the country to bridge the many divides in the country that have prevented those in the rural heartland to access benefits created by the government as well as how social issues of the urban centres could be overcome.

Sometimes he was given the green light to implement a solution that he suggested. But most of the time his solutions were taken and passed to others to implement. He suffered the disappointment in silence. While many others in his position would have complained loudly or walked away in disgust, he chose to look at the outcome positively, finding satisfaction that his ideas were being implemented to help shape the future of his country.

In an age when patriotism is more derided than admired, he has never ceased to reiterate his unwavering belief that Malaysia's greatest strength lies in its multi-cultural diversity. And he knew how that strength could be used to benefit the nation in ways unforeseen even just a decade ago.

As recently as October 2009, he wrote in his blog that Malaysia is a fortunate country.

"The population is rich in cultural diversity. The three main ethnic groups – Malay, Chinese and Indians – are the inheritors of ancient innovative civilisations that were centres of scholarship. Knowledge spurred their inventiveness and innovations long before Europe emerged from the backwardness of the Middle Ages.

"Today, China and India are again driving ahead as the engines of growth of the global economy, while the capital-rich Muslim nations of the Middle-East are being courted by countries around the world.

"With their cultural and linguistic advantages, Malaysian Chinese and Indian business people have built solid connections with their counterparts in China and India."

Mind-mapping the future

> *The future refers to that space of time that lies ahead of us. That space of time we now have ownership of. What we do with it today will determine what and where we will be tomorrow.*
>
> *Limkokwing*
> *2007*

The university that he built and continues to develop is a physical representation of what his life has been and will become. He has poured into it every ounce of his knowledge gained from the many challenges that he has overcome in his life; from a childhood when he faced and overcame hardship and poverty to earning his livelihood making the best use of his talents and succeeding with accolades and distinction. Because he endured and won many of life's battles, he is able to inspire others as well as teach the next generation.

The university is an institution of higher education but, to him, its foremost role is as a place to ignite the imagination of young people and mould them into individuals who possess a better understanding of the world and its issues.

The university is unlike any other that you will find in the world. It reflects the philosophy of its founder; a habitat for creative expression, an eco-system for exploration and experimentation that builds the confidence and develops the skills of young people. It is an institution that prefers to write its own rules because it refuses to be boxed in, categorised and controlled by old school thinking.

You are indeed doing things very differently. You are really a different university, a university that is unique, in a class of its own. I believe you are the only one that is really helping and contributing towards the success of other countries in the world today.

Dato' Seri Mohamed Khaled Nordin
Minister of Higher Education, Malaysia, December 2008

But because its programmes have to be accredited by the authorities, it struggles to stay within the norms dictated by the rules of the countries it is located in. To follow the rules and yet be innovative is something that just doesn't go together. There has to be some latitude to allow for change and transformation to take place.

Being a pioneer he has to push harder than others because it takes time and effort to get others to see the same picture that he sees. But with perseverance and determination as his close companions, he has been able to succeed where many others would have given up. What he is attempting to achieve through his university provides many cases to illustrate this point.

In all the countries that his university has established itself he works to change the mindsets of people so steeped in the old ways of doing things that they fear the change that he is bringing. They fear the collapse of the status quo and the subsequent loss of control.

But change is inevitable and it lies in the empowered minds of the next generation.

The future is with the empowered collective

American writer Malcolm Gladwell, in his book *The Tipping Point*, talks about social epidemics – the sudden popularity of products, the start of fashion trends, the drop in crime rates, among other seemingly inexplicable phenomena. The Tipping Point, he argued, is that magic moment when trends begin. He studied these events and isolated the catalysts that had direct influence on people's behaviour and often caused these epidemics. He attributed the catalysts to the 'Law of the Few' – individuals or groups of individuals that influence social behaviour to an extent where new trends begin.

Tan Sri Lim is clearly among that group of individuals who are creators of change. In Botswana, in the United Kingdom, in Malaysia, in Cambodia, wherever he has built his campuses, he began a global conversation about education. Government leaders, academics and industry leaders are beginning to see his point.

Tipping global trends in education

It is my contention that what he is doing will lead to a tipping point in global education. This will produce a ripple effect that will touch and awaken developing countries to his new vision of education. Then, the present adherence to Western models, standards and benchmarks will change as governments grow more confident and become more exploratory in developing their own routes to building the kind of human capital that they need. They will come to realise that the models created by the Western world are not meant for the economies of a developing country. The models set standards that are too lofty and will deny millions of young people access to higher education. By being unable to fulfil the standards, these young people would be doomed to be labelled as failures. They drop out of school and become unemployable.

For the developing world, the kind of education it needs has to be relevant and sustainable. They don't need to place their youths in schools for 12 years, teaching them subjects that cannot be used in the marketplace when they leave school. The manpower planning has to match the country's industry needs and economic development plans.

Speaking at a conference of Commonwealth education ministers in Kuala Lumpur in June 2009, Tan Sri Lim created a stir with his radical views on education.

He said the British system, adopted wholesale by Commonwealth countries, is not applicable to many that are struggling to develop.

This 'one-size-fits-all' solution does not take into account that other than a colonial past, most of these countries have little in common in terms of heritage and traditions with the West.

It does not take into account that in many parts of the Commonwealth, a Western-style education is accessible only to the wealthy and the privileged – in a nutshell, the elite.

This reinforced and strengthened the divide between rich and poor people within a country and between communities.

Tan Sri Lim declared that education must lie at the heart of change. Good intentions alone are not good enough.

"What we need to do…is to review, revamp and re-invent the development and delivery of education, allowing for greater flexibility and creativity. It is time for a new Commonwealth model to be considered. One that effectively accommodates the different needs of different countries; one that builds first the people and then the economy.

"This re-invention must happen if there is to be transformation so that every young person is purposefully educated and has a part to play and a stake in moving their country forward."

A model for the developing world

Through Tan Sri Lim's university, developing countries are now able to access a new model that can successfully engage its youths and empower them with the knowledge and skills they need to gain employment or create new enterprises. To the developing world, this is the means for their people to climb out of the cycle of poverty that they have been caught in for as long as they could remember.

In the earlier chapters you have seen how he injected his own ideas about the education of an individual. It has been a holistic exercise which fused the environment with events to create unique experiences aimed at

Today's young generation is a different quality of people. They are growing up in an era of technology that has enhanced connectivity and eased laborious work. It's a digital world where the word "instant" is moving from hours to minutes to seconds and now it is reducing further to nano-seconds.

Limkokwing
2009

empowering students to be the persons they want to be and to become better at what they do.

What Tan Sri Lim has attempted to do is to awaken within the youths a desire to pursue an activity that totally consumes the individual.

This brings to mind the research conducted by Malcolm Gladwell which he presented in his book *The Outliers*. It was a study of why and how people achieve success. An interesting point he made was the number of hours an individual invests in a particular pursuit. Gladwell reckons that 10,000 hours was the minimum that famous people like the Beatles, Bill Gates and everyone else who achieved success had put into their work. They were fully engaged and they were so passionate about their pursuit that they did not feel the strain of the hours they sacrificed for their projects. In investing all their time in their pursuits they honed their skills, polishing them to a perfection that brought them success.

Similarly, Tan Sri Lim has designed an environment in his campuses that encourages his students to be passionate about what they do, so much so that the many hours they commit to their pursuits become a natural part of their learning process.

In all those students that Tan Sri Lim succeeded in unlocking that passion, we will see a corps of young people emerging who will bring new understanding, innovation and exciting discoveries for the world to see.

Essentially, what he has communicated to these young people is that they can succeed in whatever they do if they apply the same convictions that have guided him to success.

How did he succeed where many others have failed? Here is my observation.

Cloning his method and style

Tan Sri Lim has never seen age as a barrier. He is very comfortable with young people. He understands them and gives them freedom to express themselves. This has often been criticised by the authorities who felt too much freedom was a bad thing. But he explained that as an institution founded on promoting creativity, its students must be given the space to explore and to experiment.

"I have students here from all over the world. They speak different languages, follow different religions and have conflicting ideologies. Yet they have never clashed. They have learnt to respect each other and this is what they take back home with them. Imagine a future with these young people at the helm of industry or government. I can foresee less conflict in the world."

Young people relish the environment at the university. They develop a love and a loyalty for the brand that is long-lasting. Limkokwing graduates now form the bulk of the university's staff. They helm many of the campus-grown business units, from web development and management to film and video content creation, design, music and sound engineering, and photography. They also manage the six faculties as well as the marketing and promotional activities.

Tan Sri Lim surrounds himself with young talent that he trained himself. He handpicked a few and despatched them to all his campuses located in eight countries.

"These young people give me the energy and focus I need to develop these campuses. They report to me every day and I know exactly what goes on at each campus. Many people are surprised that I placed such heavy responsibilities on these young shoulders.

"But people are mistaken to think that young people cannot take on heavy responsibilities. They are at an age when they are not burdened by family problems. They can travel at a moment's notice. And most of the time they enjoy the challenge and want to do well," said Tan Sri Lim.

In Cambodia is Emmeline Lyon, from the United Kingdom, who looks after the campus in Phnom Penh. Em, as we call her, had been a mainstay at Tan Sri Lim's office in Cyberjaya for many years. He was trying to train her and thought she was too playful. Em, however, has a determined streak within her and high aspirations. She hid her ambitions beneath a carefree attitude that is very deceptive.

She was a little pensive when asked to go to Cambodia because she loved being at Cyberjaya. Tan Sri Lim kept her in Cambodia to allow her to grow used to the life there. When she came back six months later she had grown so attached to the Cambodians that she was itching to get back.

"Setting up a university from scratch – from managing the first bricks that were laid, to managing a full-fledged university, with hundreds of eager young minds – is an amazing experience.

"Seeing the enthusiasm, the energy and excitement of these young Cambodians makes me feel good...makes me feel like I am doing a wonderful thing. I feel I have accomplished something great.

"The smiles on their faces, the hugs in the hallways, the fact that they don't like to leave the campus...these are the best parts of being in Phnom Penh. This is the pat on my back that I cherish. But in fact every pat that I receive rightfully belongs to Tan Sri Lim," said the loyal Em.

She said that despite a horrifying civil war, Cambodia now has a bright future with the restoration of political stability and a growing economy. It is also receiving a timely boost through Tan Sri Lim's vision and commitment to establish a facility that will help build Cambodia's much needed human resource.

Em is among the thousands of success stories of Limkokwing's alumni who find they have acquired characteristics that set them apart. They see life differently. They are not afraid to compete and feel energised by challenges.

There is Marcia Mangadi, a 20-something Motswana from Botswana, who looks after the campus in Lesotho in southern Africa. She has pictures of herself on horseback riding to remote villages to recruit students for the campus in the mountainous country. Marcia, you could say, is an old hand at this because she was among those who accompanied Tan Sri Lim to present the university's proposal to the then Botswana President

Festus Mogae to set up Limkokwing's first African campus in Gaborone.

"I was proud and happy to be part of the team but at my age I didn't realise the magnitude of the project. It only hit me a few months later when I realised that I had been instrumental in helping 12,000 Batswana obtain an education similar to what I had received," she said.

Her experience in Botswana prepared her for the tougher job in Lesotho where she was commissioned to open the university's second campus in Africa. "This time it was different because I had no team with me. I was alone when I left for this little mountain kingdom in the middle of South Africa.

"It's funny how you can be so wrong to think that countries within the same region are the same. I discovered that, like people, each country is unique. It was not easy setting up a campus in Lesotho but I kept going. I opened myself up for the learning and realised that the learning never stops. Once you know better, you do better."

She described how humbled she felt when students came up and thanked her for giving them the opportunity to get an education which put them on the path to a better life.

"I remember having to travel to the districts in Lesotho at 3,500 metres above sea level. Some places could not be accessed by cars so I had to go on horseback. There was one student who had passed with first class results but could not even afford to rent a horse to attend our interview. I went up the mountains to see this student and I am happy to say that this student is now with us.

"That was when it occurred to me that in life, we should want for others what we want for ourselves. And I must thank Tan Sri Lim for this opportunity, for seeing something greater in me than I did."

Karveen Puddoo is another 20-something Limkokwing alumnus, from Mauritius, who completed his studies in 2002. He described a conversation that he had with Tan Sri Lim. "He told me that he had a plan for me. To hear that from someone that I admire and respect moved me to become a part of the big idea that he had.

"He sent me first to Mauritius. I was just 22 years old but I welcomed the opportunity to gain the experience of promoting the university in my homeland. In the last 6 years, I have travelled to 23 countries in Asia, Africa and Europe.

"The opening of new campuses overseas and franchising our programmes abroad has brought new challenges that have developed the other side of me – in building my management and negotiation skills," he said. He was then sent to Botswana to help out at the campus in Gaborone.

He described how he received a text message from Tan Sri Lim when he was in Botswana. "He asked me to come back to KL and get ready to go to London. Within three days I was on a plane bound for London – a place I never thought I would be spending years."

Karveen has been managing the London campus with another Limkokwing alumnus Amol Gurong who is from Nepal.

In 2009, after two and a half years in London Karveen has been given a new portfolio to establish a campus in Mauritius. " It is true what Tan

Sri has been saying about designing our future. He has always told us that once we had gained our experience we should always think of going back to our countries and do something good for the nation. And now I have the chance to do this. I feel proud and very privileged to be given this portfolio."

For every story that I have given here there are thousands more as hundreds of students graduate each year and take up employment in their home countries. Just for a moment imagine this global community and the impact it will have in the years to come. These young people will rise to take their place at the top echelons of industry and government. Already we have a fresh graduate from the Maldives, who has become Asia's youngest elected Member of Parliament when he won in the recent elections held in the country. In the years to come we may yet have a country leader who had studied at the Limkokwing University. That would be interesting to watch and to learn.

These graduates are the products of a different kind of learning. While they went through the rigours of academic research and study they also participated in programmes that unlocked their talents, ignited their creativity and opened their minds to think in new ways. They learnt about opportunities and how to grasp them. They learnt the power of technology and how they need to stay abreast with changes. Their friends are from all over the world. They stay in touch in cyberspace. They form a global community that is also part of a cyberspace community.

The empowered generation

There are a lot of discussions going on around the world, especially among academics, on how to create the infrastructure that encourages creativity and innovation. There was one particularly interesting argument put forward by Professor Glyn Davis, Vice-Chancellor of the University of Melbourne, in a paper on 9 May 2005 titled *To Win Back My Youth… Encouraging Innovation.*

She said that earlier generations had simple explanations about innovation. "Innovation, they said, is what young people do. And not necessarily just an individual, but a whole generation as well. Each generation 'comes into existence' within a particular political and social moment, with shared experiences to provide some commonality in outlook."

She quoted Goethe, the German philosopher, who observed that every person's perception of the world is shaped by the experiences of youth. "Members of the same generation are linked throughout life by bonds of mutual understanding that set them apart. As a generation grows into maturity, it seeks to transform the world into its own image."

In brand Limkokwing I see that shared experience. In brand Limkokwing I see that reach into a future that promises a better world once these young people move into positions that enable them to exercise influence on others and change a world burdened by armed conflicts and violent deaths into something driven by compassion and the quest for lasting peace and greater prosperity for mankind.

It has been said that the generation born after 1982 – the Millennials – as they are known will have a positive impact on the world. We have seen that impact in the United States with the election of Barack Obama – the first black President. Young, first-time voters, made the crucial difference in the electorate that chose Obama.

In a study by Howe and Strauss, as cited by Professor Glyn, the Millennials are "on track to becoming the smartest, best-educated generation in the history of the United States. These kids are focused. Television time has decreased 13 percent while study time has increased 58 percent. Focused and determined – a 2000 survey showed 97 percent of Millennials believe in their generation's lifelong ability to improve technology, 77 percent in the ability to improve race relations and 55 percent in the ability to improve the economy."

We can conclude, just as Professor Glyn did, that we can expect current students to flood into the workplace over the coming years, brilliantly positioned to create more innovative organisations.

The future will always be about achieving the impossible. It will always be defined and designed by those with creative leadership, by those who create their own games and write their own rules. All recent phenomenal achievements have been accomplished by very young people who are fearless in their thinking.

Limkokwing
2009

As the world is rocked by problem after problem, issue after issue, it awaits the influence of the Millennial generation that will be the one to change its course. In country after country, these young people who have grown up in a different mould, who are more worldly in their lifestyle and more expressive in their opinions, either will invent the new weapons of war or, if we are fortunate, will discover the path to peace.

In many countries today, it is the powerful opinions of the youths that are making dramatic changes. In advanced countries like the United States where the culture is driven by innovation, the transition is smoother than in countries that are administered by very rigid regimes. And we continue to witness the upheavals in these latter countries that attempt to resist the change that is coming. They don't realise that they can no longer sustain their regimes in a world that is interconnected in a way like never before in the history of world.

And organisations like Limkokwing University, driven by its founder, empower the young to take control of the future of this world which is their birthright.

The University's documentation of its creative work is unparalleled. This is the third edition of Wings of Creativity that provides students better understanding of creativity and how it works through the many campaigns that Tan Sri Lim has been engaged in over the last three decades.

The accolades that recognise the talent and wizardry of Tan Sri Lim began when he was in his 20s and has not abated as he receives them from all over the world for creativity, innovation, leadership, philanthropy, entrepreneurship and globalization of education among others.

Minister of Science, Technology and Innovation, Datuk Dr Maximus Ongkili congratulates Tan Sri Lim after launching the University's Innovation Bank during his official visit in August 2009. Earlier he bestowed the title Father of Innovation in Creative Education upon Tan Sri Lim.

Tan Sri Dato' Sri Dr Limkokwing honoured as Father of Creativity and Innovation

YB Dato' Mukhriz Tun Dr Mahathir congratulates Tan Sri Dato' Sri Dr Limkokwing on being recognized by the SMI and SME community with the award.

The small-and-medium-sized industries and enterprises community recently recognised Tan Sri Dato' Sri Dr Limkokwing as Malaysia's Father of Creativity and Innovation bestowing him with a Lifetime Achievement Award at a colourful ceremony during the SMI & SME Worldwide Network Business of the Year Award annual event. At the same event Limkokwing University of Creative Technology was recognized as Malaysia's Most Popular Brand.

Heartiest Congratulations

GRADUAN GBBM JCI PUMM

Portrait of an icon of creativity & innovation

Tan Sri Dato' Sri Dr Lim Kok Wing

Artist, designer, writer, creative director, publisher, entrepreneur, film director, branding strategist, advertising guru, philanthropist, national unity campaigner, international peace advocate… the president and founder of Limkokwing University of Creative Technology wears many hats. Characteristically thought of as a pioneer and trailblazer, he has stamped his mark of excellence in many fields.

Internationally recognised for his contributions in such diverse areas as education, branding and design, SME development, and industry innovation, the 2005 Ernst & Young Entrepreneur of the Year Hall of Fame inductee has devoted a lifetime towards promoting creativity and innovation to be part of the national agenda.

His role in globalizing Malaysian education has lifted the profile of the country in the eyes of the world. Limkokwing University, now established in Asia, Africa and Europe, is a testament to his mission to empower the next generation with the skills to use the tools of the new digital era.

Part of his global initiative is to assist government leaders in developing countries as they strive for social and economic transformation – with innovation ever the central theme as he conceptualizes their future.

The inspiring leadership he has demonstrated in the past four decades makes up the essence of this publication.

Malaysia 50sen

A compilation of news articles and special features detailing the journey of a Malaysian creative genius -from humble beginnings to global icon.

Top: *Deputy Minister of International Trade and Industry, Dato' Mukhriz Mahathir congratulates Tan Sri Lim on being recognized as Father of Creativity and Innovation by the SME & SMI Worldwide Network at its Business of the Year annual event in June 2010.*

Bottom: *Over the past four decades Tan Sri Lim has been regularly featured in the media, whether through interviews, news articles or columns that he wrote. These have been compiled into a single document for easy reference.*

As a man with controversial ideas about education, Tan Sri Lim has always attracted extensive media attention.

Top: *YAM Tengku Panglima DiRaja Selangor Tengku Sulaiman Shah Alhaj ibni Al-Marhum Sultan Salahuddin Abd Aziz Shah Alhaj (on Tan Sri Lim's left) visited the location where Tan Sri Lim is planning to put up a mosque next to the University campus to facilitate Muslim students and staff.*

Middle: *The artist impression of the mosque to be built next to the campus which is being designed to include a knowledge centre amidst a huge garden.*

Bottom: *The Menteri Besar or Chief Minister of Kelantan Dato' Haji Nik Aziz Nik Mat (in turban) spent five hours touring the University campus when he visited in February 2007.*

Strategy Papers

1990–2010

Listed below are a selection of strategy papers that Tan Sri Dato' Sri Dr Limkokwing had developed in his quest to assist government leaders. His vision has always been clearly set in the future in making his recommendations to revitalize existing sectors or advocate for the inclusion of new ones.

- *Rakan Muda – galvanizing the youth of Malaysia*
- *Rakan Muda – the next phase*
- *Achieving Vision 2020*
- *Mission 2020 – the final stretch*
- *Reversing Malaysia's decline in competitiveness*
- *Reinforcing Malaysia's competitiveness*
- *Building a strong, vibrant international content creation industry*
- *Building a culture for innovation and creativity*
- *Enhancing competitiveness of Malaysian SMEs*
- *Innovating rural industry: a strategic plan*
- *Empowering 1,000,000 rural ICT internet users*
- *Moving Malaysia into an innovation economy*
- *Transformation of SMEs to MNCs: a strategic empowerment initiative*
- *Driving strategic change: building a new national mindset*
- *Strategic rebranding of Malaysia's leadership community*
- *Strengthening the vision: strengthening integrity and efficiency*
- *Engineering a safety-minded society, a civic conscious society*
- *Realising the vision: building an innovation nation*
- *Power of innovation: using it for the nation*

- *Leadership for innovation, leadership for cohesion*
- *Year of creativity and innovation 2010*
- *Roadmap for a creative Malaysia*
- *Going beyond 2020: transforming Malaysia into an innovation economy*
- *Proposal …….. of change and innovation*
- *To stay in competition, Malaysia must be driven by innovation*
- *One Malaysia: a new era of performance-led government*
- *A new era in fashion education for rural Malaysia*
- *A new generation of high-technology, creativity-driven empowerment centres*
- *Adopting the fighting spirit of a tiger: a new era in Malaysian sports*
- *Setting the leadership agenda*
- *Transforming Malaysia: doing what must be done*
- *Pivotal transformation of rural industry*
- *A strategic blueprint for Malaysia's halal industry development*
- *Halal Branding Council of Malaysia: an enduring platform*
- *Malaysia: the next quantum leap*
- *National Service: a strategic growth development programme*
- *From Vision to Transformation: Botswana*
- *Enabling innovation: Lesotho*
- *Enabling transformation, achieving Vision 2022: Swaziland*
- *Moving Cambodia forward*
- *Innovation City: a strategic development*
- *Transformation of Malaysia's creative industries*
- *Building an international education destination*
- *Malaysian airports: time for brand innovation*
- *Malaysian ports: time to innovate*
- *National Printers: the next level*

Tan Sri Dato' Sri Dr Limkokwing's endeavours and contributions are multi-faceted, spanning many business and public / community service projects. He is involved in various capacities – as Chairman, President, CEO and other executive and advisory positions on the boards of the following organisations:

Founder / President of:

- *President, Limkokwing University of Creative Technology - Malaysia, United Kingdom, Botswana, Cambodia, Indonesia*
- *President, Limkokwing Institute of Creative Technology*
- *President, Malaysian Design Innovation Centre*
- *President, Malaysian Branding & Packaging Design Centre*
- *President, Limkokwing Executive Leadership College*
- *President, Malaysian Education Promotion Council*
- *President, National Creativity and Innovation Institute*
- *President, Centre for Content Creation*
- *President, Limkokwing Film & Television Academy*
- *President, Limkokwing Institute for Tomorrow*
- *President, Think Malaysia*
- *President, Limkokwing Foundation for Creative Excellence*
- *President, The Asia Creativity Institute*
- *President, International House Kuala Lumpur*
- *President, Public Opinion & Perception Research Centre*
- *President, K-Economy Enabling Institute*
- *President, Designers' and Animators' Guild*
- *President, Malaysian World Peace Foundation*
- *President, Malaysian American Society*
- *President, Malaysian Institute of Directors*
- *Chairman, Malaysia-Europe Forum Berhad*
- *President, Images of the East*
- *Founder, Society for the Severely Mentally Handicapped*
- *Founder, Art Design Centre of Kuala Lumpur*
- *Founder, Limkokwing Institute of Creative Technology*
- *Founder, Wings of Creativity*
- *Founder, Cambridge English Centre*
- *Founder, Academy for Career Advancement*

- *Fellow, Institute of Public Relations Malaysia*
- *Honorary Chairman, 2008 Junior Chamber International Creative Young Entrepreneur Award*
- *Chief Judge, Creative Young Entrepreneur Award 2007, JCI Entrepreneur Metropolitan (Malaysia)*
- *Judge, MPA Magazine Awards 2007*
- *Adviser, Branding Association of Malaysia*
- *Adviser, National Science Centre*
- *Honorary Member, Business Initiative Directions, Madrid*
- *Member, Council of Higher Education*
- *Member, Council for Effective Communications*
- *Member, Malaysian Art & Culture Council*
- *Member, MITI Industry Excellence Award Council*
- *Honorary Member, Kuala Lumpur Malay Chamber of Commerce*

Public services - positions held (past and present)

- *President - Malaysian World Peace Foundation*
- *President - Malaysian American Society*
- *President - Malaysian Institute of Directors*
- *President - Society for the Severely Mentally Handicapped*
- *President - Council for Effective Communications*
- *Chairman, Resource & Development – Cancer Foundation*
- *Adviser - Malaysian Footwear Manufacturers Association*
- *Adviser - National Science Centre*
- *Adviser - Branding Association of Malaysia*
- *Fellow - Institute of Public Relations Malaysia*
- *Vice President - United Nations Malaysia Association*
- *Vice President - Malaysian Red Crescent Society*
- *Member - Council of Higher Education*
- *Member - Malaysian Art and Culture Council*
- *Member - Ministry of International Trade & Industry's Industry Excellence Award Council*
- *Member -National Innovation Council*
- *Member - Malaysian Business Council*
- *Member - Kuala Lumpur Malay Chamber of Commerce*
- *Member - Business Initiative Directions, Madrid*

- *Trustee - Malaysian Handicraft Development Board*
- *Trustee - National Art Gallery*
- *Chief Judge of Creative Young Entrepreneur Awards 2007*
- *Honorary Chairman, Junior Chamber International's 2008*
- *Creative Young Entrepreneur Award*
- *Judge for Malaysian Publishers Association's Magazine Awards 2007*
- *Judge of Asia Innovation Awards 2006*

Awards & Recognitions

2010

- *Commander of the Most Meritorious Order of Mohlomi(CMMOM) by HM King Letsie III, Kingdom of Lesotho*
- *CEO of The Year 2010 by The Brand Laureate, Kuala Lumpur, Malaysia*
- *Gold Award in Creative Education by Putra Brand Award 2010, Kuala Lumpur, Malaysia*
- *"Lifetime Achievement as Malaysia's Father of Creativity & Innovation" from SMI-SME Worldwide Network - 2010*
- *Global Innovation Leadership in Education" - Diamond Category at the International Quality Summit Award Convention 2010 - New York*
- *PEAK OF SUCCESS - The Bizz Awards 2010 at Houston, Texas*
- *"World's First University Founded by a Lim" by The Federation of Lim Association*
- *"Leadership in Innovation & Creativity" by Malaysia Business Leadership Awards 2010*
- *"Innovation and Creativity Award" at 1st Middle East Business Summit in Dubai 2010*
- *"CEO of The Year 2010" by The Brand Laureate, Kuala Lumpur, Malaysia*
- *Gold Award in Creative Education by Putra Brand Award 2010, Kuala Lumpur, Malaysia*

2009

- *International Contributions in 'Humanity and Philanthropy' during the 2nd Islamic Unity Conference organised by the Ramadhan Foundation, UK and the Perdana Leadership Foundation*
- *SME Recognition Awards 2009 – Platinum Award by the SMI Association of Malaysia*
- *'Worldwide Leadership in Innovative Education' by the Oxford Centre for Leadership, UK*
- *Golden Medal for Quality & Service Award 2009 from the Worldwide Marketing Organisation, Glendale, California*
- *Golden Star for Management Merit Award 2009 from the Worldwide Marketing Organisation, Glendale, California*
- *'University of the Future' from QS-Asia Pacific Professional Leaders in Education Conference 2009*

- *CEO Award for Leadership in Manpower Development Sector from International Business Review*
- *Malaysian Business Leader Lifetime Achievement Award from Kuala Lumpur Malay Chamber of Commerce*
- *Father of Innovation in Creative Education by Ministry of Science, Technology and Innovation, Malaysia*
- *Malaysia Independence Award 1957 – Strategist*
- *Distinguished World Citizen of Peace and Humanity by the Embassy of the State of Palestine*
- *Pioneering Leadership in Entrepreneurship Award ASEAN - BAC & ARFF*
- *Honorary Doctorate for Leadership in Global Education from Seo Kyeong University, Republic of Korea*
- *One of Asia's 48 Heroes of Philanthropy by Forbes Asia Magazine*
- *Lifetime Achievement Award in Human Resource Development by The Asia HRD Congress 2009*
- *"World Business Leader" by The World Confederation of Businesses, Dubai*
- *Creative Leadership in Global Education, Country Branding Award 2008-2009 by the Brand Laureate*

2008

- *Arch of Europe for Quality, Leadership, Technology and Innovation, Frankfurt - Business Initiative Directions, Frankfurt*
- *Quality Summit Award for Visionary Leadership in Innovative Education, New York*
- *Inducted into the Advertising Hall of Fame by the Association of Accredited Advertising Agents Malaysia in December 2008 in recognition of his contribution to raising the standards of creativity and in championing Malaysian talents.*
- *Innovative Leadership in Globalised Education by Accreditation Service for International Colleges (ASIC), United Kingdom*
- *Excellence in ASEAN Education Management 2008 Award by Technology Business Review ASEAN Award.*
- *Mentor Entrepreneur of the Year Award & Superior Company of the Year Award by SMI and SME Worldwide Network, Malaysia*
- *Special Achievement Award by Asia Pacific Entrepreneurship Award 2008*
- *Brand Excellence Award and Export Excellence Award (services category) – Ministry of International Trade & Industry, Malaysia*
- *Winner of "Best in Media & Entertainment" by MSC Malaysia APICTA 2008*

- *Recognition Award for Supporting Business Creativity and Innovation – Malaysian Venture Capital and Private Equity Association Award*

2007

- *Special Award for Globalising Malaysian Education by Ministry of Higher Education, Malaysia*
- *International Quality Crown Award -- Business Initiative Directions, London;*
- *Century International Quality Era Award in Platinum category, Geneva*
- *Professorship award by the Moscow Academy of the State and Municipal Management;*
- *Brand Personality Award (The Grammy Award for Branding) by BrandLaureate;*
- *Honorary Professorship Award -- Thames Valley University;*
- *Master Entrepreneur Award -- Business Summit;*
- *Century International Quality Award -- Business Initiative Directions, Geneva;*
- *Mentor Entrepreneur of the Year – SMI & SME Worldwide Network;*
- *Superior Company of the Year – SMI & SME Worldwide Network;*
- *Status upgrade to fully-fledged university.*

2006

- *International Star Award for World Quality Commitment, Gold Category – Business Initiative Directions, Paris;*
- *CEO of the Year 2006 Award by the Malaysia Canada Business Council;*
- *Honorary Doctorate of Civil Laws and Emeritus Professorship for the Chair of Innovation Management conferred by the European University, Barcelona;*
- *Asia's Most Creative Person Award by the London School of Management;*
- *Honorary Doctorate of Education -- University of East London;*
- *Lifetime Achievement Award for Humanitarian Efforts Inspiring Creativity and Innovation 2006 by Technological Business Review;*
- *Excellence in Information Technology (Multimedia Education) – Technological Business Review;*
- *Global Award for Innovation – Oxford Association of Management, UK*
- *Ernst & Young World Entrepreneur of the Year Academy.*

2005

- *Ernst & Young Entrepreneur of the Year and Master Entrepreneur of the Year;*
- *Ambassador for Peace - Universal Peace Federation and Inter-religious & International Federation for World Peace;*
- *Malaysian Peace Ambassador Award by Sun Yat Sen Centre for Peace and Education (S.E.A.).*

2004

- *Special Acknowledgement Award for role in Kuala Lumpur World Peace Conference, presented by the Institute of Public Relations Malaysia at its Krystal Awards 2004, December 2004.*

2003

- *Ad Personality of the Year awarded by the Malaysian Advertisers Association;*
- *Award for Excellence in Private Education by the National Association of Private Education Institutions, October.*

2002

- *Lifetime Achievement Award for Commitment to Education Excellence, ADOI magazine;*
- *Export Excellence Award – Malaysian Ministry of International Trade and Industry*
- *Honorary Doctorate in Design award by RMIT University, Australia, August 2002.*

2000

- *Most PR-savvy CEO of the Year 2000 award by the Institute of Public Relations Malaysia, July 2000.*

1995

- *Doctor of Letters award by Curtin University of Technology, Perth, July 1995.*

1994

- *Honorary Doctor of Laws award by the University of Hertfordshire, UK, November 1994.*

1993

- *Honorary Associate Fellow award by Auckland Institute of Technology, January 1993.*

1992

- *Honorary Fellow award by Malaysian Institute of Directors.*

1990

- *Man of the Year award by Women At Work magazine.*

Federal / State Honours

- *Honorary Title of Ahli Mangku Negara (AMN) – Order of Chivalry conferred by the Malaysian King;*
- *Dato' Paduka Mahkota Selangor – Knighthood (Dato') conferred by the Sultan of Selangor;*
- *Johan Setia Makhota (JSM) – Order of Chivalry (Third Rank) conferred by the Malaysian King;*
- *Johan Mangku Negara (JMN) – Order of Chivalry (Second Rank) conferred by the Malaysian King;*
- *Panglima Setia Mahkota (PSM) – Knighthood (Tan Sri) conferred by the Malaysian King;*
- *Darjah Kebesaran Sultan Ahmad Shah Pahang Sri Sultan Ahmad Shah Pahang (SSAP) – Knighthood (Dato' Sri) conferred by the Sultan of Pahang (First Rank)*

Tributes

Tan Sri Dato' Sri Dr Limkokwing always makes an impression on the people he meets and those he works with. They always have something to say about him on a personal level or about his endeavours. Here are a selection of these observations.

An odyssey "on a wing and a prayer"

In 1870 a conference was held in Indiana, USA, presided over by the Bishop. A scientist got up and predicted that one day men would fly through the air like birds. The Bishop was outraged. This was heresy. In the Bible, flight was reserved to the angels. With which he stormed out and went home to his two young sons. His name was Bishop Wright. His sons were Orville and Wilbur. And as history records, one fine morning on 17th December 1903 in North Carolina, Orville and Wilbur Wright did, indeed, fly through the air like birds pioneering the world's first successful flight. The plane was called the Flyer.

The genius of just two men had opened up the world to air travel which would accomplish the death of distance and make possible today's globalizing interconnected world. And successors would extend this to space travel and open up not just this planet, but the universe.

But what has this to do with Tan Sri Dato' Sri Dr Lim Kok Wing?

The invention of the first aero plane was a miraculous feat of creative technology. This calls for both vision, a leap of the imagination also combined – a rare combination, with innovation. There is one man in Malaysia whose tagline has become creativity and innovation.

Tan Sri Lim Kok Wing's parents made a happy choice of name for their son – one would say a prescient one "Kok Wing" means "glory to the country".

But even more pertinent it gave him his tag line "Wings". The title of his first advertising agency was – "Wings Creative" – It has many associations. Beginning with the story as above of the Wright brothers who invented flight. In classical legend, we had Hermes the Greek Mercury and the winged messenger of the Gods. And Pegasus, the winged horse, whose one blow with its hoof released the waters of Hippocrene, the fount of inspiration. The fount from which Lim Kok Wing imbibes freely.

Of all unlikely people, Mohamed Ali once said, "The man who has no imagination has no wings". Tan Sri Lim's career certainly took wing. As Byron said:

"Oh God it is a fearful thing
To see the human soul take wing"

The element of "soul" is the inspiration and the aspiration behind all Kok Wing does i.e. " on a wing and a power". He is you see a dangerous man – a very dangerous man. Because he is a dreamer. A day dreamer but not in the proverbial sense of Mat Jenin. More what T.E. Lawrence meant when he said:-

"Men who dream in the dusty recesses of the night, wake to find the dreams have vanished

But the men who dream by day, work to make their dream come true. They are the dangerous men".

Tan Sri Lim Kok Wing was born with one defining talent – artistic design. He became from young and still is the best graphics artist we ever had, a high flyer (to continue our analogy).

His original company became the most creative agency in Malaysia. He was inundated with awards. His reputation was global – supporting the first democratic election in South Africa – winning first prize in Hiroshima for his anti-nuclear campaign are but two examples.

It took him 30 years to build his business but it was not just an incremental effort with steady year on year improvements on the same old basic formula. It was transformational. Tan Sri is an ideas man driven by inspiration – a serial innovator. He made things happen. The latter part of the 20th century and even more the 21st has been borne in on the twin forces of globalization and technology. Kok Wing was in the vanguard of our global players until today when he more than anyone put Malaysia on the global map for creative education.

If ideas are not coupled with actions, they never get bigger than the brain cells they occupy. The action in this case was a mutually reinforcing coupling of creativity and the modernizing force of technology. The Lim Kok Wing Institute later the University of Creative Technology was breathtaking in its scope as the fertility of his imagination brought a prolific out-pouring of ideas and ambitions. It became a crowded canvas.

His was an invincible determination. It was said of him that if opportunity did not knock, he would break down the door. An all this while he was moving hearts and shaping minds ahead of his time. He fully deserved the sobriquet of Maestro.

He became ever more daring indulging a rare ingenuity which I've had occasion to call an exuberant experimentation. This was to culminate in the Limkokwing University of Creative Technology spawning its counterparts in London, Botswana, China and elsewhere creating a global scenario. He had exported his model. Back in the campus in Cyberjaya are to be found students of 140 different nationalities spanning 6 continents. Not just 1Malaysia – 1 World.

This was Tan Sri Lim's new vision – his New Age vision. He applied his redoubtable professional knowledge to build what became one of Malaysia's intellectual and creative centres – but this one is unique – one of a kind. It is dedicated to developing skilled, talented youngsters capable not only of artistic self-expression but of using the latest of modern technology. The IT revolution is unfolding at a blinding pace. What Bill Gates called the speed of light! Our best response will come once again from creative technology. Education is from the Latin edo – educere which means to draw out the latent potential and talent within an individual. Education to Tan Sri Lim Kok Wing is not just pumping in facts and knowledge. Nor is it a paper chase, but creative self-development.

Being a man of change, he is always forward looking – poised for the coming future. His University is creating the generation that will inherit 2020. Fifty per cent of the present Malaysia population is under 35.

Tan Sri Lim always conscious of that other "wing" –"Time's winged chariot hurrying near" – he wanted youth to be ready.

Let's hear what others have had to say:

Sir Francis Bacon might well have had Tan Sri Lim Kok Wing in mind when he memorably said:

"I hold every man debtor to his profession

And strive to be an ornament thereto".

"Ornament" is a true description of our subject.

Abraham Lincoln would have approved of the pace and the momentum of Kok Wing's career: "All things come to those who wait – but only what is left behind by those who hustle".

And finally back to our basic theme, with Milton:

"Headlong joy is ever on the wing".

I do not wish to presume after the testimony of such an illustrious caste. But there is one thing I might claim they can't. I am a personal friend of Tan Sri Lim – and so can verify all that has been said about him. Even all those superlatives. In fact there were not enough superlatives to do him full justice.

Datuk Dr. Paddy Bowie OBE
Managing Director Paddy Schubert Consultants

Worthy of a Nobel Prize

"I find him an extraordinary gentleman whose vision is something I have never seen anywhere in the world. His concept of university is very different. His university – what it teaches – with emphasis on creativity and innovation using technology is way, way, out of this world.

The presence of Limkokwing University of Creative Technology in Lesotho is like a miracle. When he introduced the university the things that the students were learning are quite a paradigm shift from conventional educational programmes.

For example, I never thought designing or creating games could be a profession. The entertainment industry – I never thought that it would be something that people need to go to a university to study. I come from an old school of thought where you are a doctor, a lawyer, a nurse or a teacher. So the biggest impression is that his university in Lesotho is opening new avenues or new niche areas so the Lesotho children can use their talent and creativity to get employment.

The students who study at Limkokwing University are quite different from those who are in other tertiary institutions. They are curious. They want to know more and their attitude towards their studies is different from those pursuing conventional subjects. They are interested and their curiosity is at its highest. And I think that is what education is all about for children, for learning to be made interesting for students.

Here in Malaysia he is already recognized. But in the part of the world I come from, honestly, I believe he needs a lot of recognition.

Let me give you an example of what the students in the campus of Limkokwing in Lesotho do. You may be aware that they do not carry a lot of books like in many universities. They use a laptop. The laptop is the tool that they use to learn. And that has the biggest impact because during my vacation I witnessed one of the students carrying a laptop back home in the village where there is no electricity. But he was able to show his friends, his family, everybody how or what kind of instrument they use to learn. That has really transformed the perception of Basotho parents as far as education is concerned and I think he deserves… if I were in the committee of those who award the Nobel Prize I would definitely recommend him.

I think the first thing he has done is change the landscape of education. He has shown Lesotho that we need to diversify the curriculum so that we do not only focus on the blue collar vocations but look for niche areas. Every one of us is talented. And he has shown us that the only way, the only problem we have is how to tap this talent and that is done through innovation."

H.E. Ntsebe Kokome
High Commissioner of the Kingdom of Lesotho, January 2010

"The Message Man. Malaysian advertising mogul Lim Kok Wing believes in discipline, not inspiration, in deadlines, not flexi-time... up at five, the head of Wings Advertising Agency and a bevy of other marketing communications companies has done three hours' work before the staff come in. There are meetings to attend almost every week-day night. And more work to do when he gets home. Lim goes to bed when he falls asleep."

Asia Magazine, 1985

His immense interest in all kinds of things has taken Dato' Lim Kok Wing to undertake an award-winning film on the threat of nuclear warfare, compose a popular jingle on neighbourliness and create a satirical cartoon strip about Malaysian current affairs."

The Star Newspaper, 1990

" He is a man of seemingly boundless energy, with a love for the antiquarian, the rare and the beautiful... the art and artifact gallery fulfils a long-term ambition of his to set up such an oasis of rare objects. Dato' Lim's aim is to provide the artistic community with a centre, a forum and exhibition space to foster the growth and development of art."

The Star Newspaper, 1991

"The name Lim Kok Wing, conjures awe and reverence in the minds of many. A taskmaster, he executes all with basic ingredients – consistency and an absolute commitment to excellence. A sought-after expert in the field of communications and design, winning more creative awards than any single person in Asia, Tan Sri Lim has contributed more towards building industry than anyone else."

Malaysian Institute of Directors, 1992

"The multi-talented Dato' Lim – he is an artist, cartoonist, journalist and an internationally acclaimed ad-man – has a soft spot for the unfortunate. He has probably raised as many millions for charity as he has made selling his brilliant advertising ideas. What is so admirable about this man is that his own humble past has made him very sensitive to the suffering of others."

Malaysian Tatler, 1994

"Kok Wing has odd ways of doing things but the bottom line is he produces results in whatever he does. The country needs people like him. Take his college of creative technology, I think his aim there is not so much money-making but by establishing all these links abroad he is promoting the country."

Tan Sri Mohamad Khir Johari

Former President Malaysian Institute of Directors, 1995

" His efforts in charity have been the subject of glowing eulogies in the media, of a philanthropist replete with benevolence. Indeed, Lim has probably gathered more feathers than could fit into one cap. That could explain the many hats he wears."

The Edge, 1995

"Crusaders are always in fighting mode – and their energy usually comes from emotions like anger, conviction, passion or simply a sense that a cause worth taking up has been ignored for too long. If so Tan Sri Dato' Lim Kok Wing is a crusader many times over – an many of his battles are fought outside the business arena.

Asia 21 Magazine, 1998

"Limkokwing – this name is synonymous with creativity and Malaysia has benefited, and I believe will continue to benefit from his perseverance to create a culture of quality and excellence in the country. We have some of the best well-thought out policies, some of the best infrastructure, but unfortunately because of a lack of communication skills, we sometimes have allowed this to be still of the best kept secrets. Now I am confident that with Tan Sri Limkokwing around with his skills and his team, he will help us unfold all these things we have provided for business and development in order to provide a better future for Malaysians."

Tun Dr Ling Liong Sik
Former Minister of Transport, 2000

"His work on the ANC campaign in South Africa reveals the high standard. They were well beyond international standards. I personally liked the picture of Mandela surrounded by children. I thought that was marvelous. The people of South Afirca have a lot of praise for him. He is also a very daring, very brave man. I found him to be very innovative and highly creative – a breath of fresh air. Like me he is a great believer in human resource. I see him now as a mover of education for human resource development and I think he has done very well in that respect."

Tan Sri Dr Muhammad Ghazalie Shafie
Former Minister of Home Affairs and Malaysia Commonwealth Observer for South Africa's First Elections, 2000

"It is unusual to come across creative talents who possess a commercial mind. Tan Sri Lim not only demonstrates inventive ingenuity but also is able to carry through his ideas and make them into sound business ideas. We have seen his innovation applied throughout the Wings of Creativity book. We know Tan Sri is passionate about designing his own car and we at Lotus give him our greatest support."

Mr Kevin Algood,
Managing Director, Lotus Engineering, Malaysia, 2001

"Tan Sri Dato' Lim has secured an important place for Malaysia within the global communication and design community. He has made a significant, positive contribution to his country's culture and leadership, one which has been acknowledged by Prime

Minister Dato Seri Dr Mahathir Mohamad. Tan Sri Dato' Lim has embraced his Government's vision for the future of Malaysia as a knowledge economy, driven not by commodity production but by value-added products and services."

Professor Ruth Dunkin
Vice-Chancellor, RMIT University, Australia, 2002

"Tan Sri Lim and his Institute of Creative Technology has inspired a new generation of knowledge workers, highly-skilled and capable of using new concepts and technologies to propel the country forward. He is very much a part of the government's efforts to produce a generation of k-workers, who will unleash the power of Malaysians to change the world, armed and equipped with ICT, creative and critical thinking skills, all the disciplines involving multimedia technology, educational and information content who will become the architect of a new and leading edge Malaysia."

Dato' Seri Mustapa Mohamed
Minister of Higher Education, Malaysia 2001

"The country recognizes Tan Sri Lim's strong sense of commitment and concern for youth development. His contribution to the Rakan Muda programme which invites youth to participate in self-development activities, is well appreciated by the Government. Here is a man so full of creative energy and innovative ideas. I know he really wants to see our youths take to the sky, and he works hard at it."

Dato' Hishammuddin bin Tun Hussein
Minister of Education, Malaysia, 2001

"Throughout Tan Sri Lim's years of service, he has worked selflessly to harness public support for humanitarian causes, winning their hearts and minds, getting them to understand, accept and appreciate him."

Datuk Ruby Lee
Former Secretary-General, Malaysian Red Crescent. 2002

"An industry legend, Tan Sri Lim is a communication strategist whose name is synonymous with the creative industry. From advertising, design, brand development, multimedia, publishing, media, international relations, government relations, strategic corporate communications, his achievements and contributions to the industry and the country make up a list that will probably take time to enumerate."

Shahar Noor
President, Malaysian Advertisers Association, 2003

"Tan Sri Lim was already an industry legend more than 20 years ago. His skills and capability were well-known. He helped found the local advertising business, wresting many blue-chip accounts from foreign multinational agencies. He gained respect for

local capability. He has lifted the business of advertising to new levels that has won respect for the industry."

Malaysian Advertisers' Association, 2003

"We all know that Limkokwing is a pioneer in creative education and that Tan Sri Lim Kok Wing has tirelessly advocated the need to be able to think outside the box. Long before Malaysians fully understood the term, Tan Sri Lim knew that being creative was an asset in a person. He knew about it being able to empower."

Dato' Hishammudin bin Tun Hussein
Minister of Education, Malaysia, 2003

"Tan Sri Lim is of the view that true peace means every one can live in peace. He said that the absence of war does not necessarily mean peace. Peace to him means the lives and rights of people are protected. He said that very often war results in the worsening of the quality of life followed by hunger, poverty and other problems. Because of these crises, he does not agree that war is the answer to peace."

Nanyang Siang Pau Newspaper, 2003

"Let me congratulate Tan Sri Lim Kok Wing for creating ideas. He's a man capable of churning out a lot of new ideas. Normally black is not associated with ideas as a colour but somehow Lim Kok Wing defies that. He's a man who has produced a lot of new ideas and ideas that has really excited a lot of Malaysians. So congratulations Tan Sri for what you have done. And I hope today's launch will be another milestone in your personal contribution towards the success of Malaysia."

Dato' Sri Mohd Najib Tun Abdul Razak
Minister of Defence, Malaysia
Launch of Wawasan 2020 publication, Limkokwing University, 2003

"Tan Sri Lim struck me as a very strategic, observant and intelligent man when I first met him at a promotion campaign. That was more than 14 years ago. Since then, he has been involved in other campaigns. He has contributed a lot to education and media communication. He is a very successful role model for young Malaysians."

Dato' Seri Ong Ka Ting
Minister of Housing and Local Government, Malaysia 2003

"The name Limkokwing has long been a synonym for excellence in design and innovation. I am therefore delighted it will now be borne by the Limkokwing University College of Creative Technology. This new institution will be a addition to Malaysia's tertiary education sector, strengthening yet further the country's position as a regional centre of educational excellence."

HE Bruce Cleghorn
High Commissioner of Britain, Malaysia 2004

"Tan Sri Lim through his dynamic leadership and entrepreneurship, has built Limkokwing to what it is today – a university of creative ideas that has drawn students from all over the world. They come to these shores and take back dynamic ideas to shape their industries and economies. NAPEI hopes that Tan Sri Lim will continue to inspire his team at Limkokwing to scale greater heights of achievement and acclaim to make it an organization to be emulated, not only in this contry but throughout the developing world."

Dr Hj. Mohamed Thalha

President, National Association of Private Educational Institutions 2004

Tan Sri Lim Kok Wing is a legendary character who wields a painter's brush to produce gorgeous colours at his campus. From the early start, the cartoonist turned entrepreneur had planned the university carefully. Creativity is his foundation and strategy."

Oriental Daily News, 2005

"Your university has taken me by surprise. You have taken a very practical, yet, avant garde approach to education. Here you see creativity. Here you feel creativity. I've never seen anything more inspiring."

HE Dr Ralph E. Gonsalves

Prime Minister of St. Vincent and the Grenadines, 2005

The need for new thinking, new approaches but today we are going through yet another period of transition. We are moving away from the industrial age, to communication into the information age and this requires new thinking, innovative thinking and new applications. This is largely based on more information and more knowledge.

It is important for us to realise that we need to think differently now. We cannot be conventional, we have to use new knowledge in new ways and already we see new skills being developed, new instruments, new technology being applied and part of that we saw just now on the video. Things that were impossible before are now commonplace. While we are very much taken up with the new instruments in our workplace, that are placed in our hands that can make the creativity surface. We have also to teach moral values so that these new instruments, this new power will not be abused. We hope that as we teach our students, new knowledge, new skills, we also teach them what is good, what is bad. If we do that, then all that we have learnt will contribute towards the good of the nation.

"It would not be incorrect to say the world of advertising and creativity in Malaysia would be inconceivable without the presence of Tan Sri Lim. Like the fabled Colossus, he has straddled two worlds – the world of advertising and the world of education, and Malaysia is so much richer for that."

Passions Magazine, 2006

"I am indeed, greatly encouraged by Lim Kok Wing's involvement in Botswana. I have heard it said that ordinary leaders direct, great leaders instruct but the greatest of leaders inspire. Our young people here are so inspired it is impressive."

HE Festus G. Mogae
President, Republic of Botswana
Launch of Limkokwing University Botswana, 2007

"Across the world, inspirational university leaders are in very short supply. From my very first visit to Limkokwing in KL, it was clear that at its helm is an amazing brain, namely that of Professor Tan Sri Limkokwing. He has inspired change in his university, his own country and in many other countries."

Professor Dr Michael Thorne
Vice-Chancellor, Anglia Ruskin University, United Kingdom, 2007

"This is a very impressive institution. It is obviously a creative place and everything you see has a message. Here's a world of creativity. You have everything here from hair design, fashion to animation and film"

Mel Gibson
Award-winning Hollywood Actor, Producer, Director, 2007

"Limkokwing University will prompt further change in British educational institutions as we continue to re-invent ourselves and become more relevant to today's world. In my view, Limkokwing University, with its internationally acknowledged experience in delivering skills-driven programmes, can confidently be expected to make a strong contribution to the British education sector"

Professor Dr Michael Thorne
Vice-Chancellor of Anglia Ruskin University, United Kingdom, 2007

"All Basotho are greatly indebted to Tan Sri Lim Kok Wing, President and Founder of Limkokwing University – the Global University, for this world-class institution. We are very happy that this University is now among us to provide 21st century learning environment that will develop this corps of smart, creative and techno-savvy graduates."

HE Pakalitha Bethuel Mosisili
Prime Minister, Kingdom of Lesotho,
Launch of Limkokwing University Lesotho, 2008

" Malaysia and the world should indeed, be very proud of Tan Sri Lim Kok Wing, President of the Limkokwing University for his enlightenment, vision and wisdom; for this great entrepreneur, who has made things happen and continues to make things happen in the interest of a better humanity."

Sir James R. Macham
Founding President, Republic of Seychelles, 2008

"I congratulate Limkokwing for breaking down barriers and pushing back the frontiers of international education. If international educators are to produce leaders for the 21st century, institutions of higher education must follow the lead of Tan Sri Limkokwing and equip students both on and off the campus with the tools they need to be effective world citizens."

Maurice Dimmock
Chief Executive, Accreditation Service for International Colleges (ASIC), United Kingdom, 2008

"Dr Lim Kok Wing himself had the vision to see the need where none existed. The passion to do things never been done before and the tenacity to push things forward to translate ideas into reality."

Ahmed Kathrada
Chairman, Nelson Mandela Foundation
Johannesburg, South Africa, 2008

"If Tan Sri can inspire me, he can inspire you and that is reason that we thought that by partnering with Limkokwing University is not just partnering with a university but partnering with people who mean business, we want to work with people that are innovative, people that are creative."

Youssouf Oomar
UNICEF Special Representative, 2009

"Limkokwing is known for its extraordinary way of defining education away from the norm. Tan Sri Lim's visionary leadership in developing creative and innovative-inspired education to prepare the younger generation with in-demand skills for the 21st century has shaken up the traditional education establishment by designing one university that is anything but traditional"

HE Kennedy Jawan
High Commissioner of Malaysia to Botswana, 2009

"Despite its relatively short history, Limkokwing University has been on the frontline of globalization, opening campuses in UK, China, Indonesia, Africa, and Cambodia. A most accomplished university, you have truly globalised education."

Dr Sung Min Kim
Chairman, Seo Kyung University South Korea, 2009

"One year has passed since Limkokwing University established itself in Maseru with the grand mission of developing a new generation of human capital equipped with skills of new technology and creative thinking capabilities. Limkokwing University Lesotho has provided the 21st century learning environment to develop this corps of intelligent, creative, and techno-savvy Basotho graduates.

And I am very certain that soon the country will receive the boost it needs when these skilled and creative Basotho graduates. We sorely need their skills and knowledge to take Lesotho's economy to the next level. It is time the world saw Lesotho is our investment in the future where our youths, empowered with the right skills, knowledge and attitude will lead Africa to greater integration with the global economy."

Dr Mamphono Khaketla
Minister of Education and Training, Kingdom of Lesotho, 2009

"He has invested the time and money to make this campus the most hi-tech institution of higher education in Botswana.

He has brought Botswana to the world and the world to Botswana through the website that has over 108 million hits a year from 190 countries worldwide. The biggest promise he made was to build the human capital for Botswana to plan its way forward. Today this has come true at this graduation. Through their creative and innovative ideas they can build for Botswana the products and services that the world will desire."

"Three years ago the Limkokwing University became a part of our education landscape. Three years later, today, we are graduating creative thinkers, injecting them into the lifeblood of the Botswana economy. Three years from now I believe there will be change in the way Botswana responds to challenges."

HE Festus G. Mogae
Former President of Botswana
Graduation Ceremony at Limkokwing University Botswana, March 2010

"Tan Sri Lim Kok Wing is not known only in Malaysia but he is a man who is talked about outside Malaysia, in different countries, for his creativity and his innovation which exceeds the borders of Malaysia. He has put into practice a new system of education in Limkokwing University and other campuses of Limkokwing overseas.

I was amazed actually to see more than 140 countries representated at the Limkokwing University campus in Kuala Lumpur. "

HE Abdelaziz Aboughosh
Ambassador of Palestine, 2010

"I think that Tan Sri Lim Kok Wing has done his part to improve creative technology in the whole country. I believe also that the government already recognizes Limkokwing University as one of the universities that help to build the creative industries in Malaysia."

Senator Tan Sri Datuk (Dr) Jins Shamsudin
A legend of the Malaysia film industry, 2010

"I believe that Tan Sri Limkokwing himself is a person who has been very consistent and has been very firm in translating ideas into reality. Tan Sri has made a big impact in changing of all those involved in the education industry. As Malaysians we should be grateful that we are gifted by God to have a person like Tan Sri Lim Kok Wing. I believe Tan Sri has come through a very long process, moving from strength to strength, learning from his weaknesses, and transform all those weaknesses into strengths.

Datuk IR. Idris Haron
Former Deputy Minister of Higher Education of Malaysia and Member of Parliament, 2010

"A man with vision, a man who is able to transform anything that he does today with passion, with conviction, and that's what is Limkokwing University today. He is able to actually bring Limkokwing University from zero, literally, to a globalized university that we have known today and has already surpassed more than 150 countries. Tan Sri Limkokwing has actually put up a number of initiatives to encourage both the public sector and the private sector to undertake innovation and to transform ourselves. In SMEs, for example, Tan Sri Limkokwing himself has worked together with SME Corp Malaysia to drive innovation, trying to make think differently."

Dato' Hafsah Hashim
CEO of SME Corporation, Malaysia, 2010

"He has made things that were mundane before into a fine art. I was very impressed when I went round his university to see his museum. I was actually struck to find so many of the government campaigns for nation building, had his hand in it. And I think he did most of them pro bono."

Toh Puan Dato' Seri Hajjah Dr Aishah Ong
Chairman, Health Promotion Board, Ministry of Health Malaysia, 2010

"You can not talk about Tan Sri Lim Kok Wing without talking about the university he built. He has built an exciting, interesting, refreshing, energetic university. And he identifies the university with innovation and creativity.

It's like his laboratory, his building, his ideas about creativity and innovation. I think Limkokwing University has shown the evidence that it has attracts good brains, good students, it has produced graduates that are welcomed in the market place. If the measure of an outcome is the measure of the success it certainly is an indication. I think Tan Sri Lim is the kind of restless person like all creative and innovative people are, who will not stop reflecting and suggesting and questioning and innovating and challenging and his passion of creativity and innovation.

I think the likes of Tan Sri Lim Kok Wing should not only play a more important role but should be encouraged and given the platform and encouragement and the support, to help, to assist, to be partners with the government, with the industry, with whoever is interested to build a new Malaysia strongly based upon, supported by creativity and innovation."

Dato Dr Syed Ahmad Hussein
CEO Malaysia Qualifications Agency (MQA), 2010

"I think it is through Tan Sri's efforts that people understand what creativity and innovation is. People no longer think that creativity or innovation is something that's just theory, something that's on paper. It is something that people know that has a lot of value in it. His thinking towards humanitarianism, peace, harmony, and I think these are the things that encompass the whole holiness of persons, not just one aspect of creativity or innovation, but something that ges far beyond."

Gan Chin Kew
Managing Director of Red Tomato Magazine, 2010

"I think I've never met someone who's more creative than Tan Sri Lim and he has the ability to look at situations and improvise upon them so that you all can see a way forward. Creativity, does not only deal with a certain type of discipline. It involves society as a whole and in very many different sectors of what a society is involved in. In terms of getting the people to feel a sense of warmth there is a creativity that is required to move something in motion. Likewise, if you're talking about commercialization or product branding, I think he's very, very strong in that and I might add, even though I do not have personal experience of this matter, I do know that even in the area of politics Tan Sri has also been very helpful in making politicians become a bit more creative in a positive sense especially in reaching out to the people at large."

Dato' Syed Amin Aljeffri
President, Kuala Lumpur Malay Chamber of Commerce, 2010

"Not only has the government recognized him, I think the Malaysia Book of Records has also placed some of the records of Tan Sri Lim Kok Wing's University in the Malaysia Book of Records, like having the most number of international students in universities. In fact he has a lot of, accomplishments and recently we also have listed some new records of Tan Sri Lim Kok Wing's University in our latest edition."

Datuk Danny Ooi
Managing Director, Malaysian Book of Records, 2010

"Malaysia has many innovative thinkers in many fields, in medicine, in media, in advertising, in academia, judiciary, industry. Tan Sri is certainly one of them. A leader. When you sit with him in a meeting you can tell he is always leaps and bounds ahead of all of us. When it comes to a problem, he cuts the Gordian knot with lightning speed. And he comes out with a solution, often an unorthodox solution. Yes, certainly he is a guru of lateral thinking. There is so much we can learn from him, there is so much he has contributed, there is so much more he can continue to contribute to the development of Malaysia."

Philip Mathews
Former Assistant Director General ISIS Malaysia, 2010

"I think he works smart and I believe he also works hard. I understand that he's a very light sleeper and that he's a strong taskmaster. I believe he is quite an innovative and creative person in his own ways I think this is very evident over the last 3 decades of his work, in building up the university for example. I would recognize him as among the people who have contributed to thinking out of the box. I think his contribution is well appreciated among the ordinary Malaysian citizens as well as intellectuals, and academicians, who have seen his approach and in venturing beyond our shores to have campuses elsewhere. His contribution is not only national but also global."

Dato' Hajeedar Hj. Abdul Majid
Hajeedar & Associates, 2010

"He's a very exceptional gentleman. His mind is always working all the time. And he's thinking of ways and means of how to improve society and how to create a generation of very talented people. And the talented people are the ones who're supposed to inherit the future and to shape the future. So his mind works all the time thinking of very, very creative and innovative ways of educating the next generation.

When leaders like Tan Sri Lim Kok Wing become the paradigm's pioneer and establish universities which focus on creativity, then we'll create new opportunities for individuals to discover undiscovered talent; to bring forth the hidden talents; to hone or improve or sharpen and expand and enhance existing talents, and then to combine various kinds of talents founded on the arts and the sciences to move forward."

Professor Dato' Ibrahim Ahmad Bajunid
President, Malaysian Association of Leadership Management, 2010

"Tan Sri, I would say is the guru of innovation. His work, his whole life is dedicated to creating the kind of mindset that people in Malaysia understand that it is a creative and innovative mind that can create new things, beautiful things, and change the world. I think Tan Sri has devoted his entire career to changing the way people think, the way people do business. Tan Sri foresees a lot of what normal people don't. He's so farsighted. He sees beyond. He sees thirty years, fifty years or a hundred years to come. This is what this wonderful mindset can teach us, can create in us. Through innovation you really see things differently."

Dato Lewre Lew

President, Branding Association of Malaysia, 2010

"Tan Sri's creativity and innovation certainly has a great impact on the younger generations particularly, Malaysians in understanding the importance of creativity and innovation needed to place Malaysia on a very important status in the world. Tan Sri is not just outstanding on his innovations, he is also guiding the younger generation to understand branding so they can uplift their standards of living.

Ultimately I think the developing nations will adopt Tan Sri's vision in moving their economies to the next level through the capability of their skilled human capital."

Dato' Dr Chin See Keat

Founder, Malaysian Retailer Chains Association, 2010

"Speaking about Tan Sri Lim Kok Wing, I must say that he is one of the rare individuals that I have met over the years who is extremely talented in many ways. I regard Tan Sri Lim Kok Wing as a mentor, in fact, he is a role model not just for young people but for all Malaysians.

I think Tan Sri Lim Kok Wing has made an impact on most Malaysians, be it directly or indirectly. He was behind a lot of the major campaigns that our country was organizing over the past twenty years. So I think in one way or another, Malaysians have been positively influenced by Tan Sri Lim Kok Wing. He has put Malaysia on the world map. I think that is the greatest contribution that an educationist can ever make."

Eric Chong

Founder & CEO, Erican International, 2010

"The desire to innovate, rarely, if ever, occurs to people who are in their comfort zones. Innovators are almost always found at the cutting edge, where they deploy resources and create mechanisms to push the boundaries.

It is for this reason that I would like to pay tribute to such a person that is Tan Sri Dato' Sri Dr Limkokwing. A man I applaud for his ceaseless pursuit of innovation and the proof of his success in constant re-invention, not only himself, but in his passion at Limkokwing University that bears both his name and philosophy.

He himself is a role model of innovation, and an inspiration to others in innovative education, where his life exemplifies the characteristics of an innovator, one who never rests, always challenging the norm, pushes past boundaries and never takes the easy way out."

Tuan Haji Fadillah bin Yusof
Deputy Minister of Science, Technology, and Innovation Malaysia, 2010

"I really believe that Tan Sri Lim Kok Wing has influenced the thinking of government people, private sector people, the educationists that we have to be creative, we have to be innovative. He should be made a Malaysia's Creativity Personality of the year or of the decade or something, I do not know. But what is important is the recognition by people that he has contributed a lot. Limkokwing University is hardly 20 years old but it's already the biggest globalized university in the world."

Dato' Sulaiman Osman
Deputy Chairman, University Council of Limkokwing University, 2010

"Tan Sri Lim Kok Wing is a person who exudes enthusiasm. You can count on him in providing a breath of fresh air in whatever he does because he tends to bring creativity and innovation to the fore. Yes, without a doubt, I think Tan Sri Lim has made a great impact as a champion of innovation and creativity. In Malaysia, the name Limkokwing is synonymous with creativity and innovation and a lot of young CEOs or even the more matured ones look upon Limkokwing for instance to provide new ideas as well as direction in how to move their programmes forward with creativity. Tan Sri Limkokwing is actually a role model for the young people on creativity and innovation. He has proven himself and is a good role model for everyone to follow."

Shameem Bt Abdul Jalil
Board Member (Asia) Global Alliance for PR & Communication Management
Lugano, Switzerland, 2010

In 2005 Tan Sri Lim won the coveted Ernst & Young Entrepreneur of the Year award. He was recognised for his work in improving international humanitarian relations, building human capability and enhancing cross-cultural understanding of the world. In June 2006 he was inducted into the exclusive World Entrepreneur of the Year Academy in Monte Carlo, Monaco (reserved only for country winners of the Ernst & Young Entrepreneur of the Year).